"As the modern teaching of the Enneagram is rapidly clarify identity, what the Calhouns and Loughriges have done in *Spiritual Rhythms* is nothing short of remarkable. This fresh and timely contribution to the Enneagram's tradition offers a seamless integration of faith and identity. Engaging, compelling, and courageous, *Spiritual Rhythms for the Enneagram* provides practical application on some of the Enneagram's more under-explored concepts. There's no doubt the depth of spirituality embodied in the author's personal lives animates these pages with profound clarity, offering contemporary applications for an ancient tool."

Christopher L. Heuertz, founding partner of Gravity, a Center for Contemplative Activism, author of *The Sacred Enneagram*

"*Spiritual Rhythms for the Enneagram* is a unique contribution to Enneagram literature. The authors invite us to experience the Enneagram in a contemplative, healing way. Through Scripture, penetrating questions, and spiritual practices appropriate to each Enneagram space, they call us to a richer, deeper self-awareness. This is not a book to guzzle. It is a book to digest slowly. It is a meal to consume alone or with friends. It is a feast for the soul."

Alice Fryling, author of *Mirror for the Soul: A Christian Guide to the Enneagram*

"The journey that this new transformative work on the Enneagram invites you to take will change you . . . for good. With practice in the spiritual rhythms, you will not only know where you identify on the Enneagram, but will become an expression of the beauty and life that that number is meant to reveal to the world. The authors bring their personal journeys, extensive study, pastoral experience, and Enneagram expertise to this book. If you embark on this journey you will become more of who God created you to be and do."

Sibyl Towner, codirector of The Springs Retreat Center, coauthor of *Listen to My Life*

"I am deeply indebted to Doug and Adele Calhoun, for they introduced me to the Enneagram. They gave me hope that the wayward motivations of an Eight to control and confront could be redeemed into the desire to serve and release the potential in others. The Calhouns and Loughriges have laid out a process of harmonizing your head, heart, and gut into wholeness. If you truly want to fulfill the potential for which you have been made, this is the book for you. You will need to marinate in the carefully structured exercises and stories. Yet what awaits you is a treasure-trove of discovery that will set you free to flow in the stream of God's original design. Great payoff requires great investment."

Greg Ogden, author of *Discipleship Essentials*

"For me, identifying my Enneagram type was like the dog who caught the car—now what? I knew there was more than just becoming a better version of myself. Thanks to *Spiritual Rhythms for the Enneagram* I now know and appreciate concepts like head, heart, and gut IQs, spiritual rhythms and the Ignatian practices of discernment, and consolation and desolation. This handbook serves as a trusted advisor, reflecting the four authors' life experiences and deep expertise. I now have an inspiring resource for *how* to return to my true self."

Joan O. Wright, O'Sullivan Wright Inc.

"*Spiritual Rhythms for the Enneagram* is an accessible volume that will take your understanding of the nine personality types to the next level. In beautifully written prose, the authors present useful concepts and skills that will help you better understand yourself and others—equipping you to gracefully navigate the complexities of life."

Kimberly June Miller, counselor, author of *Boundaries for Your Soul*

"As valuable as this book is for getting an in-depth view of each Enneagram type, it is an essential resource for understanding how the head, heart, and gut can work together, empowered through spiritual practices to have dynamic, harmonious relationships. In these pages, you will find a variety of ways to discover more deeply who you are, are not, and who you can love more fully. The depth of information and the comprehensive resources make this a unique Enneagram handbook that you will want to reference often. I use the insights and practices in these chapters every single day in my relationships with family and friends as well as in spiritual direction, teaching, and team building. This is the Enneagram book I have been waiting for—applying what is in these pages will change your relationships and your life."

Mary Albert Darling, associate professor of communications, Spring Arbor University

"This book makes a wonderful contribution to the deeper understanding of the ancient tool of the Enneagram. Doug and Adele and Clare and Scott masterfully weave deep insight along with helpful spiritual direction and application on every page. *Spiritual Rhythms for the Enneagram* is not just an invitation to gain more information but an opportunity for personal transformation as well. I encourage you to not only read this book but allow it to read you!"

Joe Walters, executive director, Potter's Inn Soul Care Institute

"A fantastic book! The authors of this comprehensive handbook deliver on their promise to help readers answer next-steps questions. The embedded narratives allow readers to go beyond system and theory to experience an embodied Enneagram. This useful resource provides practices and pathways for my own continued spiritual transformation and in my work with others. Exceptional!"

Nina Barnes, vice president of student life, University of Northwestern-St. Paul, conflict coach, spiritual director

"What a welcome contribution to the literature on the Enneagram, particularly from the Christian perspective! *Spiritual Rhythms for the Enneagram* delivers on its commitment to answer this important question: I know my number; what do I do now? It does so in a clear, accessible, and practical way. Their deep work on the Harmony Triads is both newsworthy and noteworthy. Congratulations to the four authors bringing forth this important material and doing so with one voice."

Ginger Lapid-Bogda, author of *Bringing Out the Best in Yourself at Work*

"The first thing that struck me in reading this comprehensive dive into Enneagram awareness, practice, and spiritual literacy was the section on empathy and the way aspects of ourselves are reflected in our resistance and openness to others. The authors understand the humbling truth that as we awaken together, it's much less easy to hide from our egotism! Savor this guide because there is an abundance of solid practices to support your development. Using the Harmony Triads and their understanding of timeless religious wisdom, the Loughriges and Calhouns have generously offered countless reflections to digest and deepen communion with ourselves, others, and the God who is One."

Leslie Hershberger, Enneagram/integral course developer of Coming Home, editor of *IEA Nine Points Magazine*

SPIRITUAL RHYTHMS

FOR THE

ENNEAGRAM

A Handbook for Harmony and Transformation

ADELE *and* DOUG CALHOUN

CLARE *and* SCOTT LOUGHRIGE

Foreword by JEROME WAGNER

IVP Books

An imprint of InterVarsity Press
Downers Grove, Illinois

InterVarsity Press
P.O. Box 1400, Downers Grove, IL 60515-1426
ivpress.com
email@ivpress.com

InterVarsity Press® is the book-publishing division of InterVarsity Christian Fellowship/USA®, a movement of students and faculty active on campus at hundreds of universities, colleges, and schools of nursing in the United States of America, and a member movement of the International Fellowship of Evangelical Students. For information about local and regional activities, visit intervarsity.org.

All Scripture quotations, unless otherwise indicated, are taken from The Holy Bible, New International Version®, NIV®. Copyright © 1973, 1978, 1984, 2011 by Biblica, Inc.™ Used by permission of Zondervan. All rights reserved worldwide. www.zondervan.com. The "NIV" and "New International Version" are trademarks registered in the United States Patent and Trademark Office by Biblica, Inc.™

While any stories in this book are true, some names and identifying information may have been changed to protect the privacy of individuals.

Cover design: David Fassett
Interior design: Jeanna Wiggins

Images: gold background: © studiocasper / E+ / Getty Images
abstract blue background: © kostins / iStock / Getty Images Plus
blue painted background: © Pobytov / DigitalVision Vectors / Getty Images

ISBN 978-0-8308-3600-0 (print)
ISBN 978-0-8308-7121-6 (digital)

Printed in the United States of America ⊗

Library of Congress Cataloging-in-Publication Data
Names: Calhoun, Adele Ahlberg, 1949- author.
Title: Spiritual rhythms for the enneagram : a handbook for harmony and
*   transformation / Adele Ahlberg Calhoun and Doug Calhoun, Clare Loughrige*
*   and Scott Loughrige ; foreword by Jerome Wagner.*
Description: Downers Grove : InterVarsity Press, 2019. | Includes
*   bibliographical references.*
Identifiers: LCCN 2018054465 (print) | LCCN 2019002585 (ebook) | ISBN
*   9780830871216 (eBook) | ISBN 9780830836000 (pbk. : alk. paper)*
Subjects: LCSH: Christianity—Psychology. | Enneagram.
Classification: LCC BR110 (ebook) | LCC BR110 .S69 2019 (print) | DDC
*   155.2/6—dc23*
LC record available at https://lccn.loc.gov/2018054465

| P | 30 | 29 | 28 | 27 | 26 | 25 | 24 | 23 | 22 | 21 | 20 | 19 | 18 | 17 | 16 | 15 | 14 | 13 | 12 | 11 | 10 | 9 | 8 | 7 | 6 |
| Y | 44 | 43 | 42 | 41 | 40 | 39 | 38 | 37 | 36 | 35 | 34 | 33 | 32 | 31 | 30 | 29 | 28 | 27 | 26 | 25 | 24 | 23 | 22 | 21 |

Thank you to the Enneagram teachers who have mentored us and generously shared their wisdom with us, and to the courageous souls who attend our workshops and then do the work that brings harmony to their lives and this world.

This book is our response to the question, "I know my number. What do I do now?"

CONTENTS

FOREWORD
Jerome Wagner

WHEN I FIRST LEARNED THE ENNEAGRAM from Father Robert Ochs, SJ, while studying theology in the early '70s, there was nothing written about the Enneagram. We only had mimeographed handouts. When I did my dissertation research in psychology on the Enneagram, there was still nothing written about it. Because it was passed on through oral tradition, I suggested to my dissertation committee that I list phone numbers in place of a bibliography. Surprisingly, they failed to see the humor in that suggestion. Now, in 2018, there are a plethora of Enneagram books and resources available in the market and through the internet. Apparently, there have been no thoughts about the Enneagram that have not been transcribed or recorded.

And so you ask: Do we really need another Enneagram book on our bookshelves? And I would answer, Yes—this one! It adds material and insights that other books don't have. Is the Enneagram a fossilized framework etched in stone to be passed on dogmatically as is? Or is it a living system that can grow and develop with additional accretions and insights? I think the latter is the case.

For example, in my early courses on the Enneagram, we didn't consider the Harmony Triads. While not unique to this book, these thoughtful connections are elaborated and vividly presented here. Combined with the three centers—physical or gut (GQ), emotional

(EQ), and intellectual (IQ)—the Harmony Triads are quite useful additions for understanding our own style, favored center, and connection to styles in other centers. It's a very helpful integrative approach.

Also, people ask: Now that I know my type, what do I do with it (or myself)? After reading *Spiritual Rhythms for the Enneagram*, you will know. There are numerous reflection questions to help you further your knowledge of yourself and your style, along with suggestions about how to apply this knowledge to your personal transformation.

I've had the honor of having Adele and Doug Calhoun and Clare and Scott Loughrige as participants in my Enneagram Spectrum Training and Certification Program. These authors, ministers, and spiritual directors take their place in a long line of spiritual guides. They incorporate the insights and practices of Evagrius Ponticus, the fourth-century desert father and spiritual director; Ramon Llull, the twelfth-century Franciscan theologian who endeavored to integrate Christianity, Judaism, and Islam in a comprehensive Enneagram-like figure; and Ignatius of Loyola, the fifteenth-century founder of the Society of Jesus and a renowned retreat director.

Spiritual Rhythms for the Enneagram is a very creative and comprehensive presentation of this system with an easy blending of psychology and spirituality. Karl Popper, the philosopher of science, said the highest status that a scientific theory can attain is not yet disconfirmed. So the latest theories about the Enneagram will be replaced by more adequate theories. Apparently science (and the Enneagram) require humility. That's what a community of knowers is all about. We share our insights with the community; they reflect on them and test them against their experience, contributing their reflections and conclusions; and thus wisdom grows. Adele, Doug, Clare, and Scott have given us much to think about and profit from. We will all benefit from their diligent work.

INTRODUCTION
You've Got Harmony

With God's help, I shall become myself.

SOREN KIERKEGAARD

THE ENNEAGRAM OPENS YOU to an extraordinary view to the truth about you. It can help you recognize your unique melody as well as where you are off-key internally and relationally. The Enneagram reveals your tempos, soloist agendas, and dedication to your "playlist." Still, discovering the truth of your number can never encompass who you are. Nor does it automatically change you or your relationships. Relational repairs and healthy interactions take intention and attention. Enneagram insights have to be applied to the rhythms and grooves of ordinary daily lives to bring transformation and harmony.

The Enneagram comforts and discomforts. It names how we default and defend ourselves from truth—especially truth about ourselves! Jesus continually struggled with people who were closed to new truth about God and themselves. During his last hours with his followers, Jesus said, "I have much more to say to you, more than you can now bear" (John 16:12). Jesus' friends just weren't prepared to hear truth that contradicted their agendas and self-understanding. Two thousand years later, we are no more prepared to bear and practice truth than Jesus' disciples were,

For us personally, God graciously used the Enneagram in our lives to get around our defenses and blind spots so we could *practice* truth. The Enneagram revealed the reality of our inner discord and its effect on others. Knowing our Enneagram number gave us eyes to see how image, wounds, lies, triggers, and default responses shaped us every bit as much as our faith. Yet, recognizing our number was just the beginning of a journey that is changing us and our ability to love God and neighbor as we love ourselves.

At Enneagram training events, people often ask, "What do I do now that I know my number?" *Spiritual Rhythms for the Enneagram* is our answer to that question. Each chapter invites you to search through the stories of every number to find yourself and learn empathy for others. We offer spiritual practices that create space to develop new patterns of relating with God, yourself, and others. Our desire is for you to partner with the Spirit of Truth in doing the work that helps you live into the glorious person God created you to be. Dig in and grapple with the beautiful and uncomfortable truth that can set you free. You are more than your Enneagram type.

HOW WE LEARNED THE TRUTH ABOUT OURSELVES

Jalaluddin Rumi asked, "Why do you stay in prison when the door is so wide open?" Truth can be hard to bear. It can take time . . . especially if it is about *you*! Each of us can vouch for our own resistance to truth.

Authors Doug and Adele have served together in ministry for decades. They have read their Bibles, prayed, counseled, mentored, preached, and taught others "truth." Yet for years, Adele couldn't get Doug to see how his clenched jaw, harsh tone, and steely eyes leaked anger. And he couldn't convince her that she interrupted *a lot*. They both resisted the other's perspective. Even though Doug knows and loves Adele better than anyone else, she discounted what he said with three easily accessed defenses: "I do not interrupt (denial). I like to jump into conversations and take part (rationalization). You can speak up if you want to (blame)." Adele simply didn't want to change the fantasy in her mind that she was a great listener. Doug also patently denied that anger was part of his story. After all, he never raised his voice or hit anyone! How could he be angry? We both recognized the disharmony in our relationship, but we were oblivious and unwilling to bear inconvenient truths that could bring harmony.

More than twenty-five years ago, authors Clare and Scott planted a nondenominational, charismatic church. As young senior pastors, they dedicated themselves to teaching people how to "Love the Lord your God with all your heart and with all your soul and with all your strength and with all your mind" (Luke 10:27). Clare was definitely driven and all in. She recalls her rationale at the time this way: "I am wired to move, motivate, and activate. I'd auto-matically seize the day, move things forward, and ask questions later. I'd say, 'We're made for this!,' and 'Let's just do it.' I was blind to how my passion fueled overwork and impatience."

Scott, on the other hand, was wired to slow things (and Clare) down. He could moderate, regulate, calculate, and frustrate Clare. He would say, "Hang on, let's not rush into anything; let's make this work for everybody." This slow-it-down energy could default into peace-at-any-price or I-will-not-be-moved leadership. Running on automatic, we each lived our own version of sheer youthful enthusiasm, which kept fantasies intact and uncomfortable truths at bay.

For the four of us, the Enneagram opened a new way to live. Writing together allowed us to blend four voices of varied timbre, experience, and expertise. We let go of soloing on our Enneagram number and synchronized the intelligence of Adele's Four, Scott's Nine, Doug's One, and Clare's Three. This led to a creative, mediating, reforming, and effective four-part harmony—which, as it happens, is at the heart of the Enneagram approach we want to share with you.

Clare is the visionary who recognized the connections between theologians Ignatius of Loyola, Evagrius Ponticus, and Ramon Llull, and articulated this expression of the Harmony Triads with Ignatian spirituality (more on that later). She and Scott offer an accredited, certification training for learning the Enneagram with Harmony. Doug and Adele are experienced pastors and spiritual directors who offer training in spiritual practices, the Ignatian Spiritual Exercises, the Enneagram, and the Enneagram with Harmony. They are thought partners in developing and cowriting the material in this book. Scott, Clare, Doug, and Adele employ Harmony Triad principles in their work with individuals, organizations, and in leadership development.

HEAD, HEART, AND GUT INTELLIGENCE

Intriguing current research suggests human beings are created with head, heart, and gut intelligence. Your gut and heart each have a vast neural network just like your brain. In fact, your gut and your heart can "know" things before your brain does. We call the three intelligences *IQ* (Head Intelligence), *EQ* (Emotional/Heart Intelligence), and *GQ* (Gut Intelligence). In the therapeutic community the term *Emotional Intelligence* (EQ) generally includes the capacity to notice, control, and express your emotions in judicious and empathetic ways. Here, we use *EQ* to describe the intelligence of the Heart Triad as the capacity to feel and take cues for relating from the responses of others.

We believe the intelligences of IQ, EQ, and GQ line up with the way you were designed. You were created to love God, neighbor, and self with all your heart effect, gut strength, and mind thoughts. Loving is the most difficult spiritual work any of us have to do. Loving is intensely practical work that ripples out and affects neighbors near and far.

The Enneagram reveals that each Enneagram Triad has a preferred way of relating in the world. Numbers Five, Six, and Seven trust their head intelligence. Numbers Two, Three, and Four trust their heart intuitions. Numbers Eight, Nine, and One trust their gut instincts. Yet nature, nurture, and trauma can shut down one or more of these intelligences, so we continually solo on one default intelligence. When that happens, we undernourish or dismiss parts of ourselves that can bring harmony.

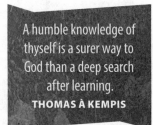

A humble knowledge of thyself is a surer way to God than a deep search after learning.
THOMAS À KEMPIS

THE TRIADS

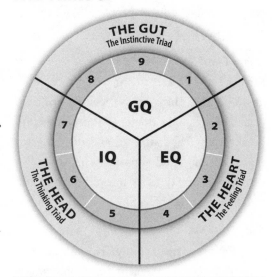

Figure 1. The Harmony Triads, detailing the three Enneagram intelligences and their numbers

When each Enneagram number learns to integrate head curiosity, heart emotions, and gut instincts, we respond to love and work in richer, healthier, and more harmonious ways. The Enneagram invites you to investigate the discord that puts you out of tune. It suggests that to experience the music of life in its fullness, you need to trust something besides your solo part.

Harmonious relationships aren't a result of everyone seeing things "my way" or doing things "my way." Harmony comes from trusting that the head and the gut enrich what the heart brings. Still, some of you trust one of these intelligences more than the others. As you look at the head, heart, and gut triads (fig. 1), which one do you favor?

Head Triad

IQ people protect themselves from the vulnerability of heart feelings by moving into their *heads*. They engage the world through mental activity, knowledge, and planning for contingencies. They trust reason and brain power, dismissing heart people as lightweights and gut people as reactionary.

Heart Triad

EQ people trust *heart* connection more than anything else. They rely on feelings and relationships to guide them. When connection breaks, they feel distressed and do things to regain affection and approval. They may also dismiss gut reactions as too judgmental and find head people unfeeling.

Gut Triad

GQ people react instinctively. They know in their *gut* whether they like someone or if something is good or bad. Trusting their gut more than anything or anyone else makes it easy to jump in or pull away without a second thought. In the heat of the moment, gut people can judge head people for their slow deliberations and heart people as too concerned about what people think.

Harmony in relationships depends on integrating and appreciating our head, heart, and gut.

TRADITIONAL ENNEAGRAM THEORY

While traditional Enneagram theory is built on these three centers of intelligence, it doesn't provide ways for every number to access them. Looking at the traditional Enneagram diagram (fig. 2), with arrows indicating directions of disintegration and integration, you'll notice that the arrows do not connect every number to head, heart, and gut. Numbers Two, Four, Five, and Seven access only two types of triad intelligence rather than three. Five and Seven are two-headed and without a heart. Two and Four are two-hearted and without a head.

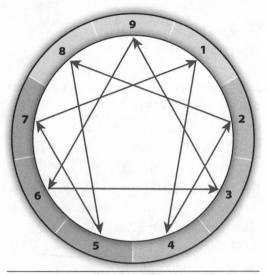

Figure 2. The Traditional Enneagram

THE HARMONY ENNEAGRAM

To address this issue, the Harmony Enneagram (fig. 3) reimagines the connecting lines to create three balanced triangles: Eight, Two, and Five; Nine, Three, and Six; and One, Four, and Seven. The Harmony Enneagram takes the music of your automatic intelligence—be it head intelligence (numbers Five, Six, Seven), heart intelligence (numbers Two, Three, Four), or gut intelligence (numbers Eight, Nine, One)—and integrates the voices of the other two intelligences.

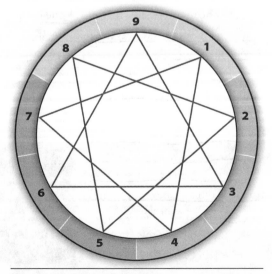

Figure 3. The Harmony Enneagram

Every number is connected to two other intelligences, even if you have dismissed or don't trust one or both of them. Integrating gut, heart, and head creates capacity to see and respond with more than your single center of intelligence.

Drawing on the harmonies of your head, heart, and gut triad can create new, life-giving neural pathways that override habitual default reactions. In the face of decisions and interactions, take a moment to notice:

- ▶ What does your head (IQ) think?
- ▶ What does your heart (EQ) feel?
- ▶ What does your gut instinct (GQ) know?
- ▶ What harmony comes from these three ways of knowing?

Practicing awareness of your IQ, EQ, and GQ can develop new patterns of knowing and loving. When you are stuck in a single number and default way of knowing, you push your way of seeing the world onto others. If they resist your view, you get triggered and try to control and coerce reality to fit your agenda. When you do that, you end up on your edge—you quite literally fall away from your God-given center to the edginess of your ego.

The virtues and vices diagram (fig. 4) shows that when you are centered, you have access to nine virtues—virtues found in God. Out on the edge, you are stuck in a single type and are far away from the center and every other number. Harmony Triads move you from your edgy addiction to a single way of knowing and being toward integration and the ability to receive reality as it is. It offers each number a way to return to your true, centered self by accessing head, heart, and gut intelligences. As you integrate your harmony numbers, you learn to love God, self, and others with all your head, heart, and gut strength.

David Daniels, a Stanford psychiatrist and founding member of the International Enneagram Association, states, "Just 'studying' the Enneagram is not enough to create transformative personal change. . . . In order for us to actually experience personal growth, it's necessary to interweave consistent and dedicated 'practice'—process—with the study of great content. . . . The Enneagram of Harmony Triads are the key to development."

Our Harmony Triad (fig. 5) gives each Enneagram type a name that integrates their three

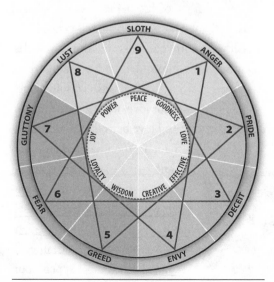

Figure 4. Virtues and Vices

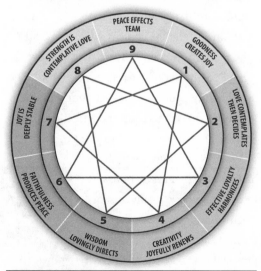

Figure 5. Balanced Intelligence

centers of intelligence. It is a vision of what wholeness and freedom can look like for you.

HISTORICAL HARMONIZERS

Where did the Harmony Enneagram come from? Our Enneagram teachers, mentors, and friends span sacred, secular, and psychological approaches. We are deeply grateful for their wisdom and insights. We root our understanding of Harmony intelligence in Evagrius Ponticus (AD 345-399), Ramon Llull (1232-1315), and Ignatius of Loyola (1491-1556). These men wrote of spiritual solutions that address our blindness and addiction to self. They cared that people discern their call and purpose. To do that meant learning to distinguish when they were following God's Spirit and when their actions were ego driven. We believe their combined insights are useful to all who seek self-awareness and desire to love with all of who they are.

TRANSFORMATION AND HARMONY

God is the original harmony of three in one. This divine chorus of Father, Son, and Holy Spirit exists in an eternal concert of giving and receiving, honoring and loving. And you are designed for harmony in this concert too! The breathtaking good news is that your vulnerabilities, brokenness, mistakes, and addiction-to-self are real-time opportunities to practice harmony.

We all say things we wish we hadn't said. We don't do things we intend to do. We sow discord when we want to create harmony. Dallas Willard wrote, "Projects of personal transformation rarely if ever succeed by accident, drift, or imposition." Transformation depends on attention and intention. We have to make space in our lives for the Spirit of Truth to transform us through our sin.

How do we do this? How do we know if we are beautiful, competent, successful, or strong? Are we the story we tell ourselves? Are we who others say we are? Does our best or worst day determine the truth of us? Few of us wake up in the morning and decide to torpedo our relationships and spread disharmony. But who are we when we do that? Are we who we think we are? Are we who our hearts feel we are? Are we who our gut instincts shout we are?

How do we keep becoming ourselves as God intended and harmonize internal voices and outer relationships? Jesus might answer, "'Love the Lord your God with all your heart and with all your soul and with all your mind and with all your strength.' . . . [And] 'Love your neighbor as yourself.' There is no commandment greater than these" (Mark 12:30-31).

What matters most is being open, vulnerable, and able to connect with others using your IQ, EQ, and GQ. Jesus knew how to do this. He practiced loving God, friends, and enemies with every fiber of his being using his head, heart, and gut. His emotional intelligence (EQ) overflowed with compassion and love. His wisdom (IQ) confounded and brought truth. His deep gut strength (GQ) wasn't afraid to feel pain and sacrifice for love. Jesus gave his life to create harmony and love between us all.

We who are made in the image of God are meant to use our three intelligences just as Jesus did. Sometimes we are nurtured in ways that naturally help us unfold, open, and love with heart, mind, and gut strength. When this happens, our

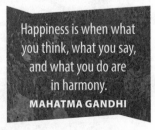

Happiness is when what you think, what you say, and what you do are in harmony.
MAHATMA GANDHI

HISTORICAL CONNECTIONS

EVAGRIUS PONTICUS

This early church father provided guidance on how to move from the old sin nature to the new Christ-in-me nature. Evagrius was a theologian, philosopher, contemplative, and scientist. He believed the spiritual life could be advanced by understanding Pythagorean mathematics and astronomy. He used numbers to express the orderliness of creation. Evagrius recognized patterns that sabotage the ability to love God and neighbor. These patterns include eight or nine signature sin motivations or energies, such as intemperance, pride, deceit, envy, avarice, fear, gluttony, lust, and sloth. You will recognize these "vices" in the Enneagram.

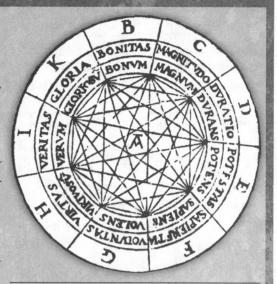

Figure 6. Ramon Llull's Diagram

RAMON LLULL

This twelfth-century Franciscan theologian developed diagrams of three overlapping triangles to explain how to move from vice to virtue (see fig. 6). His diagrams are prototypes for our Harmony Triads. They align with Evagrius's understanding of signature sins as well as Ignatius's Exercises for Spiritual Discernment.

IGNATIUS OF LOYOLA

This priest and theologian was a soldier and man of the world before he became a man of faith. While in his mid-forties he founded the Society of Jesus, also known as the Jesuits. Their mission was to take faith, hope, and love wherever the need was greatest. Ignatius developed his Spiritual Exercises to help his followers discern what God was calling them to do. Ignatius taught that wise discernment depended on the Holy Spirit's motions of the soul. This movement registered in the intelligences of head thoughts, heart feelings, and gut instincts.

Evagrius, Llull, and Ignatius all focused on how to bring God's own harmony out of scattered, compartmentalized, discordant, and ego-driven selves. Their intent was to help us love God, neighbor, and self with all our heart, mind, and gut strength. They are the chords in our harmonizing history—#kindredspiritsall.

---

brains create neural pathways to our prefrontal cortex where love, joy, gentleness, connection, and more originate. Sometimes the opposite happens: we are turned out of people's hearts and betrayed in ways that trigger our amygdala (the brain's seat of emotional reactions). The amygdala protects us by downloading a slew of chemicals, creating neural pathways that automatically defend. We pack our vulnerability away. We close rather than open. We fight, we flee, or we freeze. The neural pathways we need to give and receive love don't develop.

Think of neural pathways like this: when we walk through the same forest day after day, we wear down a path in the ground. In the same way, habitual thought patterns wear a path in the brain. Under stress, we don't think about which path to take. We automatically follow habit. Spiritual practices are one way the Spirit of Truth creates new neural pathways that renew our minds (see Romans 12:2). Old defensive paths and habits give way to loving with our entire being.

Doug, a One on the Enneagram, has learned to move from gut anger to an easy goodness. Adele, an Enneagram Four, can access her dismissed gut intelligence, show up with conviction, and not be cowed by what people think. Clare, a classic Three, can retrieve her head harmonizer and put loyalty before striving and driving. And Scott, our peaceful Nine, can tap into his EQ and wade into the messy work of negotiating harmony rather than defaulting to a duck-and-cover strategy. Yes, we fail at loving God, neighbor, spouse, boss, and enemies. But we keep on practicing because we know God wants us to embody divine harmony. God wants us to *be* the harmony we want to see in the world.

Most of the divisions, fractures, and disharmony in systems and relationships are rooted in the defensive reactions of our false self. We are eager for you to learn how to turn off your default, autopilot false self and become the unique person God had in mind before time began. *Spiritual Rhythms for the Enneagram* is our attempt to help you reclaim the harmony of your beloved, multifaceted, made-in-the-image-of-God self.

automatically. Without spiritual rhythms that integrate broken and dismissed parts of ourselves, we play one string of the instrument that is us, instead of the full chord. The spiritual rhythms in this book are ways we pay attention to what Ignatius of Loyola calls the Spirit's *motions of the soul*. Ignatius believed direction, growth, and presence came through noticing the Holy Spirit's movement in your head thinking, heart feeling, and gut instincts.

If you are making a decision, a pros and cons list might be part of the Spirit's motion in your IQ. God-given desire and delight might register in your EQ. And God's passion and vision might manifest as deep GQ knowing. The point is to pay attention to what Ignatius terms *desolations* and *consolations* in your head, heart, and gut. True consolations lead toward God and love of neighbor. False consolations lead away from God and love. Desolations can be signs you are headed in the wrong direction, but they might also nudge you to turn to God.

Ignatius taught that both desolations and consolations could reveal blindness, triggers, fragility, and habitual sin patterns. They could alert you to inner harmony and/or discord, shame, and judgment. Noticing the Spirit's motions in your soul was part of divine guidance that could lead to inner freedom to love well God, neighbor, and self.

God's purpose is for *you* to be fully alive to loving God, neighbor, and self. To be awake to God's purpose takes awareness. Awareness doesn't require equipment, money, or a PhD. Awareness takes a body that is awake and alert to what is happening—even if feels awful. Noticing takes a mind willing to see how the best and worst of times can hand us truth.

HARMONY AND SPIRITUAL RHYTHMS

A healthy psyche that can give and receive love doesn't happen

The glory of God is man [and woman] fully alive.
SAINT IRENAEUS OF LYONS
(WITH OUR ADDITION)

SECTIONS IN THIS BOOK

Each chapter offers questions and spiritual practices to help you reflect on the Holy Spirit's movement in your head, heart, and gut. As you do these exercises, dig in and participate with what the Good Spirit is doing in your life. No matter what you see, the Spirit is ready to guide you through the beauty and grime of your life and transform you "from one degree of glory to another" (2 Corinthians 3:18 ESV).

Resist the urge to hurry through the chapters. Your soul needs time and space to feel safe in order to come out of hiding. The point is not to "finish" a chapter but to partner with the Holy Spirit for growth and transformation.

Each chapter is divided into sections that build on one another.

Section 1: Who Am I and Who Am I Not. This section asks you to identify the words that shape the narrative you tell yourself about you.

Section 2: True Self and False Self (see Key Terms for further definition of these terms). This section will help you recognize compulsive and impulsive reactions that stem from your ego, as well as responses that arise from love of God, others, and self. When you can recognize that you have fallen into your false self, you can choose transformation. You can learn and practice another way of responding.

Section 3: Harmony. This section provides ways to integrate IQ, EQ, and GQ responses and intelligences into your default patterns of interaction. Harmony creates a vision of who you can be in FLOW (see Key Terms for further definition), when you love God, self, and others from all your gut strength, all your heart feelings, and all your mind. This is the gift of your Harmony Triad.

Section 4: Healing Childhood Hurts. Richard Rohr says, "If we do not transform our pain, we will most assuredly transmit it." This section is intended to help you process past pain, defense structures, dismissed parts of yourself, and childhood lies. Processing is not navel gazing. It is not introspection. The Holy Spirit is your guide as you journey through your past. Partnering with God's healing Spirit might give you compassion for where the child inside you is still acting out and making important decisions today. With the Spirit's help, you can engage with the traumatized places inside you and reclaim lost ground that brings inner freedom.

Section 5: Discernment: Desolations and Consolations. Jeremiah 6:16 states, "This is what the LORD says: 'Stand at the crossroads and look; ask for the ancient paths, ask where the good way is, and walk in it, and you will find rest for your souls.'" This section will help you listen to the movement of the Holy Spirit in your heart feelings EQ, mental thoughts IQ, and gut instincts GQ. It will help you learn to discern your purpose and make life-giving choices.

Section 6: Spiritual Rhythms. Spiritual transformation is a two-part invention. You intentionally and attentionally partner with and notice the Holy Spirit's motions in your soul. Spiritual practices don't work like a drug—"Here, take this; it will make you better." Spiritual practices fit your particular circumstances and season. They make space for God in the reality of what is. This section provides spiritual rhythms that address the compulsions, vices, and wounds of each number that hijack our journey of growing into the likeness of Jesus. Paul says, "Speaking the truth in love, we will grow to become in every respect the mature body of him who is the head, that is, Christ. From him the whole body . . . grows and builds itself up in love, as each part does its work" (Ephesians 4:15-16). God's Spirit partners with us for growth but we have work to do. The Spiritual Rhythms section provides practices, relationships, and experiences that can make space for God and grow you into healthy maturity. Explore exercises that act like mental floss to clear out the crud in your neural pathways and default reactions. Work on triggers that Enneagram expert Jerry Wagner calls "blind spots and hot spots."

Section 7: Empathy. This section is designed to help you grow in empathy for each number. It aims to help you understand your personal biases and provides stories and practices that help you see others from God's perspective. When you resonate with how the divine compassion of God looks at others, you can bring empathy into your interactions with them.

Every chapter introduces you to a host of ordinary people who are learning how to create harmonious relationships out of their inner discord and pain. Their stories are raw and real. Reading their stories may tap into your own triggers and pain. Notice your responses. When do you numb, avoid, or judge? Can you give your full attention to the pain that is present and let it lead you to truth? These narratives can give you hope as you watch people move from

▶ blocked and defended to open and receptive;

▶ judgment to empathy;

▶ false self to true self;

▶ distraction to present to God, self, and others; and

▶ disintegration to integration.

Were it not for the guidance of the Spirit of Truth, the four of us would still be blind to how our giftings and passion can wound us as well as others. We assure you, the journey out of shame, guilt, and default triggers into your true, beautiful, created-in-the-image-of-God self is worth all the time, discomfort, and inconvenient truth. This is your path to freedom. (See Soul Resource 12.)

Soul Resources. These helpful resources are found at the back of the book. Think of them as hidden treasure that can bring harmony to your work and love. You don't need to finish the book before you comb through these resources. In fact, we suggest you begin with the first Soul Resource, "STOP for Harmony," right away. Then ask the Holy Spirit to guide you to the other Soul Resources as you work your way through the chapters. If a particular resource feels inviting or challenging, that may be the one for you. Notice both resonance and dissonance. Don't work through the resources as a to-do list. A Soul Resource that is flat for you now could be what you need next month! Let the Holy Spirit lead you. You can use these resources alone with God or process with a spiritual friend or spiritual director.

HOW TO USE THIS BOOK

Who Is This Book For?

This is not a basic introductory text for the Enneagram. It is for those who want to grow, transform, and bring health into their loving and life. The sections in each chapter are distilled Enneagram wisdom around the specific topics mentioned above. The book can be used by the following:

▶ Individuals interested in reading and engaging in practices around their three harmony numbers and finding ways to integrate them. We hope you will read all the numbers and then work with the empathy sections for each type.

▶ Groups interested in processing the Harmony Triad journey together. You will find tips on how to use this resource with a group in Soul Resource 12 at the end of the book.

▶ Spiritual directors, healthcare professionals, coaches, and pastors seeking to help their clients integrate and grow in awareness, healing, and love of God, others, and self through practices, questions, and exercises; those seeking to bring God's presence and empathy to disharmonious people and systems.

Where to Begin

The first chapter begins with the Gut/Body Triad because the body gives so many signals about our heart and head. For instance, simply slowing your breath can help you think with a clearer IQ and make you more present to God and others while using your EQ. Still, there may be good reasons to begin with another Triad. If there is trauma in your body, you may want to get grounded in your heart space first and begin with the Heart Triad. If you feel safest to begin with your own number and its harmonies, that's okay. If you sense a resistance to one of your three intelligences, you may want to begin there. However, if your head and heart are disconnected, you may want to begin with the Gut/Body Triad as it will ground you in exploring your disconnect. When in doubt, begin with the chapter that calls to you.

What If I Don't Know My Number?

If you have picked up this book as an Enneagram newbie and don't know or aren't sure of your Enneagram number, you have options. We have put them in the order we most recommend.

1. Since the Enneagram began as an oral tradition, we believe the best way to find your number is take time to explore each number with a spiritual director, soul friend(s), coach, or other trusted companion. Start with one of the centers (head, heart, or gut) and spend a week to a month with each of the three numbers. Where does the number resonate with you? What do you resist or judge in the number? How does your understanding of this number change as you sit with it? As you try on each number, invite the Spirit to reveal truth through the spiritual rhythms you engage.

2. Choose a number and work through its chapter. When you are finished, re-read the description of that number on its chapter title page. On a scale of one to ten, how does it fit you? Write that number on the side. Continue through other numbers doing the same.

3. Read through the descriptions of all the numbers on their chapter title pages. Notice which numbers resonate with you. Don't automatically choose one number. Focus on at least three numbers and then take your time trying on each one. Soul Resource 11 has some more helpful tips.

4. There are many online Enneagram assessments. While these can be useful, they do not guarantee a correct diagnosis since the results depend on how you answered the questions (e.g., Were you able to respond beyond what is expected of you in your family of origin, work place, or culture?). If you are determined to take an online assessment, we recommend Dr. Jerome Wagner's Enneagram Assessment available at www.wepss.com. The test is available for a

fee and provides information about your ability to access your head, heart, and gut intelligences. It is well worth your investment.

Read All of the Chapters

Each of us has experience with the sins and virtues, as well as the strengths and weaknesses, of every number. They are common to all humanity. Thus every chapter offers you a way to understand yourself and your relationships. Chapters not in your Harmony Triad are designed to help you find empathy for people in that space and also recognize where that number shows up in you.

Each chapter is divided into bite-sized readings that include motions of the soul exercises (indicated by ▶▶▶), Scripture engagement, and prayer practices. People have different capacities and paces for inner work. Experiment. Do what works best to keep you aware and engaged in reflection and spiritual rhythms. Try working through one section a day or a couple of chapter sections in a week. The number of exercises you do at one time depends on you. The point is to notice how the Spirit moves in your soul to give you truth about who you are—*not* simply to finish the book.

You may not fit perfectly into one of the harmony triangles. You can be very strong in a number and not in your Harmony Triad. Don't worry. Try on your Harmony Triad numbers. Maybe you have undernourished or dismissed a center of intelligence because of past experiences. See if you can get to know what you don't know.

If you are tempted to skip over chapters that don't apply to you, we encourage you to engage your IQ, EQ, and GQ to help you pursue God's empathy for every number. If you don't have the patience to tackle all the questions in every chapter, read all the stories that apply to a number. Then move to the Empathy section where the questions are designed to help you make space for God so you can notice your judgment of others and where you are being invited to view others through God's eyes.

Harmony Triads invite you to savor the goodness of your created being. Our hope is that as you integrate loving God, self, and others with all your head, heart, and gut that your relationships and your world will shift toward harmony. We celebrate how the Holy Spirit will help you release old patterns of reacting and decision making so you become all you were meant to be.

KEY TERMS

These words are deliberately used throughout this book. These terms help you access harmony, help bring intention to your awareness, and help you replace default practices with new responses. Practice makes permanent.

Consolations: Ignatius of Loyola used the word *consolation* to refer to the Holy Spirit's motions in our head, heart, and gut intelligences. Discerning the Spirit's motions of our soul through head thoughts, heart feelings, or gut inspirations creates an inner environment where guidance and discernment are possible. Ignatius urged believers to follow John's advice: "Do not believe every spirit, but test the spirits to see whether they are from God" (1 John 4:1). We move in the right direction when our choices lead toward God and bear the fruit and consolations of love, joy, peace, patience, presence, and union with God. God's Good Spirit leads people to "interior freedom from sin and disordered loves so that we can respond more generously to God's call in our life."

Desolations: Ignatius used the word *desolation* to refer to how the Holy Spirit reveals sin, distress, vice, and disharmony through head thoughts, heart feelings, and gut instincts. Desolations are a useful part of discernment. Desolations can lead us toward our need for God. Ignatius suggests that desolations can act like "spoiled children" or a "false lover." Desolations can sow doubts, confusion, and insecurity, as well as willfulness or will-lessness. It is important to notice that desolations that feel bad may actually be an invitation to depend on God.

Dismissed childlike self: As children, many of us learned to depend mostly on one of our three intelligences. We may have been rewarded for thinking (IQ) and penalized when we got emotional (EQ). So we learned to dismiss the heart's way of knowing. Or we may have been punished for big gut reactions (GQ) such as anger and encouraged to be quiet and read, so we dismissed GQ instincts as bad. Or it wasn't okay to have fun or ask questions, so we dismissed our IQ and tried to please people with EQ.

Integrating the dismissed parts of our childlike selves is part of learning to love with all our head, heart, and gut strength.

False self: Our false self is the compulsive, ego-driven, old nature. It is the deeply entrenched, externalized identity comprised of roles, personas, masks, and achievements. This automatic self is deeply egoistic and addicted to itself. The false self bases its worth almost entirely on thoughts about our body, job, education, clothes, money, car, performance, success, and more. The false self is competitive, fabricated, and grandiose. When triggered, it poses, postures, spins, hides, defends, judges, deflects, pretends, manipulates, and fears. Vices such as anger, envy, sloth, deceit, gluttony, pride, avarice, fear, and lust describe the false self behavior.

FLOW: This acronym and word captures the inner rapport and practices that weave head, heart, and gut intelligences together with love of God and neighbor. When you are in FLOW, you are:

> **F**ree—able to let go of false self reactions
> **L**oving
> **O**pen to your head, heart, and gut
> **W**ith God and reality as it is

Jesus talked about rivers of living water *flowing* out of those who trust him (John 7:38), and living water opens you to flow with God's presence. FLOW is being awake to God and self, being open and aware. When you say a wiser word than you know, when you are more loving than you feel, when you are triggered and still kind, and when you move from discord to harmony, you are in FLOW with God the Father, Son, and Spirit. When you constrict and tighten around default patterns of anxiety, fear, shame, anger, sloth, or envy, you close the FLOW to virtue and presence. Noticing where you are open or closed brings discernment and is foundational for transformation.

Harmony Triads: Each Enneagram number has an automatic center of intelligence that is found in the head, heart, or gut.

▶ Gut/Body Intelligence (GQ) includes Eights, Nines, and Ones.

▶ Heart Intelligence (EQ) includes Twos, Threes, and Fours.

▶ Head Intelligence (IQ) includes Fives, Sixes, and Sevens.

Harmony Triads connect your automatic intelligence with your other two centers of intelligence, even if you have undernourished or dismissed them. They create head, heart, and gut connections between numbers Eight, Two, and Five; Nine, Three, and Six; and One, Four, and Seven. Integrating gut (GQ), heart (EQ), and head (IQ) creates capacity to interact with multiple centers of intelligence. It also reflects the trinitarian and harmonic nature of God. Harmony takes you from compulsive to centered, from automatic to adept, and from fixation to freedom.

IQ, EQ, and GQ: These are the three intelligences and ways of knowing. They are shorthand for the intelligence quotients of head thoughts (IQ), heart emotions (EQ), and gut instincts (GQ). Head, heart, and gut all have neural receptors that respond to outside stimuli. Each of us tends to prefer or trust one or two of these intelligences more than the other(s). Harmony Triads provide pathways to integrating IQ, EQ, and GQ so that you grow in empathy and love for God and neighbor.

Motions of the soul: Ignatius uses the term *motions of the soul* to refer to God's movement in the head, heart, and gut. The Spirit's interior movement gives you the ability to love God and neighbor with your entire being: heart, mind, and gut strength. Integrating the trinity of head, heart, and gut intelligence leads to what Ignatius calls "discernment of spirits" (see 1 John 4:1). When you pay attention to gut wisdom and perspective, heart emotions and affect, and head cognition and imagination, you open yourself to more than one way of knowing and choosing. Integrating head, heart, and gut intelligence helps us "choose life so that we and future generations may truly live" (Deuteronomy 30:19, our paraphrase).

Presence: When we use the word *presence* we are referring to your ability to be present to God, self, and others with your IQ, EQ, and GQ. Who you are and what you present shapes your story with its reactions, emotions, thoughts, motives, and actions. To change these default settings you need to be present to and aware of them. You cannot change what is outside your awareness. To explore how practicing the presence of God can move you from edgy addiction to harmony with God and neighbor, see Soul Resource 8.

STOP: STOP is an acronym that can give you awareness of default reactions. STOP can return you to presence with God and others so you have freedom in the moment to make a different choice. STOP is a sign in the moment to:

See—Ask the Spirit of God to give you eyes to see and ears to hear more than what your particular number automatically sees and hears.

Trigger—Notice without judgment. What just happened in you?

Open—Open your head, heart, and gut. Breathe into your harmony and loosen the constriction around your false self and its need to automatically react.

Presence—Intentionally return to being present to God, yourself, and others.

This practice is core to your use of the Enneagram. We encourage you to use Soul Resource 1 in conjunction with every chapter as it gives STOP practices for each number.

True self: Your true self is your true, Christ-in-me self. It is the beautiful person that has existed in the mind of God from the beginning. You cannot earn your true self, for the reality of it emerges from union with God. It has nothing to do with performance or roles. It is not an image you construct or acquire. Your true self is humble, restful, open, and vulnerable. It is present to God and reflects God. It is present to others and receives others. Your true self knows its belovedness. It can give and receive love, and it expresses itself in a life of freedom and virtue.

PART I

THE GUT TRIAD:
Eights, Nines, and Ones

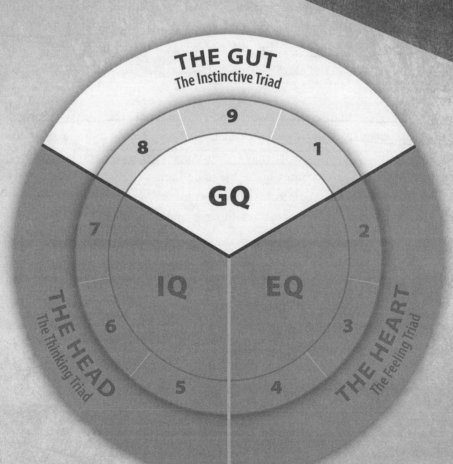

THE GUT
The Instinctive Triad

9

8

1

GQ

7

2

IQ

EQ

6

3

THE HEAD
The Thinking Triad

5

4

THE HEART
The Feeling Triad

We start this book with the Gut Triad because presence, awareness, and spiritual practices all begin in the body. You not only have a body; you *are* a body. Your body is your soul's address. Your subconscious and unconscious manifest in your body. Your body constantly signals what is going on in your heart and even your mind. In fact, there are more neurons sending information from your body (GQ) to your brain than vice versa. We believe starting in the body can give access to head and heart. However, if you have experienced body trauma, it can be difficult and painful to begin with and integrate body GQ. Take your time and feel free to begin your exploration of the Harmony Triads with head IQ or heart EQ if that feels safer to you.

THE GUT TRIAD HAS INSTINCTUAL OR GUT INTELLIGENCE (GQ)

Eights, Nines, and Ones perceive or filter the world through their basic gut instincts. This triad knows things in their bones. They say things like "I have a gut feeling . . ." Gut intelligence types bring passion and energy to their lives. They are independent people who embody agency and power. Gut people remind us that "your bodies are temples of the Holy Spirit" (1 Corinthians 6:19). As living temples, Eights reflect God's justice, Nines reflect God's peace, and Ones reflect God's goodness. The virtue of Eights is innocence, the virtue of Nines is action, and the virtue of Ones is serenity.

GQ

Healthy gut people can discern how much force, power, autonomy, and passion are required in any given moment. They are aware of their intensity and can monitor their instinctive responses so their power is user-friendly and their goodness is easy goodness. They embody Ephesians 3:20-21: "Now to him who is able to do immeasurably more than all we ask or imagine, according to his power that is at work within us, to him be glory in the church and in Christ Jesus throughout all generations, for ever and ever! Amen."

GUT DEFENSIVE POSTURE

When unhealthy gut people can't control reality, they convert their frustration into anger. This dominant fixation on anger brings energy and gives them a sense of strength and power. Eights express anger. Nines have stubborn, passive-aggressive anger. Ones suppress their anger, and it leaks out in criticism and resentment.

EXPERIENCING THE SACRED

Gut types often connect with God through their bodies. Kneeling, lifting their hands, walking, dancing, singing, experiential worship, and stillness are all body sensations that open this triad to God, life, and others. The body can answer the questions, "How am I?" and "How am I being touched or moved?" The body knows! Offering our bodies to God is a spiritual act of worship (see Romans 12:1-2).

EIGHTS

Strength Is Contemplative Love

I am not interested in power for power's sake; but I am interested in power that is moral, that is right, that is good.

MARTIN LUTHER KING JR.

I am an independent, vigorous person who is comfortable taking the lead. I want to be respected for my strength and dependability, and that is more important than being liked. I am a no-nonsense go-getter who values honesty and faithfulness. I have no room for people who choose to be weak. But I will crusade for those who are weak without choice. I will defend people I care about at any cost. I resist taking orders from people I don't respect or agree with. I will make my opinion known, my presence felt, and challenge the status quo. I want to fight injustice. I am direct, confrontational, decisive, and courageous in the heat of battle. And I can create my wars. Some people may think I'm bossy, controlling, and ready to grab others' power. But I don't want them to have power over me. I am known for having the last word.

WHO I AM AND WHO I AM NOT

Eights bear the image of God as strong. Your life resonates with Isaiah 1:17:

> Learn to do right; seek justice.
> Defend the oppressed.
> Take up the cause of the fatherless;
> plead the case of the widow.

Strength is inevitably part of your story. Stories about who we are and who we are not shape what we do, who we become, and where we get stuck. Eights have a <u>narrative about being tough, strong, and decisive</u>. You skip over the chapters of your life about tenderness, weakness, or vulnerability. This section gives you awareness of some words that shape the narrative of an Eight.

▶▶▶ **BELOVED EIGHTS**

Spend some time with the words below that describe who Eights are and are not. Circle the characteristics that resonate with your journey. Star words that express your gifts. Underline words that describe parts of your personality that are unusable by God in their present form. Put a checkmark beside characteristics that you *celebrate*.

Eights Descriptive Words List

I AM		I AM NOT	
strong	passionate	weak	ambivalent
powerful	energetic	impotent	phlegmatic
magnanimous	impulsive	small	procrastinator
self-sufficient	hardworking	needy	easy going
independent	industrious	dependent	lazy
assertive	forceful	push-over	shy
confrontational	intimidating	avoidant	meek
challenging	aggressive	wimp	timid
revolutionary	fearless	slave	fearful
in charge	hard	subordinate	soft
in control	rough	helpless	smooth
my way	tough	accommodating	bleeding heart
boss	invincible	subservient	vulnerable

➤ Which words reflect the image of God in you?

➤ Which words are you most attached to? Addicted to? Compulsive about?

➤ Which do you resist and judge the most?

➤ If you opened up to the words you resist without judgment, how might your life and relationships shift?

➤ Journal about the words that reflect how God's strength and power affect you.

▶▶▶ **GETTING TO KNOW EIGHTS**

This Eight shares how she began to know things in her body when she was three years old. She knew something others did not: "I am the one who knew bigger was better." Notice how this awareness shapes her narrative.

> My first memory attached to my gut intelligence is the Christmas I turned three years old. That year, the one big gift I received was a large doll. She was about three feet tall (she was as tall as I was!), had dark hair and dark eyes, and had a red dress. I named her "The Child" and she never had any other name! I distinctly remember feeling more powerful than and superior to my older sister, who had received a normal-sized baby doll as her gift. In my mind, it was simple: I had a child, she had a baby. Obviously, bigger was better. I don't remember that we ever talked about it or fought about it; it was just something I *knew* was true in my gut—my doll was better than my sister's.

➤ What does "The Child" story bring up in you?

➤ What is your memory of your first Eight experience?

➤ What is it like for you to know something is true instinctively and in your gut?

TRUE SELF AND FALSE SELF: THE POWERFUL PERSON

Who we are or are not comes with expression and energy. The attitudes, behaviors, and motivations of beloved Eights convey powerful energy. Your true self emerges from union with God. It is not built by powering up and balancing the scales of justice. Your false self is the compulsive, deeply entrenched, old nature—the psychological or ego self that is constructed on a complex mixture of nature, nurture, and agency. This section will help you begin to recognize compulsive and impulsive false self reactions, as well as true self FLOW that loves God, others, and self.

True Self Eights: Sacred Strength

Eights are designed to reflect God's strength and passion. A true self Eight has user-friendly power and intensity that serves the marginalized and needy. Eights are resourceful, decisive, and assertive. You drive hard, live large, initiate, champion, and take risks that can be noble and heroic. Passionate, earthy, and at home in the world, your presence says, "I am here!" Beloved Eights are comfortable wielding power and being in control. You prefer respect to approval. You don't need to fill every leadership vacuum. When Eights live present to God, others, and self, you are warm, powerful,

Breath Prayer ┃

In silence and solitude, ask God to help you see yourself clearly. Begin with breathing. Breathe in: "Made in God's image," and then breathe out: "I am not God." Spend a few minutes with this breath prayer. Feel the goodness and freedom of being made in God's image; feel the liberty of letting God be God. Breathe this prayer in and out throughout the day.

empathetic, independent, and vulnerable. As a leader, you are decisive and think about how much strength is needed in any given moment. Centered Eights embody God's sacred strength.

False Self Eights: Constrict in Control, Aggression, and Lust

Compulsive false self Eights over-identify with being strong and in control, which makes your energy user-unfriendly. Constricting around default and repetitive patterns of anger and control, you deny weakness and avoid vulnerability. This instinctive, reactive self finds it hard to soften and trust others. In your false self, Eights are unaware

of how you can be aggressive, confrontational, oppressive, self-centered, self-righteous, domineering, insensitive, and prone to excess. Although lust is the vice of the Eight, we use this word to reflect the intensity or force that drives the Eight to power up and take control. These lusty, tough, bossy, "go big or go home" personalities often get things done through intimidation and autonomy rather than collaboration. You take on injustices with your own brand of justice. Eights who can't be the boss or lead the charge may act out or pull away. If you can't call the shots, direct the program, right the wrongs, and have *the* last word, you may take your marbles and leave.

►►► TRUE OR FALSE SELF

As you think about your true and false self, consider these questions. Notice what comes up for you; notice without judgment. What questions particularly invite you to jot down or journal responses?

➤ How do true self Eight characteristics show up in your relationships with others?

➤ Where do false self Eight qualities show up in your relationships with others? How does anger show up? ("I've had enough!") How does guilt show up? ("I haven't done enough!") How do you pull away or act out when you don't have control?

Gut Reactions to Gain Control

This reading highlights the disciples' gut reaction to people they couldn't control, and Jesus' response to resistance. Notice who he "rebukes."

As the time approached for him to be taken up to heaven, Jesus resolutely set out for Jerusalem. And he sent messengers on ahead, who went into a Samaritan village to get things ready for him; but the people there did not welcome him, because he was heading for Jerusalem. When the disciples James and John saw this, they asked, "Lord, do you want us to call fire down from heaven to destroy them?" But Jesus turned and rebuked them. Then he and his disciples went to another village. (Luke 9:51-56)

1. When does "calling down fire" show up as your go-to, ego response?

2. Who are the Samaritans in your life that trigger you to power up? How easy would it have been for you to just go on to another village?

3. Jesus didn't rebuke those who didn't welcome him. He rebuked the Eight-like, call-down-fire reaction from his own followers. What might true self Eight energy look like in this instance?

> ➤ What makes you constrict your muscle (power and control)? What is a cue to relax your muscle?

> ➤ How do you feel the difference between centered, true self energy and edgy, false self energy?

HARMONY: STRENGTH IS CONTEMPLATIVE LOVE

Eights are often thought of as the powerful number, but you are much more than just one number! You bear the image and harmony of a three-in-one God. When beloved Eights are present to their head and heart intelligence, they harmonize and FLOW with the contemplation of Fives (IQ) and the care of Twos (EQ). This section creates awareness of how FLOW is the unique gift of the Harmony Triads.

In harmony and FLOW, an Eight's instinct for justice flows with thoughtfulness and compassion. Your just action rights the wrongs in ways that respond wisely to need and oppression with the IQ of a Five and express sacrificial love of others with the EQ of a Two.

►►► MORE THAN A TYPE

This Eight shares how she detached from the addiction to power and opened to the wisdom and will of another. When lusty, earthy Eights embrace your compassionate strength (EQ), you become approachable, protective, and nurturing. When you integrate your thoughtfulness (IQ), you slow down to observe. "Ready, *fire*, aim" transforms into "Ready, *aim*, fire." No longer relying solely on your gut instincts (GQ), you become discerning. Notice how this Eight integrates her head and heart intelligence with her gut intelligence.

> As a child, I needed to protect and guard myself. Weakness made me vulnerable and put me in a place where someone could (or would) use my words or emotions against me. This threat and the unconscious belief that people were against me made me confrontational and angry with others. It also made me deny the soft part of my feelings and emotions. The Harmony Triads gave me tools to integrate a Two's warmth with my power. The Fives' detachment helps moderate my passionate gut responses. Silence, solitude, and breath prayer "unhook" me from anger and need to control.

> ➤ When do you ignore tenderness and vulnerability in the heat of the moment? How could a warm-hearted response actually express your user-friendly strength?

> ➤ How do you ignore the time it takes to think things through and instead go with your gut? How might slowing down and waiting connect you to love of God and neighbor, as well as help you get the job done?

> ➤ Imagine yourself tempering your energy for justice with contemplative love, an energy that produces warmth rather than heat. What do you see?

▶▶▶ **GQ, EQ, IQ**

This directing and challenging Eight courageously embraces contemplative waiting (IQ) and love (EQ). Notice how the willingness to pause warmed her actions with wisdom and care.

> My father's death shut down my Two heart center and the deep, loving side of me. I wanted to be able to love, but love seemed lost to me; so I pushed full steam ahead. When I tried to reach out to people, they would walk away. Right now, as a relationship fails, I sense God's invitation to wait and observe (IQ) with love (EQ). I am not to plow through and shut off love. I am to contemplate what is and not react. Harmony Triads help me realize I have GQ, IQ, and EQ within me. God created me to be a whole person. What a gift! I am an Eight coming alive to all that is possible.

➢ When Eights engage their head, they observe, detach, and moderate their gut agency to learn more about an issue. Where do you see IQ in yourself?

➢ When Eights engage their heart, they see people and events with compassion and not just as problems to be solved. Where do you see EQ in yourself?

➢ What is it like for you to have IQ, EQ, and GQ?

Reactions to Wrongdoing

In this story, Jesus tells us about how enemies sabotaged a man's harvest. Notice the distinction between the responses of the man and his servants.

> Jesus told them another parable: "The kingdom of heaven is like a man who sowed good seed in his field. But while everyone was sleeping, his enemy came and sowed weeds among the wheat, and went away. When the wheat sprouted and formed heads, then the weeds also appeared.
>
> "The owner's servants came to him and said, 'Sir, didn't you sow good seed in your field? Where then did the weeds come from?'
>
> "'An enemy did this,' he replied.
>
> "The servants asked him, 'Do you want us to go and pull them up?'
>
> "'No,' he answered, 'because while you are pulling the weeds, you may uproot the wheat with them. Let both grow together until the harvest.'" (Matthew 13:24-30)

1. Who do you identify with in this parable?

2. When have you wanted to power up to destroy evil?

3. How are you with waiting and letting things unfold when something bad is happening? Can you imagine acting like the man in this story? What is it like for you?

HEALING CHILDHOOD HURTS: OPENING TO INNOCENCE

Children are wired for resilience. Still, residual childhood distress can leak into adult Eight relationships. Eight children can lose the message, "The world can be trusted." The default message you can learn is, "Don't trust; don't show weakness." To survive, you toughened up and pushed back. Your defenses protected and mitigated against connectedness and thoughtfulness.

When these messages get triggered in adult Eight interactions, then raw, ragged, unprocessed pain can erupt and sabotage the FLOW of an Eight's loving strength. Suddenly a needy four-year-old inside you begins to act out and call the shots. Defaulting to the false self, Eights can get stuck on the edge of intense anger, lust, and powering up. These controlling and visceral gut instincts are not necessarily the same things as feelings. They arise almost unbidden and seek to dominate rather than connect. Eights who think it is weak to process past pain, defense structures, and childhood lies need to hear how much courage it takes to explore these things. It is part of healing and growth in loving God and others and self with your whole self—head, heart, and gut.

The Harmony Triad offers a way for Eights to partner with God's healing presence and reclaim your virtue of innocence. Innocence is disarming, vulnerable, and noncontrolling. Innocence can be reclaimed again and again.

> ### Prayer of Ignatius of Loyola
>
> *Allow this prayer of Ignatius of Loyola, which addresses the heart, head, and gut energy of the Enneagram Triads, to become your prayer.*
>
> *It is my will to win over the whole world, to overcome evil with good [GQ], to turn hatred aside with love [EQ], to conquer all the forces of death [GQ].*
>
> *Take, Lord, and receive all of my liberty, my memory, my understanding [IQ], and my entire will, All I have I call my own.*
>
> *You have given all to me. To you, Lord, I return it.*

▶▶▶ RECEIVING THE DISMISSED CHILDLIKE SELF

Receiving your dismissed child can heal and help you recover the innocent and trusting part of you again. Remember, within every passionate and gutsy Eight there is a tender, caring Two who wants to connect with others and wonders if your big emotions exclude you from love. There might also be a private little Five who is detached and unwilling to share your time and energy with others. To recognize where you dismissed your childlike self, pay attention to where you may have ignored tenderness (EQ) and thoughtfulness (IQ).

In this story, look for the heart-full, Two inner child who couldn't trust her vulnerability to others. Be curious about how she dismissed her larger-than-life Eight because it wasn't "safe" to use her voice and show up.

My long battle with my GQ began when I was five. I would "sense" that something was right or wrong and would say so. The authorities (parents, grandparents, aunts, uncles, pastors, church leaders, and teachers) told me I didn't know what I was talking about. I couldn't know because girls/children/women didn't have wisdom to know anything that didn't come from a man. If I tried to share a feeling, I was told, "Don't feel like that." I knew in my gut that they were *wrong*! But if I led with my gut anger and confrontation, it just led to deeper rifts in relationships. So my everyday life became a persistent battle of holding back my gut instincts to be "nice." Being alienated from and dismissing my Eight self was exhausting. Sometimes I just wanted to hide.

➤ What might it be like to have an embattled narrative shape you? What do you dismiss and hold on to?

➤ Within the Eight, there is a Five child who hides and wonders, "Do I have energy for this?" Where does this message show up in your life?

➤ Within the sometimes bullying Eight, there is a gentle heart who wonders, "Will I be loved or rejected?" Notice when your inner child asks this question.

►►► JOURNALING YOUR DISMISSED CHILDLIKE SELF

Integrating and accessing your head and heart can help you moderate the strength of your responses. Accessing your heart (EQ) softens your strength, making it user friendly. Integrating your head (IQ) slows down instinctive reactions. Checking out what your heart feels and your head perceives gives you more than instincts to work with on your path to harmony.

Journal about what you did with tenderness that made you feel weak or vulnerable. Courageously explore when you began to defend yourself with an inner hustler that just muscled through. This is hard work. Feel free to choose among the questions and return to other questions at another time.

➤ What is your story about finding the world untrustworthy? What default reactions and triggers of your childhood self still operate today?

➤ Where do you dismiss your power or overpower because of anger or past trauma? What is causing you to muscle up right now? What is that about? If you softened to nurture yourself and others, what might happen?

➤ Where has your trust been repaired/healed or increased/solidified?

Eights tend to be playful and tender with children. What would it look like for you to open up to the childlike innocence that makes you less intimidating to others and gives you the hearing you want?

Immediate and intense Eights have a default stance of "just do it." You find God's invitation to wait frustrating and difficult. Waiting feels like a waste of time and sabotages control. Thus spiritual practices of waiting and slowing put beloved Eights in a place to know who you are when you can't be in control. It may be helpful for you to read the chapter "Invitation to Wait" in *Invitations from God* by Adele Ahlberg Calhoun.

When you feel your inner hustler bullying, pushing, and charging ahead, consider the possible collateral damage. How much intensity do you really need to use? What might unfold if you slowed down and took a pause? This week practice intentionally slowing. Drive more slowly. Talk more slowly. Eat more slowly. What happens as you open and create some space around what you are doing? Notice how slowing moderates your intensity.

DISCERNMENT: CONSOLATIONS AND DESOLATIONS

Ignatius of Loyola taught that God's Empowering Spirit moves in all three centers of intelligence—head, heart, and gut. When making a decision, Ignatius suggested noticing your consolations and desolations by asking: What does my heart feel? What does my mind think? What does my gut sense?

Consolations point Eights toward God's presence and a power that doesn't force or coerce you. Consolations are evidence that an Eight is heading in the direction of GQ agency that IQ ponders how to stand in EQ solidarity with others. Desolations such as shame, lust, and anger distort the FLOW of God's strength. Desolations alert Eights that you have fallen into your false self and lost inner freedom to discern well. (More information on Harmony Triad discernment is found in Soul Resource 5.)

Eights experience consolations such as sacred strength, contemplative power, insightful justice, compassionate confidence, warm direction, detached decisions, enlightened courage, and holy

Healing Prayer

When Eights process your wounds in the presence of a God who is strong enough to lovingly hold you—intensity, lust, anger, and all—you open yourself to change. Healing prayer can help Eights recover your childlike innocence and give you access to emotions other than anger.

This is a way to do healing prayer on your own. Relax into silence and solitude. Breathe deeply. Don't force it. Become present to God and yourself. Ask God to show you where you need ongoing healing. Wait quietly for God to bring a past sorrow or trauma to mind. When something comes to mind, follow this simple trail of healing prayer.

* *Imagine yourself and Jesus back in the memory. Get your bearings. Where is Jesus? Where are you?*

* *What are you feeling? (mad, shamed, weak, powerful, vulnerable, alone, or something else)*

* *Do these feelings remind you of a time you had similar reactions? You can go with Jesus to that place and time or stay where you are.*

* *Continue to name what you feel in your experience. Ask Jesus if these feelings point to a lie you began to believe at that time. Give it a name.*

* *What is Jesus saying to you about this lie? Listen. Is there an image, word, or phrase that he speaks to you?*

* *Repeat the truth you have heard from Jesus about yourself gently and frequently. Let the truth be an antidote that lets the pain go into Jesus and sets you free.*

vulnerability. Consolations can lead Eights to relinquish control and trust that God is at work in what is. This is freedom.

Eights experience desolations such as lust, arrogance, domination, bullying, insensitivity, forceful confrontation, powering up, self-righteousness, judgment, control, excess, and anger. These desolations leave you bound.

▶▶▶ PRESENT TO WHAT'S HAPPENING INSIDE

Both desolations and consolations can give us a thread to follow that leads toward love of God, neighbor, and self. Here we focus on consolations and desolations particular to Eights. This Eight is studying the map of his soul. He notices signposts of desolation in his messy life that block discernment. Notice how the consolations and desolations of this Eight direct him toward healing and God.

> My life right now is messy and chaotic. Relationships are broken and tense. I don't like this uncomfortable and uncontrollable place (desolation). So I automatically block what I don't want to see. Which also means I miss seeing some good things God provides in the mess. When I remember that my defense mechanism of denial is at the bottom of my resistance, I remember that I can choose to open my eyes and ears in the chaos and be present to what is (consolation). When I am in presence, I'm not trying to control and I see more. But being present is challenging for me. I need my EQ and IQ to pull me away from the edge of ruthless strength and center me in receptivity and gratitude (consolation).

> When is your instinctive response to desolation "messy and chaotic"?

> Name a current desolation. Check God's motions in your gut. Is your gut just mad and pushing against your desolation? How is the desolation leading you to God?

Prayer Practice for Waiting

God waits. And so do we. Waiting is especially hard for Eights who resist this daily given. When you wait or go slow, breathe deeply into your inability to control time. Breathe in: "God you are here." Breathe out: "I have strength to wait." Let this breath prayer open you in developing the muscle of patience. To fight waiting doesn't make things move faster. Something unexpected might happen if you wait for God to show up.

▶▶▶ DESOLATION AND DENIAL

Defensive and aloof Eights have the default defense mechanism of denial. Denial refuses to admit the truth about oneself. Denial protects Eights from being vulnerable or accountable. Early on, Eights denied your need of others and took responsibility for protecting yourself by acting strong and autonomous. You denied the presence of helplessness, weakness, subordination, and tenderness and treated these traits as though they did not exist. But they do exist in us all. Without judgment, notice where you constrict in desolation and denial.

➤ Looking back on your life, when has denial kept you stuck and unable to move forward? How has denial impacted your decision making?

➤ Where does your body hold the denial of pain and frustration? What do you want to do with that denial?

➤ How does revving up serve or hinder the FLOW of strong love for God and neighbor? How can awareness of this help you choose what to do?

▶▶▶ CONSOLATIONS AND INNOCENCE

The Spirit's invitation to consolation engages heart presence that feels for others as well as head presence that tells an Eight's inner hustler to "take a time-out!" Engaging EQ and IQ helps Eights get reacquainted with your inner, innocent child—the one who knows how to play and trust. Innocence is open and teachable. It accepts that others may know better than you.

God's Spirit calls Eights out of denial into innocence that depends on and is vulnerable to others. Vulnerability takes real strength. It's not wimpy. Don't deny that recovering innocence is important. It matters as much as changing the world, landing the deal, and passing the legislation. The world needs leaders who are "as shrewd as snakes and as innocent as doves" (Matthew 10:16).

➤ Describe a situation in which the Holy Spirit invited you out of denial and into an innocence that trusts others. What happened? What consolations came to you?

➤ When has innocence helped you FLOW with trusting, user-friendly strength?

SPIRITUAL RHYTHMS FOR EIGHTS

He (Jesus) is the one we proclaim, admonishing and teaching everyone with all wisdom, so that we may present everyone fully mature in Christ. To this end I strenuously contend with all the energy Christ so powerfully works in me. (Colossians 1:28-29)

Eights are equipped to "strenuously contend." Your energy makes you a dynamo. It is your great gift. Paul says that this energy is not an end in itself. Your energy exists for the sake of others. It is not about you alone. Practicing the wise use of your energy creates new neural pathways. As you "contend," partner with the Spirit to become "mature in Christ." Discernment takes spiritual maturity. It is not the same thing as to blast off. Attending to the Spirit's motions in your soul on a daily basis matures and ripens an Eight's fruitfulness so you have strength to lovingly and wisely direct.

These spiritual rhythms are all ways Eights can lean into God's invitations to transformation and mind renewal. Not every practice will be the one for you. Say yes to the practices that best capture your desire to be with God right now.

▶▶▶ PRACTICING PRESENCE: EIGHTS

Re-read the FLOW definition in the Key Terms section. Notice the presence of Trinitarian harmony.

> Father, Son, and Spirit belong and flow together.
> Head, heart, and gut belong and flow together.
> Faith, love, and hope belong and flow together.

Divine harmony calls Eights to intentionally practice integrating your force with IQ and EQ so your power reflects God's own sacred strength. Let the following meditative prayer move through your entire created being so it holds you together. Staying with this prayer for a season can help Eights lead with EQ and IQ.

Find a comfortable and awake position. Remember that the Spirit of God dwells within you and prays for you. Ask God to give you an open and receptive head, heart, and gut.

Gut Presence: Put yourself in the presence of the Spirit. Fill your belly with breath. Notice what is happening in your body without judgment. Let your body tell you what it knows. Is there something your body wants to do in this prayer? Do that. Experience your force—your big energy. Give thanks for your ability to "strenuously contend." How and when does your body react rather than let vulnerability in? Where do you push in or lash out before observing?

Heart Presence: Put yourself in the presence of Jesus. Breathe into your heart space. Feel your tenderness. Notice your heart's need to be held and cherished. Breathe in and create even more space around your heart. Notice your childlikeness and kindness. Invite self-compassion. Welcome softer emotions; name them and breathe: "I can trust you." Tell Jesus what in you needs some care, a kind word, or a soothing touch. How does Jesus respond to you?

Head Presence: Put yourself in the presence of the Wise Creator. Breathe into your magnificent mind. Breathe into your head and shoulders. Feel their weight and tightness. Breathe into your intellect. Observe your life in the body. What does your head tell you? What is it like to trust information and perspectives rather than your gut instinct? Is there a place where your gut goes "Ready, *fire*, aim"? Ask your head to show you how to go "Ready, *aim*, fire."

Pray into your Harmony:
Strength Is Contemplative Love
"Strength is contemplative love" is a breath prayer that helps you engage the life-giving intellect of Fives that can hold things loosely, observe, detach, and learn more about an issue before reacting; as well as the tender heart of Twos that is loving, nurturing, warm, and able to connect with how others are feeling.

Memorizing this prayer brings awareness of what is most true about you to real-life situations. You are more than your type. Breathe it in as you

> Human progress [Five IQ] is neither automatic nor inevitable.... Every step toward the goal of justice [Eight GQ] requires sacrifice [Two EQ], suffering, and struggle; the tireless exertions and passionate concern of dedicated individuals.
>
> **MARTIN LUTHER KING JR. (WITH OUR ADDITIONS)**

prepare to take the field, scale the mountain, launch the company, lead the board meeting, or face the music. Anytime you feel yourself get triggered and are tempted to forget who you are, breathe "strength is contemplative love." Let go of the constriction around power and control that keeps you stuck in your gut. Open to the FLOW of God's loving power. Then call on all your God-given strength.

FLOW Practice for Eights

In FLOW, Eights are **F**ree, **L**oving, **O**pen, and **W**ith. You stand in the presence of the three-in-one God and integrate heart and head with your strong effort. Strength gets channeled through the Christian virtues of faith, hope, and love. When you notice that you are constricting and stuck in powering up, when you tighten around leading and grab the helm, this is the moment to breathe and ask the Spirit to give you inner freedom to stay with and open to your head and heart. Ask, "How much force or energy do I need to keep love flowing as I get this job done?" Feel the freedom to dial it back. At the end of the day, log what happened when you were not in FLOW. Celebrate when God's strength flowed through you. Confess when it didn't. Begin again tomorrow.

Practice Confession

Vulnerability and transparency about who you are connects you to God and others. Confess your:

- *Vice of self-reliance and lust:* ask God and a trusted accountability partner to help you make the journey to vulnerability and innocence.
- *Anger:* "I've had enough." Name where you have lashed out or backed out. Ask God to help you send your energy in the direction of love.

- *Guilt:* "I haven't done enough." Ask God for grace to see when "this is enough."
- *Shame:* "I am too much; I am too brash, lusty, driven, vengeful . . ."

Receive words of assurance: "Before a holy and righteous God, as God's Beloved Eight, you stand completely in the clear."

Breath Prayers

Notice your magnificent breath. Feel the oxygen fill your lungs and lift your chest. Follow your breath in and down. Take time to notice what is happening in your gut. Feel the strength of your created life as you breathe in: "You have formed my inward parts; I am powerfully and wonderfully made . . . may my soul know that very well." Spend a few minutes with this breath prayer. Follow your breath to trust that you don't have to be the all-powerful Creator.

Keep breathing into your body. Breathing in from the soles of your feet, fill your belly with breath, and continue breathing to the crown of your head. Feel your experience. Breathe into your head, your heart, and your gut. Without judgment, notice whatever comes up. If memories come, welcome them with your wise, loving strength. Stay with them. Take action to stay inside and hold yourself in a loving way.

- ❖ *Inhale: "Made in God's image."*
  Exhale: "I am not God."
- ❖ *Inhale: "God, you are here."*
  Exhale: "I have strength to wait."
- ❖ *Inhale: "Strength is,"*
  exhale: "contemplative love."

Practice the Presence of People

Moderate your gut reactions to people by being present and listening until they stop talking.

> ▶ When you want to get the job done, you can run over others. Let the people in the room matter. Take a moment to see them. Say their names to yourself with kindness.

> ▶ Notice when people seem threatened or overwhelmed by you. Is that the response you want them to have? Ask some trusted friends or colleagues, "What is it like to be on the other side of me?"

> ▶ In conversations, make sure you have heard a person before you launch in and hold forth. Ask them, "Did I get what you are saying?" Ask, "Is there more?" When they say "no more," you have practiced their presence.

> ▶ When you have no more bandwidth for practicing the presence of people, offer an explanation. Say "I need to focus," or "I'm in a groove; can I get back to you to-morrow?" or "Sorry to be abrupt. I can't focus on anything else. I'm under a self-imposed (or real) deadline."

Practice Trusting

Trust something besides you and your gut. Take a risk—risk is the other side of the coin of trust.

> ▶ Ask God for the grace to appreciate and trust heart people and their emotions. Validate someone's emotions.

> ▶ Ask for humility to learn from head people who don't see things as instinctively as you do. Validate someone's ideas.

> ▶ Let go of control, join in, be a participant, and trust that things can unfold in a good way, even if you aren't leading, because God is present.

> ▶ When you want to act like an independent operator or when you don't want to be told what to do by anyone, you are on your edge, trusting yourself alone. What is God wanting to say to you about this? How can you trust enough to collaborate with someone rather than go it alone?

Practice Empathy and Understanding

Your strength and gifting to serve the marginalized, oppressed, and needy becomes more powerful when packaged in empathy and compassion.

> ▶ Express heart concern for others as you take on the world. Relationships don't work without empathy and compassion.

> ▶ Notice when your energetic or over-bearing presence dismisses what others think and feel. Apologize and say, "I didn't mean to come on so strong. What am I missing here?"

> ▶ When you listen to people's stories and opinions, be curious and use your IQ, EQ, and GQ. Monitor your gut reaction to challenge and debate. You don't need to power up. How could you have a good conversation without being threatening?

Practice Detachment

Detach from your agenda, plans, and way.

> ▶ Detachment is the gift of your head IQ. When you are so attached to your ideas, expectations, and leadership that you can't open and let go, it's time to pray: "God, your will; nothing more, nothing less, and nothing else." This prayer loosens your muscle and constriction around control.

▶ Detachment opens a space to hear or create something new.

▶ Step back and consider how much you need to force your agenda. Less just might be more.

▶ Detach from the need to have others be as committed to success, truth, or perseverance as you are. They have their own attachments.

Blessing for the Beloved Eight

As we close this section, take time to breathe in this blessing and create space in your soul.

May the Holy Three bless your vulnerable journey home to your true self.

May God the Father give you wisdom to understand that strength is made perfect in weakness.

May the heart of Jesus infuse and compel your heart's passions, helping you to be tender with yourself.

May the Holy Spirit ground you with patience to wait for all that will be accomplished in you.

May the sacred strength of the Trinity lead you on your road, empowering you and loving you.

Empathy for EIGHTS

You may not control all the events that happen to you, but you can decide not to be reduced by them.

MAYA ANGELOU

Children need to find their caretakers trustworthy. Eights had caregivers that undermined their trust. To survive, they had to toughen up. When we understand how the power-and-push strength of an Eight developed, we create space for empathy. Here you can explore your responses to Eights and how you might grow in empathy, seeing them as God does.

Empathy is a true self response that harmonizes and breaks down the we/they divide. You may think Eights are like hit-and-run drivers who knock you down and keep going. Or you may love their intensity, entrepreneurial passion, and no-nonsense ways. Understanding how an Eight's lust for power and intensity developed can create compassionate and empathetic interactions with them.

This Eight describes how shame around her gut responses caused her to dismiss her true self. Sit with this story. Allow compassion for this powerful, vulnerable Eight to rise in you.

When I was in kindergarten, my best friend was killed. My parents pulled me away from my siblings and explained what happened. They also told me that I was not to talk about it. I was not allowed to go to my friend's funeral. She was gone—no goodbye, no closure, no way to process what had happened. I still feel the knot of unfairness in my gut; to behave this way toward someone I loved dearly. I was sad, angry, and frustrated, and had nowhere to go with all those emotions.

My father was a profoundly damaged Eight, and I lived in horror that I might be like him. Even when my Eight brother's gut responses were approved and applauded, I didn't want to be an Eight. Their deep, brazen, gut reactions to my Eight-ness made me feel guilty about my strong presence. To survive, I functioned as a deformed Two until my mid-thirties. The depths of family misogyny and patriarchy that dismissed my female Eight are bottomless. It has taken a long time to accept that being a strong Eight is a gift from God.

1. As you consider the Eight story, notice:
   - What are you thinking about this Eight?
   - What are you feeling about this Eight?
   - What is your gut instinct about this Eight?

2. When have you constricted around something not being fair? How have you wanted to make it right?

3. How does an Eight's intensity mitigate against connection and trust, torpedoing empathy? How can this give you empathy for Eights?

UNDERSTANDING THE DEFENSE MECHANISM OF DENIAL

Another Eight explores the formation of her defense mechanism.

When I was about eight or nine years old, I was in the back seat of the car while my dad was driving under the influence. I wanted to be afraid, but I refused. I denied my feelings and vulnerability, put on my armor, and developed an unconscious belief that it wasn't safe to rely on others to protect me. I protected myself. I denied my vulnerability and powered up to stay in control. As a teenager, I lost respect for my dad and became verbally challenging. As conflict escalated, I dismissed and guarded my heart. It hurt too much to want love from someone who wasn't capable of it.

1. This Eight denied her vulnerability in order to "stay in control." What do you want to say to this Eight?

2. Get inside this Eight's story. When have you dismissed your heart out of fear or hurt? What was it like for you?

3. How might you join the Holy Spirit by praying for an Eight you know?

RELATING TO AN EIGHT

We find grace to see things from an Eight's point of view when we remember that under the tough exterior of an Eight is a tender child who powered up to protect themselves.

- Eights can seem brusque; don't take it personally. They aren't trying to hurt you and are unaware that they have.

- If you feel hurt by an Eight, tell them. Eights trust and respect people who stand up for themselves, so meet them with intensity and truth.

- Honor the courage it takes for Eights to show up with gentleness and vulnerability. Speak your appreciation, but don't gush or flatter.

- Eights often look like they don't need or want affection, but brief purposeful signs of affection are welcome.

- Eights can feel like it is "me against the world." Show them you are on their side by being responsible and with the program.

- Don't make excuses or spin the truth. Eights have a nose for BS.

- Eights like to battle injustice. They have compassion for true weakness and/or limitations, but they have no patience for self pity. If your need is genuine, they will help.

The following list summarizes key characteristics of Eights. Consider your responses to these characteristics.

- *Authentic, true self:* Powerful, strong
- *Compulsive, false self:* Lustful
- *Virtue leading back to true self:* Innocence

- *Personality style:* Challenger
- *Work style:* Insister, asserter, decisive
- *Leadership/action style:* Director
- *Thinking style:* Dialectical
- *Relational style:* Decider
- *Relationships:* Challenging
- *Core motivation:* Power, control
- *Negative fixation:* Anger, guilt
- *Narrative:* "I've had enough," "I haven't done enough"
- *Communication:* Blunt, direct, truthful
- *Eight with a Seven wing:* More joyful, responsive, extroverted
- *Eight with a Nine wing:* More calm, relaxed, receptive
- *Basic fear:* Lack of control, independence
- *Basic desire:* To be strong, in control
- *Drive:* To resist vulnerability, to exercise power and control

Based on the description above:

1. How does it feel to be an Eight? Which descriptors give clues on how to relate to Eights?

2. Is there a better way to say what is true of Eights?

3. Eights are intense and like energetic exchanges. What is it like to meet the strength of an Eight with your own gut intensity and strength?

4. Eights want to be appreciated for their ability to lead and accomplish. How can you express your appreciation for an Eight?

NINES

Peace Effects Team

We can never obtain peace in the outer world until we make peace with ourselves.
DALAI LAMA

I am a mediator who feels most comfortable when I bring peace and harmonize people. I naturally see everyone's side in a conflict and how each perspective is worthy of consideration. I recognize people's agendas, and my diplomacy helps them make peaceful resolutions. Negotiating peace and accommodating the feelings of others matter more than my own feelings. Dismissing my ideas, opinions, and feelings can make me appear passive or indecisive, but I prefer to save my decisiveness for the important issues. I tend to keep my anger in check. Expressing it is so unpeaceful. I don't like confrontation and discomfort in relationships. I am adaptable, calm, nonjudgmental, and supportive. If I can see myself in all nine types, this may be my style.

WHO I AM AND WHO I AM NOT

Nines bear the image of God's own peace. Your life resonates with Isaiah 26:3: "You (God) will keep in perfect peace / those whose minds are steadfast, / because they trust in you."

Peace and stability are inevitably part of your story. Stories about who we are and who we are not shape what we do and where we numb and do *not* do. Nines often tell a story about how accepting, good-natured, and relaxed you are. You see yourself as chill and diplomatic, and you skip over the chapters of your life about passive-aggressiveness or numbing out. This section gives you awareness of some words that shape the narrative of a Nine.

►►► BELOVED NINES

Spend some time with the words below that describe who Nines are and are not. Circle the characteristics that resonate with your journey. Star words that express your gifts. Underline words that describe parts of your personality that are unusable by God in their present form. Put a checkmark beside characteristics that you *celebrate*.

Nines Descriptive Words List

I AM		I AM NOT	
peaceful	stable	frantic	erratic
harmonious	avoid conflict	hassled	conflicted
fair	patient	biased	pushy
comfortable	ecumenical	edgy	bigoted
serene	inclusive	driven	excluding
relaxed	cool	energetic	hotheaded
easygoing	laid back	ambitious	Type A
balanced	calm	imbalanced	upset
easy	accommodating	aggressive	controlling
noble plodding	uninvolved	quick	passionate
unflappable	uncommitted	emotionally expressive	decisive
unexcitable	creature of habit	nervous	unpredictable

> ➤ Which words reflect the image of God in you?

> ➤ Which words are you most attached to? Addicted to? Compulsive about?

> ➤ Which words do you resist and judge the most?

> ➤ If you opened up to the words you resist without judgment, how might your life and relationships shift?

> ➤ Journal about the words that reflect how God brings you calm.

►►► GETTING TO KNOW NINES

This Nine shares the journey that began when he was in elementary school. Early on, this Nine discovered some things felt right. He knew in his body that inclusion and bringing peace was internally satisfying and outwardly empowering. Experiences that mediate and bring peace still form his life story today in his work as a colead pastor.

> Growing up, I was good at sports and liked to be one of the team captains so I could pick the players I wanted. I remember picking the players nobody else wanted because I could sense the fear and anxiety of the kids picked last. I enjoyed challenges; but most of all I enjoyed bringing peace to those who could find experiences like this unpleasant. I felt responsible for dispelling their panic and agitation. I didn't want the bullies on the field to dominate the nobodies. And it seemed right to include the overlooked and marginalized on my team. I could sense in my body when things were equal and all was well. The opposing team always seemed at peace with it as well. No conflict. No problem.

➤ How does this story invite you to understand what makes this Nine tick?

➤ What is your memory of your first Nine experience?

➤ What is it like for you to sense you can bring everyone together? What happens in your gut space?

TRUE SELF AND FALSE SELF: THE PEACEFUL PERSON

Who we are or are not comes with expression and energy. The attitudes, behaviors, and motivations of beloved Nines convey peaceful presence. Your true self emerges from union with God. It is diplomatic and engages in the love and service of God and neighbor. Your false self constricts around default and repetitive patterns of inertia, procrastination, and stubbornness. This section will help you begin to recognize compulsive and impulsive false self reactions, as well as true self FLOW that loves God and others and self.

True Self Nines: Sacred Peace

Nines show us God's peace. You are accepting, trusting, stable, good-natured, kind-hearted, relaxed, easygoing, and supportive. Your self-effacing and non-judgmental approach to others creates acceptance and ease. In conflict, true self Nines release your agenda and work for a win-win solution. Your easygoing manner makes collaboration natural. When Nines are present to God, you FLOW with grace, support, and compassion, and are patient with tasks and relationships. Unflappable Nines bring mediating energy to conflict and peace issues. You engage and feel your heart. You engage your head and bring stability without indecision. Nines embody an indomitable and all-embracing divine harmony that brings sacred peace. Uniting people, healing conflicts, and bringing effective calm, you offer your virtue of action.

Breath Prayer

In silence and solitude, ask God to help you see yourself clearly. Begin with breathing. Breathe in: "Made in God's image," and then breathe out: "I am not avoidant or asleep." Spend a few minutes with this breath prayer. Feel the goodness and freedom of being made in God's image; feel the liberty of being actively engaged and awake. Breathe this prayer in and out throughout the day.

False Self Nines: Constrict in Avoidance,
Sloth, and Passive Aggression

Non-transforming Nines disconnect. When inner and outer conflict becomes too overcharged or demanding, you abdicate responsibility. You pull the plug on connection; or seeking peace at any price you merge with others' ideas and opinions. You no longer pay attention to your needs, feelings, or anger. When Nines are numb to the presence of God and others, you become indecisive, spaced out, apathetic, undisciplined, unassertive, passive-aggressive, and stubborn. False self Nines neglect your desires, shut off emotion, disappear, and act like everything is fine. This leads to the Nine's vice of sloth and procrastination. The false, automatic self of the Nine says "whatever." A Nine in a "whatever" state can lose touch with your essential self.

▶▶▶ TRUE OR FALSE SELF

As you think about your true and false self, consider the following questions. Notice what comes up for you; notice without judgment. What questions particularly invite you to jot down or journal responses?

➤ How do true self Nine characteristics show up in your relationships?

➤ Where do false self Nine qualities show up in your relationships? How does anger show up? ("I am running out of energy" or "I've had enough.") What do you do to lower your desire to withdraw?

➤ What makes you constrict and shut down your gut power and agency? What is a cue to open and show up with your presence?

➤ How do you feel the difference between centered, true self energy and edgy, false self energy?

HARMONY: PEACE EFFECTS TEAM

Nines are often identified as the peaceful number, but you are much more than just one number! You bear the image and harmony of a three-in-one God. When beloved Nines integrate your EQ and IQ, you harmonize with your peace flowing effectively like a Three (EQ) and building a team like a Six (IQ). This section creates awareness of how FLOW is the unique gift of the Harmony Triads.

In harmony and FLOW, a Nine's instinct for unity flows with loyalty and effectiveness. Your peace initiatives bring people together in ways that form alliances with the IQ of a Six and effectively negotiate harmony with the EQ of a Three.

▶▶▶ MORE THAN A TYPE

This story describes how a Nine integrates EQ, IQ, and GQ in ways that help her show up like a Three, and trust curiosity and questions like a Six. Integrating heart and head intelligence gives this overly-merging Nine the ability to voice her opinions and act. Do parts of her story resonate with you?

My goal for years was to keep the peace; keep everyone happy. I tried to shield everyone around me from pain, disappointment, or trouble. I would give to their needs first. I would deny myself and forget about me in a futile attempt to keep everyone around me happy. When I'm unaware, I can't name what I want; I look for what others want. Ask me what I think, and I will remain silent and give the impression that I am in agreement. My husband says I am "benign." I want to do more than be a Nine! The Harmony Triads are helping me welcome my head and heart. I look for ways to connect with feelings and thoughts that belong to me. I check with my EQ and ask, "How do I feel about this?" I check with my IQ and ask, "What do I think about this?" I pray for the Holy Spirit to enlarge my heart and head and ground me in truth. I don't want to live on my edge and numb out. I want to breathe and practice and integrate. It's all so new, and I can fall into sloth, denial, and resistance. It's an effort to stay in FLOW. The Harmony Triads are helping me see that there is so much more to me than just Nine-ness. I have access to the commitment of a Six and the efficacy of a Three. I have just tripled in size!

To Avoid or Engage

Sometimes avoidance and inaction masquerade as peace. In this reading, Jesus addresses the false self that makes excuses to avoid action. Consider where you might use inaction to sidestep getting involved.

Jesus replied: "A certain man was preparing a great banquet and invited many guests. At the time of the banquet he sent his servant to tell those who had been invited, 'Come, for everything is now ready.'

"But they all alike began to make excuses. The first said, 'I have just bought a field, and I must go and see it. Please excuse me.'

"Another said, 'I have just bought five yoke of oxen, and I'm on my way to try them out. Please excuse me.'

"Still another said, 'I just got married, so I can't come.'

"The servant came back and reported this to his master. Then the owner of the house became angry and ordered his servant, 'Go out quickly into the streets and alleys of the town and bring in the poor, the crippled, the blind and the lame.'

"'Sir,' the servant said, 'what you ordered has been done, but there is still room.'

"Then the master told his servant, 'Go out to the roads and country lanes and compel them to come in, so that my house will be full. I tell you, not one of those who were invited will get a taste of my banquet.'" (Luke 14:16-24)

1. What comes up in you as you read Jesus' words?

2. When have you been apathetic or ambivalent regarding important invitations?

3. How engaged and awake are you to opportunities and open doors? Where might you use excuses to avoid decisiveness?

> ➤ When do you avoid assertiveness? What benefits could be gained from moving in EQ confidence that helps you be productive?

> ➤ Where do you fall asleep to your thoughts, ideas, or disappointments? How could IQ alertness wake you from sloth and help you be vigilant in serving the common good and getting the job done?

> ➤ Imagine tempering your attachment to peace with energy for effectiveness like a Three and faithful participation like a Six. What do you see?

▶▶▶ EQ, IQ, GQ

This Nine has awakened to how his false self sits in the driver's seat. He intentionally invites his proactive EQ and persistent IQ to take a turn at the wheel. How does this story help you recognize IQ and EQ in your life?

Dealing with Distractions

Nines are easily distracted. This reading describes how both over-promising and being distracted by multiple things can derail action and follow through. Notice where decision and action are part of fitness for service in God's kingdom.

As they were walking along the road, a man said to him, "I will follow you wherever you go."

Jesus replied, "Foxes have dens and birds have nests, but the Son of Man has no place to lay his head."

He said to another man, "Follow me."

But he replied, "Lord, first let me go and bury my father."

Jesus said to him, "Let the dead bury their own dead, but you go and proclaim the kingdom of God."

Still another said, "I will follow you, Lord; but first let me go back and say goodbye to my family."

Jesus replied, "No one who puts a hand to the plow and looks back is fit for service in the kingdom of God." (Luke 9:57-62)

1. To be human is to be distracted, but Nines have a way of taking distraction to another level. Where do you see lack of focus and neglect of responsibility costing you valuable opportunities?

2. The people in this story care about the needs of others to their own detriment. Where might your own needs and desires go unmet as you focus on everyone else's needs?

3. How do the words of Jesus in the passage invite you to awaken and engage rather than fade away?

I was in the middle of a passel of kids. My older siblings were louder, bigger, and demanding. My younger siblings were needier. I tried to appear as though I didn't want or need anything. I would go along to get along with everyone, because the chaos and conflict could silence me. My default behavior was "duck and cover" instead of showing up and naming my desire. Over the last fifteen years of working with the Enneagram, I have seen how much I need my EQ and IQ to keep me out of procrastination, conflict avoidance, and numbing out. At work, I intentionally show up with a desire for impact and legacy (EQ). This requires perseverance and longevity for the sake of the team, like a Six (IQ). When I notice that I am passive-aggressive with my wife, I practice EQ (effectiveness) and openly share my feelings, including anger, which used to go unexpressed. The Harmony Triads remind me to be seen (EQ) and stay faithful to the process to the end (IQ).

➤ When Nines engage their head, they moderate their gut and are able to observe, wake up, and persist through circumstances. Where are you aware of IQ in yourself?

➤ When Nines engage their heart, they moderate their laid-back gut and become efficient and confident. Where are you aware of EQ in yourself?

➤ What is it like for you to have IQ, EQ, and GQ?

HEALING CHILDHOOD HURTS: OPENING TO ACTION

Children are wired for resilience. Still, residual childhood baggage and lies can leak into adult Nine relationships. Nine children can lose the message, "Your presence matters." The default message you can learn is, "It's not okay to assert yourself." To cope, Nine children avoid conflict, fade into the background, and try not to make waves. These defenses mitigate engagement and passion. Do any of these messages resonate with you?

When these messages get triggered in adult interactions, then raw, ragged, unprocessed pain can erupt and sabotage the FLOW of a Nine's peace. Suddenly a needy four-year-old inside you begins to power down. Your false self gets stuck on the edge of sloth, indecision, and anger. When Nines partner with God's healing presence, you move back to your center

> ### Prayer of Ignatius of Loyola
>
> *Allow this prayer of Ignatius of Loyola, which addresses the heart, head, and gut energy of the Enneagram Triads, to become your prayer. Pray the mind, heart, and strength of the Trinity into your life and interactions.*
>
> *May it please the supreme and divine Goodness to give us all abundant grace [EQ] ever to know His most holy will [IQ] and perfectly to fulfill it [GQ].*

and reclaim your virtue of action. Action empowers your efforts to heal and bring shalom to your environments. The Harmony Triad offers a way for Nines to be curious about childhood trauma, defenses, and dismissed needs that shape your relationships today, so you learn to calmly take action.

▶▶▶ RECEIVING THE DISMISSED CHILDLIKE SELF

Receiving your dismissed child can heal and give you freedom to wake up and engage your life! Remember, within every cooperative and self-effacing Nine there is an energetic, competitive, and charismatic Three who wants to be up front and applauded for your skill and achievements. There can also be a little anxious, fearful, and doubting Six who doesn't trust your inner authority and is looking for a way to be safe in a dangerous world. To recognize where you dismissed your childlike self, pay attention to where you may have ignored agency (EQ) and courage (IQ).

In this story, this Nine begins to integrate his loyal and persevering Six inner child with his producing and achieving Three inner child.

> As a child, my older brother had many struggles. So when my mom became pregnant with me, she had a lot of anxiety. She told me the last thing she wanted was another struggling, hard-to-handle child. Her concern was so extreme she considered terminating her pregnancy in spite of her religious convictions. She was relieved that I came into this world with a peaceful presence. That presence was cheered at home. During childhood, long drives in the back of the Buick would turn chaotic with four young children and no seat belts. My grandfather often asked, "Where's Scotty?" It was his way of complimenting and encouraging my peaceful presence in the back seat. Still, that peaceful presence can go too far. My wife says that I can turn a mountain into a molehill.
>
> Outside my home, I was encouraged to let my EQ energy fly. Succeed! Be in charge! Be captain, collect trophies, make honor roll, and win the championship! But always bring that peaceful Nine energy home at day's end. Loyalty from the IQ space was also a core family value. But voicing fears of the Six space was for other families, not ours. Acting to integrate Nine, Three, and Six has been transforming and freeing. I resonate with Paul's words from Philippians 3:13-14 (paraphrased): "not that I have already attained it, but I press on toward the mark of the high calling of Jesus Christ."

As you read the questions below, notice where you sense God's invitation to more deeply receive your dismissed child. Write down any new insights and awareness. You are doing important and integrative work here.

➤ This Nine grew up in a family that didn't want too much energy and action from him. How does this resonate in you?

➤ Underneath the duck-and-cover Nine, you can find an energetic and assertive Three heart who wants to know, "Can we please get something—anything—done?" Where does this message show up in your life? How do you dismiss your heart?

➤ Underneath the pulse-absent Nine is a vigilant and fearful Six who wonders, "What might come next?" or "Is it safe to be here?" Notice when your inner child asks this question. Where do you dismiss your head?

▶▶▶ **JOURNALING YOUR DISMISSED CHILDLIKE SELF**

Integrating and accessing your EQ and IQ can help you wake up and discern how much chill you need in any given moment. Getting reacquainted with your competency (EQ) and confidence can change potential energy into kinetic energy that makes things happen. Integrating preparedness (IQ) and concern for others helps you FLOW with faithfulness that serves the common good.

Name and journal some of your defensiveness and anger. Courageously explore when you began to disappear, procrastinate, and pull away from others. Use your IQ and EQ to help you understand. Feel free to choose among these questions and return to other questions at another time.

➤ What is your story about finding the world chaotic? How do you resist chaos? How do you get passive-aggressive when you are pushed to do something you don't want to do?

➤ What default reactions and triggers of your childhood self still operate today? Where do you dismiss your energy or desires because of anger or past trauma?

➤ Ask God to help you return to your virtue of action. Open to and explore your childlike gusto that fully engages life. This week, keep track of times you channeled your energy from procrastination to action. What do you notice?

➤ Where has the importance of your presence been repaired/healed or increased/solidified?

Non-controlling Nines have a default stance of "everything is fine" or "I will not be moved." When Nines are stuck in your false self, it can be difficult to get you up and running. God's invitation is to break free from merging with others and embrace your own healing so you can name and own your desires and agendas. The invitation to participate in your own healing is central to a Nine's transformation. It may be helpful for you to read the chapter "Invitation to Participate in Your Own Healing" in *Invitations from God* by Adele Ahlberg Calhoun.

When your gut instincts tighten because you sense someone is trying to control you, don't default to stubborn, reactivity energy. Open. Cross-check your instincts with EQ and IQ. Are you sure people are wanting to control you? What conversation can you initiate about this? Ask God for grace to stay present and active in the dialogue. Notice what happens when you show up with your whole self and engage with others.

DISCERNMENT: DESOLATIONS AND CONSOLATIONS

Ignatius of Loyola taught that God's Guiding Spirit of wisdom moves in all three centers of intelligence—head, heart, and gut. When faced with a decision, Ignatius suggested noticing your consolations and desolations by asking:

What does my heart feel? What does my mind think? What does my gut sense?

Consolations point Nines toward God's presence and a peace that can hold in the storm. Consolations are evidence that a Nine is heading in the direction of IQ service and EQ initiation and collaboration. Desolations of procrastination, disappearing, and "whatever" alert Nines that you have fallen into your false self, which confuses the FLOW of divine peace with passivity. False peace is not discerning or healing. (More information on Harmony Triad discernment is found in Soul Resource 5.)

Nines experience consolations such as open adaptability, active peace, bold support, patient energy, nonjudgmental engagement, team harmony, and self-forgetful achievement. This is your freedom.

Nines experience desolations such as sloth, indecision, spaciness, disconnection, apathy, lack of discipline, passivity, stubbornness, narcotization, and immovability. These desolations leave you bound.

▶▶▶ PRESENT TO WHAT'S HAPPENING INSIDE

Both consolations and desolations point toward the purpose for which Nines were created. Below we concentrate on consolations and desolations particular to you. This Nine studies the map of his soul and notices signposts of desolation that numb him to reality. What responses block his journey toward presence?

As a child, I was told I had a calming, peaceful presence, and that I was adaptable, stable, and responsible (consolation). I did and do like being chill. I try to ignore any anger inside me and others. I become numb or passive-aggressive. I'm not sure why I never see it coming. One minute I'm fine, but then conflict gets too intense, and I disappear (desolation). When I feel

Healing Prayer

When Nines engage and seek grace from God's peace-giving Spirit, you receive grace to stop numbing and procrastinating when you don't like what's happening. Instead of being slothful, you embrace your virtue of action and you co-create with God a narrative of freedom and cure.

This is a way to do healing prayer on your own. Relax into silence and solitude. Breathe deeply. Don't force it. Become present to God and yourself. Ask God to show you your desire for ongoing healing. Ask God to bring to mind a past sorrow that is still being transmitted. Be still and wait. When something comes to mind, follow this simple trail of healing prayer.

❖ *Imagine yourself and Jesus back in the memory. Get your bearings. Where is Jesus? Where are you?*

❖ *What are you feeling? (numb, angry, calm, stubborn, dug in, unmoved, overwhelmed, or something else)*

❖ *Do these feelings remind you of a time you had similar reactions? You can go with Jesus to that place and time or stay where you are.*

❖ *Continue to name what you feel in your experience. Ask Jesus if these feelings point to a lie you began to believe at that time. Give it a name.*

❖ *What is Jesus saying to you about this lie? Listen. Is there an image, word, or phrase that he speaks to you?*

❖ *Repeat the truth you have heard from Jesus about yourself gently and frequently. Let the truth be an antidote that lets the pain go into Jesus and sets you free.*

overwhelmed by constant responsibility and being on, I want to push back and say, "I'm done with this! Let someone else do it!" When I am awake to my angry resistance, it can alert me that I have choices. I can appear, show up, stay in the game, and invest in relationships or what I don't want to do. If I do this, things go much better (consolation).

> When does "conflict get too intense" and induce desolation in you?

> Pay attention to the Spirit's motions in your heart and head. Are you trying to avoid your desolation through distraction and/or doing something else? How are you opening to the consolation of a peaceful place that is found on the other side of conflict?

Prayer Practice for Conflict

Nines in particular don't like conflict. You want misunderstandings to go away or fix themselves on their own. This strategy never works. So when you have to engage in conflict, intentionally breathe deeply into your dis-ease and resistance. Breathe in: "God is engaged." Breathe out: "I can engage." Let this breath prayer open you to God and the moment. Something unexpected might happen if you are present.

▶▶▶ DESOLATION AND NARCOTIZATION

When reality bites, Nines want to narcotize. When Nines feel cornered by conflict, unwanted expectations, and deadlines, they instinctively numb themselves to avoid their discomfort. This defensive move is called *narcotization*. A Nine will relieve tension with the anesthesia of peace at any price. Narcotization can also be recognized by passive-aggression that says, "Nothing's wrong!" and then finds strategies that avoid others. Some Nines will pursue conflict if they feel it is the only way back to peace. Without judgment, notice how avoidance, escape strategies, and numbing show up in you. Stay with one or two of these questions and let the truth settle in.

> When have you powered down or ignored reality to keep the peace? When does sloth show up with "It's all good," "I'm fine," "whatever," or "It's not on me"?

> How does your body constrict in desolation? Where do you carry your anger when people try to get you to do something you don't want to do?

> How do a Nine's defenses constrict your ability to discern?

> Are there defenses besides narcotization that block your discernment?

▶▶▶ CONSOLATIONS AND ACTION

For a Nine, the Spirit's invitation to consolation often means engaging heart and head presence that acts responsibly. Your IQ, EQ, and GQ harmony is designed to help you wade into conflict with strength, action, and loyalty. This is who you are. Notice when the Spirit invites you into the consolation of making peace.

Nines are consoled as they follow God's Spirit out of sloth into action. Action keeps Nines awake to how your presence actually makes a difference in the world. Peace initiatives large and small are one way Nines FLOW with divine shalom. Your peaceful presence can change the atmosphere in a room or the course of history.

➤ Describe a situation in which you felt the Holy Spirit inviting you out of apathy to be an "instrument of God's peace," as prayed by St. Francis of Assisi. What happened? What consolations came to you?

➤ When has action helped you stand in FLOW that peacefully loves God with your heart, soul, strength, and mind?

SPIRITUAL RHYTHMS FOR NINES

Make every effort to live in peace with everyone and to be holy; without holiness no one will see the Lord. (Hebrews 12:14)

Nines can be slow to show up and act. Yet these Bible verses suggest that peace is more than lack of tension. Peace stems from effort that pursues and chooses to "turn from evil and do good" (Psalm 34:14). Making every effort to live a life of peace means engaging spiritual practices that transform your default reactions and gut instincts so new neural pathways of holy responsiveness are created.

Attending to the Holy Spirit's motions in the soul on a daily basis provides Nines with guidance about where you need to step up, encourage, and mediate. The Spirit's movement within you helps Nines integrate so your peace effects the team.

These spiritual rhythms are all ways Nines can lean into God's invitations to transformation and mind renewal. Not every practice will be God's invitation to you. Say yes to the practices that best capture your desire to be with God right now. Saying yes to these invitations requires attention and intention.

▶▶▶ PRACTICING PRESENCE: NINES

Re-read the FLOW definition in the Key Terms section. Notice the presence of Trinitarian harmony.

Father, Son, and Spirit belong and flow together.

Head, heart, and gut belong and flow together.

Faith, love, and hope belong and flow together.

Divine harmony calls Nines to presence that makes every effort to seek peace and pursue it. Nines who practice the presence of God and others with head, heart, and gut lean into wholeness. Let the following meditative prayer move through your entire created being so it holds you together. Staying with this prayer for a season can help Nines access their EQ and IQ, bringing stability to gut instinct and reaction.

Find a comfortable and awake position. Remember that the Spirit of God dwells within you and prays for you. Ask God to give you an open and receptive head, heart, and gut.

Gut Presence: Put yourself in the presence of the Spirit of Peace. Breathe into your gut space. Notice what is happening in your body. Notice without judgment. Let your body tell you what it knows. Is there something your body wants to do in this prayer? Do that. Experience your peace; give thanks for your calming nature. How and when does your body close down and constrict rather than let love in? Where do you fade out before taking note of your opinion, need, and desire?

Heart Presence: Put yourself in the presence of Jesus. Breathe into your heart space. Feel your tenderness. Notice your heart's need to be held and cherished. Breathe in and create even more space around your heart. Notice your own needs. Invite self-compassion. What inside you needs to speak up, show up, hear a kind word, feel a soothing touch, or place a healthy boundary? Let Jesus hold these things in his heart. How does Jesus respond to you?

Head Presence: Put yourself in the presence of the faithful God who is on your side. Move your head around on your shoulders. Feel its weight and tightness. Breathe into your intellect. Observe your life in the body. What does your head tell you? What is it like to trust questions, information, and perspectives rather than your gut instinct? What questions would you like to ask your heart space? What is it like to trust your heart's instinct to do something?

Pray into Your Harmony: Peace Effects Team

"Peace effects team" is a breath prayer that helps you engage the life-giving heart of Three with its confident, efficient, magnetic action. It also engages the life-giving head of Six that observes, questions, and loyally perseveres in serving what is good and right in the world.

Memorizing this prayer brings awareness of what is most true about you to real-life situations. You are more than your type. Breathe this prayer when you engage evasive maneuvers, face a challenging conversation, want to go it alone, or need to act on a difficult problem. Anytime you are triggered and tempted to constrict and tighten around your need for autonomy, breathe: "peace effects team." Then call on your God-given gifting to enact divine peace.

FLOW Practice for Nines

In FLOW, Nines are **F**ree, **L**oving, **O**pen, and **W**ith. You stand in the presence of the three-in-one God and integrate head, heart, and gut in your loving. You also relate with the three Christian virtues of faith, hope, and love. When you notice that you are constricting and stuck in avoiding conflict, when you tighten and pull the plug to disconnect, this is the moment to breathe and ask the Spirit to give you inner freedom to show up and reclaim your energy as a person of peace. Notice that freedom flows when you are with what is, when you can say "I disagree" as well as "I agree." At the end of the day, log when you resisted welcoming reality and lost FLOW. What happened when you were in FLOW? Celebrate when

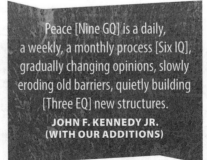

Peace [Nine GQ] is a daily, a weekly, a monthly process [Six IQ], gradually changing opinions, slowly eroding old barriers, quietly building [Three EQ] new structures.

**JOHN F. KENNEDY JR.
(WITH OUR ADDITIONS)**

God's peaceful presence flowed through you. Begin again tomorrow.

Practice Naming Your Desire

If "peace at any price" is your motto, it will be hard to know what you need and desire. If you numb to the impact of life, it will be hard to feel alive. Practicing the presence of your desires is one way to stop merging with others and remain true to who you are.

▶ When someone asks you "Do you want to . . ." use this simple scale to help you recognize what you want: "No" is minus one. "I don't care" is zero. "Yes" is plus one. Pick your number. Voice your desire.

▶ You can also use a ten-point scale to measure desire. If one is the lowest level of desire and ten is the highest, where are you landing? Work with friends or your partner. Agree to do what the one with highest score of desire wants.

▶ When you recognize a desire, don't close it down. Hold the desire before God without demand. In the space between desire and demand, listen to the motion of the Spirit in your EQ, IQ, and GQ. What do you hear? What desires are being fulfilled in you right now? Thank God for them. How could naming some desires actually give you direction and energy?

Practice Confession

Vulnerability and transparency about who you are before God and others is part of transformation and connection. Confess your:

▶ *Vice of sloth:* when you procrastinate, perseverate, and avoid both good and bad things.

▶ *Narcotization and apathy:* when you check your energy at the door.

▶ *Detachment:* admit when your detachment is simply a way to avoid discomfort, conflict, and the present reality. Admit when you attach to something else to avoid what needs doing.

▶ *Avoidance:* when you avoid conflict and hard conversations.

Breath Prayers

Notice your magnificent breath. Feel the oxygen fill your lungs and lift your chest. Follow your breath in and down. Take time to notice what is happening in your heart. Feel the strength of your created life as you breathe in: "You have formed my inward parts; I am peacefully and wonderfully made . . . may my soul know that very well." Spend a few minutes with this breath prayer. Follow your breath and remember you don't have to be the all-peaceful Creator.

Keep breathing into your body. Breathing in from the soles of your feet, fill your belly with breath, and continue breathing to the crown of your head. Feel your experience. Breathe into your head, your heart, and your gut. Without judgment, notice whatever comes up. If memories come, welcome them with your peaceful effective action. Stay with them. Take action to stay inside and hold yourself in a loving way.

❖ *Inhale: "Mighty God."*
   Exhale: "Prince of Peace."

❖ *Inhale: "Made in God's image."*
   Exhale: "I am not avoidant."

❖ *Inhale: "God is engaged."*
   Exhale: "I can engage."

▶ *Disappearance:* when you disappear rather than being fully present.

▶ *Anger:* both passive and explosive.

▶ *Merging:* acting as if your lives is not as significant as the lives of others.

▶ *Stubbornness:* when you dig in and refuse to move.

Receive words of assurance: "The God of peace sees you, hears your voice, forgives your hiding, and bids you come."

Practice the Presence of Yourself

Recognize your disengagement. Throughout the day, pay attention to your level of awareness, energy, awake-ness, and engagement with what is going on.

▶ Are there times of the day that you are most alert and present? Times you are not?

▶ What people and events make you want to disengage? Dig in? Merge?

▶ Nines can become asleep to their own needs. Where are you dismissing what you are feeling or thinking?

▶ The Spirit of God within you is present to everything that is going on. Notice where the Spirit might be inviting you to wake up to you.

Practice Participating in Your Own Healing

When Jesus heals people, he tends to ask them to participate in their healing. A man with a withered hand is told "stretch out your hand." A man who has been an invalid for thirty-eight years is asked, "Do you want to get well?" What do you want? Do you want to stay the same or become more emotionally healthy and whole? If you do, it will mean partnering with the Spirit for transformation.

▶ Name some part of your personality that is unusable by God in its present form. Do you want that to change? If so, what are ways you can enter into the healing process? Healing prayer? Counseling? Spiritual direction? Coaching? Spiritual friendship? Justice work?

▶ Employ your gut action to choose involvement in your own journey. Refuse to be a bystander in transformation and healing.

▶ Bring your heart feelings and your head fears to the Healer. Imagine Jesus speaking truth to your feelings, fears, and lies. What do you hear? Participate with the Healer in developing new responses.

Practice Loyalty and Assertion

Your strength and gifts of diplomacy and inclusion become more powerful when integrated with EQ assertion and IQ loyalty.

▶ Let people hear your heart and see you act. Don't withdraw.

▶ Express your insights. Encourage and build into others.

▶ Stick with what is hard for the sake of growth in yourself and others.

▶ Listen to people and situations with IQ, EQ, and GQ. Remember peace effects team.

Practice Spiritual Direction or Spiritual Friendship

Ask a spiritual friend and/or a spiritual director to help you tend your desires and pay attention to feelings and motivations you have submerged. Let them accompany you and your soul as you seek to know God and yourself. Directors and friends can help you listen for the voice of God within so you come alive to all God has for you. In this safe place of noticing, your interiority can open to new graces. You can develop new neural pathways instead of merging with others and going with the path of least resistance.

Blessing for the Beloved Nine

As we close this section, take time to breathe in this blessing and create space in your soul.

May the Holy Three bless this all-inclusive journey home to your true self.

May God the Father direct you with courage and insight as you consider your next steps.

May the heart of Jesus draw forth and encourage your heart's desire to make a difference.

May the Holy Spirit ground you and empower you with the initiative to activate all that is meant to be accomplished in you.

May the sacred peace of the Trinity that passes all human understanding lead you on your road while on this journey, upholding you and loving you.

Empathy for NINES

Peace is not the absence of conflict, but the ability to cope with conflict by peaceful means.

RONALD REAGAN

Every child should be able to know their presence matters. In childhood, Nines may have lost this message. They may have had caregivers who gave the message that it was not okay to assert themselves. To survive, they suppressed their desire to be seen and became the backdrop in the family. Here you can explore your responses to Nines and how you might grow in empathy and see them as God does.

Empathy is a true self response that harmonizes and breaks down the we/they divide. We may find that Nines check out and refuse to work through relational issues. Or we may love that Nines are easier to get along with than any other number. Understanding how Nines became uber-peaceful can open compassionate and empathetic interactions with them.

This Nine describes her journey. See if you can enter into the story and engage your understanding heart.

> Children were to be quiet. When there was conflict, I wanted to be in another part of the house. I never felt the freedom to express Three energy. I could never show off, or be the center of attention, or acknowledge and express my feelings. I was never asked about my ideas, dreams, hopes, and fears. I was there and not there. At school I fit in with various crowds but was never part of any. I didn't participate in clubs or sports. In class I was quiet and never gave an answer even if I knew it. Speaking up was agonizing and expressing an opposing opinion was impossible. I took a dance class when I was five. The teacher made me feel talented; but after one class, I quit. I didn't want to be the center of anyone's attention. Now I feel disappointed and wonder why.

This Nine learned to *not* show up, follow through on activities, pursue interests, or share thoughts. Internalizing the subtle message to *not* be in the forefront left her in a space of inaction. Sit with this Nine's story.

1. Allow compassion for this peaceful, merging Nine to rise in you.

   - What are you thinking about this Nine?
   - What are you feeling about this Nine?
   - What is your gut instinct about this Nine?

2. When have you had your presence dismissed? What was it like for you to fall asleep to your talents or identity in a group?

3. Why do you think Nines find it easier to disappear and let others shine rather than shine themselves?

UNDERSTANDING THE DEFENSE MECHANISM OF NARCOTIZATION

Another Nine describes her journey to integration and empathy. Notice how this Nine repressed her gifting to bring peace.

> As far back as I can remember, my Nine was trying to keep peace and calm because my environment was not peaceful. My dad was a hard worker and physically present but found it hard to show affection. He was never abusive, but his anger had a short fuse that came with spanking and yelling, which upset Mom. She would hush us and beg us to be good so Dad wouldn't get angry. After one of Dad's outbursts, my mom took my sister and me and drove off. Because I

wanted Mom happy, I would do anything to keep the peace. We never talked about feelings—good, bad, or indifferent. No one ever asked what was going great and/or troubling us. The message was, "Children should be seen but not heard." I took that to mean, "Don't ever be seen or heard." I wasn't given permission to be angry, but I am angry a lot. I numb out so that I don't feel it.

1. What connections and resistances are you feeling with this Nine?

2. Get inside this Nine's story. Can you recognize how her anger at not being seen led her to narcotize?

3. How could you demonstrate that God's active peace shows up in a way that invites a Nine to show up too?

4. How might you join the Holy Spirit by praying for a Nine you know?

RELATING TO A NINE

We find grace to see things from a Nine's point of view when we remember that under the placid, diplomatic exterior of the Nine is a forgotten child that went with the current to survive.

- Because Nines sometimes merge with the perspective of others, ask them questions about their ideas, opinions, and needs, respecting their individuality.

- Nines crave peaceful environments, so minimize chaos and unpredictability.

- In a meeting or at an event, Nines can fade into the background. Appreciate them and respond to them when they speak.

- It can seem like Nines waste time on things that don't have to be done now to avoid doing what should be done now. Nagging them will likely make them move slower. Directly and non-confrontationally ask Nines about their timetable and encourage them when they get things done.

- Nines may resist exerting physical energy. Invite them to do something with you that involves movement.

- When you experience a Nine pushing down anger or digging in, tell them you want to understand what is going on.

The following list summarizes key characteristics of Nines. Consider your responses to these characteristics.

- *Authentic, true self:* Peacemaker, harmonizer
- *Compulsive, false self:* Slothful, procrastinating
- *Virtue leading back to true self:* Action

- *Personality style:* Accepting
- *Work style:* Diplomatic
- *Leadership/action style:* Mediator
- *Relationships:* Accommodating
- *Core motivation:* Power, control
- *Negative fixation:* Anger, guilt
- *Narrative:* "I've had enough," "This is too much"
- *Communication:* Easygoing
- *Nine with an Eight wing:* More assertive, confrontational, energetic
- *Nine with a One wing:* More objective, critical, task oriented
- *Basic fear:* Loss, separation
- *Basic desire:* Inner stability, peace of mind
- *Drive:* To avoid conflicts, have peace, preserve the status quo, resist tension

Based on the description above:

1. How does it feel to be a Nine? Which descriptors give clues on how to relate to a Nine?

2. Is there a better way to say what is true of Nines?

3. Nines are laid back and like to keep the peace. What is it like to meet the calm of a Nine with your own gut harmonizing diplomacy?

4. Nines want to be appreciated for their ability to lead through mediation. How can you express your appreciation for their peacemaking initiatives?

ONES

Goodness Creates Joy

Nothing so needs reforming as other people's habits.

MARK TWAIN

I am very conscientious and want to be a good person. I want to be grounded, ethical, ordered, and work for the good of those around me. At my best I can be very insightful and discerning. I have high standards. I can spot when something is wrong and will work hard to make it better. I enjoy seeing something done right, and I will put aside my needs to get a job done in the best possible way. I am committed to making things better. I have a hard time when people don't have that same standard for their work. When people expect a handout or are irresponsible, I get resentful. I have a strong inner critic who is quick to voice "shoulds" and "oughts." This makes it hard for me to be vulnerable and admit I am angry or have made a mistake. After all, anger and mistakes aren't "good." Some people say I can be controlling, rigid, perfectionistic, and anal-retentive. I take myself very seriously. Fairness and correctness are at the top of my list. If it's not right, I will reform it, clean it, restructure it, and do whatever it takes to make it better.

WHO I AM AND WHO I AM NOT

Ones bear the image of a good God. Your life resonates with Luke 18:19: "No one is good—except God alone."

Goodness is inevitably part of the One's story. Stories about who we are and who we are not shape what we do and don't do, who we become, and where we stall out. Ones typically tell a story about fairness and how you make things better or right. You can skip over chapters of your life about your judgmentalism, anger, or resentment of rule breakers. This section offers awareness of words that shape the narrative of a One.

▶▶▶ BELOVED ONES

Spend some time with the words below that describe who Ones are and are not. Circle the characteristics that resonate with your journey. Star words that express your gifts. Underline words that describe parts of your personality that are unusable by God in their present form. Put a checkmark beside characteristics that trigger you.

Ones Descriptive Words List

I AM		I AM NOT	
good (very)	dependable	bad	undependable
right	professional	wrong	amateur
upright	committed	licentious	uninvolved
moral	careful	immoral	careless
righteous	persistent	unethical	quitter
just	critical	unjust	tolerant
principled	strict	lawbreaker	forgiving
upstanding	opinionated	loose	tolerant
firm	organized	wishy-washy	disorganized
fair	meticulous	arbitrary	impulsive
ethical	high standards	unethical	slipshod
idealistic	standard bearer	realistic	compromising
responsible	thorough	irresponsible	haphazard
reliable	tidy	fair-weather friend	sloppy

➤ Which words reflect the image of God in you?

➤ Which words are you most attached to? Addicted to? Compulsive about?

➤ Which words do you resist and judge the most?

➤ If you opened up to the words you resist without judgment, how might your perceptions and reactions shift?

➤ Journal about the words that might expand your awareness of God's acceptance of you with all your foibles.

▶▶▶ **GETTING TO KNOW ONES**

This One shares early memories, where he learned he'd better get things right because everything was going to be evaluated. Constant critique made this child want to be perfect to avoid judgment. It also created a habit of seeing "bad" in others.

> I grew up living close to my grandparents, aunts, and uncles. Once a month we had lunch and then hung out. I remember how, on the drive home, I listened to and later engaged with my parents in critique of my cousins' behavior. Their "bad" behavior was linked to my aunts' and uncles' "bad" parenting. These conversations played into my desire to be the good kid/person/parent who got everything right. It also gave me the paradigm for judging others and imagining how to improve them! Seeing how to "help" others be better is my curse and my gift.

➤ What does this One childhood story bring up in you?

➤ What is your memory of your first One experience?

➤ What is it like for you to know in your gut that something can be better? How does this manifest in your body center?

TRUE SELF AND FALSE SELF: THE GOOD PERSON

Who we are or are not comes with expression and energy. The attitudes, behaviors, and motivations of beloved Ones carry reforming presence that makes things better for others. Your true self emerges from union with God, not from perfect lives. True self Ones affirm the good you see. When improvement is needed, you are patient with yourself and others. A One's false self is the compulsive, deeply entrenched, old nature that constricts around ensuring that everyone does everything right. It is the psychological or ego self that is constructed on a complex mixture of nature, nurture, perfectionism, and free will. This section will help you begin to recognize compulsive and impulsive false self reactions as well as true self FLOW that loves God, others, and self.

True Self Ones: Sacred Goodness

Ones are designed to display God's goodness. This core goodness works for and recognizes the innate dignity of others. True self Ones are altruistic and not ambitious for yourself. You give unstintingly for the betterment of the world and inspire others to reach their potential. Healthy Ones are conscientious, responsible, and dedicated to a life of service and integrity. You have an easy goodness that sees beyond what is wrong to what really matters. True self

> **Breath Prayer** ▶
>
> *In silence and solitude, ask God to help you see yourself clearly. Begin with breathing. Breathe in: "Made in God's image," and then breathe out: "I am not the judge." Spend a few minutes with this breath prayer. Feel the goodness and freedom of being made in God's image; feel the liberty of letting God be God. Breathe this prayer in and out throughout the day.*

Ones are hard working, discerning, and willing to accept and forgive imperfections in yourself and others because you know perfect is as temporary as dew. Still, your commitment to nudge an imperfect reality into a better place often brings God's goodness and blessing to others. Centered Ones serve as sacred crusaders, bringing out the good in all things.

False Self Ones: Constrict in Anger, Judgment, and Resentment

Under stress, Ones lose touch with your own goodness as well as the goodness of others. The world becomes rife with imperfections. Errors and misguided people hit Ones in the gut, and your instinctive response is to take control and make things right. You become "good in the worst sense of the word," a phrase popularly attributed to Mark Twain. You micromanage, blame, control, stifle spontaneity, and constrict around *oughts* and *shoulds*. When mistakes are unacceptable, an unhealthy One's internalized critic becomes resentful, deadly serious, and hypersensitive to criticism. To defend yourself from the scalding "bad" within and without, you become angry. Since it's not "good" to express anger, Ones sublimate and stuff your anger so you won't look "bad." But your suppressed anger leaks out in not so subtle ways: criticism, judgments, and clear-cut directives.

> #### ▶▶▶ TRUE OR FALSE SELF
>
> As you think about your true and false self, consider your passion for the right way and your desire to control things to make that happen. Notice, without judgment, what comes up for you as you answer the following questions. Jot down and/or journal your responses.
>
> ➤ Where do true self One characteristics show up in your relationships?
>
> ➤ Where do false self One qualities show up in your relationships? How does anger show up? ("This isn't right! This isn't fair!") How does guilt show up? ("I've screwed up again. I'm no good!") How do you act when you don't have control or things don't go your way?
>
> ➤ Where does your body constrict when you are angry? What does it feel like when you are able to relax and accept things as they are?
>
> ➤ How do you feel the difference between centered, true self energy and edgy, false self energy?

HARMONY: GOODNESS CREATES JOY

Ones are often identified as the good number, but you are much more than just one number! You bear the image and harmony of the three-in-one God. When beloved Ones integrate your IQ and EQ intelligence, you harmonize and flow with Four creativity and Seven joy. This section creates awareness of how FLOW is the unique gift of the Harmony Triads.

In Harmony and FLOW, a One's instinct for making things better reflects creative openness and awareness of nuance with the EQ of a Four and considers how to make this enjoyable and life-giving to others with the IQ of a Seven.

▶▶▶ **MORE THAN A TYPE**

This story describes a One who is learning his connection to his Four EQ and Seven IQ. This One is moving from constricting rigidity and having to be right to a place of freedom and trust in divine goodness that lets him receive other perspectives like a Seven. Relaxing the need to be definitively clear about everything, like a Four, opens this One to an easier goodness. As you read the following, consider which parts of the story resonate with you.

For decades, I lived with an internal tension of anger—which I could not admit to myself, let alone anyone else. Growing up, every single thing I did was critiqued or corrected by

Expecting a Reward

Jesus tells a story about two brothers; the elder brother is dutiful and does what he ought. The younger brother disrespects his dad, asks for his inheritance, and leaves home. When he blows everything he has and hits bottom, he comes to his senses and returns home. We pick up the story as the son kneels before his father.

"The son said to him, 'Father, I have sinned against heaven and against you. I am no longer worthy to be called your son.'

"But the father said to his servants, 'Quick! Bring the best robe and put it on him. Put a ring on his finger and sandals on his feet. Bring the fattened calf and kill it. Let's have a feast and celebrate. For this son of mine was dead and is alive again; he was lost and is found.' So they began to celebrate.

"Meanwhile, the older son was in the field. When he came near the house, he heard music and dancing. So he called one of the servants and asked him what was going on. 'Your brother has come,' he replied, 'and your father has killed the fattened calf because he has him back safe and sound.'

"The older brother became angry and refused to go in. So his father went out and pleaded with him. But he answered his father, 'Look! All these years I've been slaving for you and never disobeyed your orders. Yet you never gave me even a young goat so I could celebrate with my friends. But when this son of yours who has squandered your property with prostitutes comes home, you kill the fattened calf for him!'

"'My son,' the father said, 'you are always with me, and everything I have is yours. But we had to celebrate and be glad, because this brother of yours was dead and is alive again; he was lost and is found.'" (Luke 15:21-32)

1. When have you felt that you haven't been rewarded or noticed for doing the right thing?

2. Where do you gain your sense of value from comparing yourself to others (especially their faults)?

3. What prevents you from recognizing all the love that is yours already and being able to join the party?

my parents. Every minute I lived on the edge of their disappointment and judgment and therefore anger. My beloved wife very patiently and kindly pointed out the signs of anger in my life. But I steadfastly refused to believe that a "good" person like me could possibly be angry. I didn't shout. I didn't lose my temper. I didn't hit; so therefore I couldn't be angry! Encountering the Enneagram was the God moment that pulled back the veil and gave me courage to see the reservoir of anger inside me. This awareness began to change me in virtually everything.

Connecting to my Harmony Triad of Four EQ and Seven IQ also helped me. Fours can hold the tension between light and dark, and good and bad without compromising their authenticity. They long to maintain connection even when they disagree. Integrating this EQ was and is a huge thing for me. I never thought I was creative until I saw how the creative Four showed up in my cooking. Now, let's be clear, I use the right pan or knife. But I rarely follow the recipe. I make up my own version and feel great freedom to express myself in creating delicious meals for family and friends. The gift of the Seven IQ also helps me take myself less seriously and be curious about others' opinions. Doing this takes me beyond my gut instinctive judgment. Integrating my Four and Seven has dramatically changed my spiritual journey and my ability to lean more fully into who God has made me.

➤ When do you simply judge reality and refuse to engage your thinking (Seven IQ)? When does your critical spirit drown out nuanced awareness and compassion for others (Four EQ)?

➤ When you do get stuck in getting things just right, how can a Seven's IQ of levity open you to divergent opinions and balance the goodness you bring? Imagine tempering right or wrong dualisms with head curiosity and heart kindness. What happens?

➤ Where might admitting you might be wrong open pathways for connection and relationship?

▶▶▶ IQ, EQ, GQ

This One describes her discovery of One, Four, and Seven integration. In accessing her Harmony Triad, her dominant One style becomes even *better* through embracing the playfulness of the Seven IQ and the originality of the Four EQ. What resonates with you?

One of the greatest revelations of the One, Four, and Seven Harmony Triads was awareness of how I pushed aside soul desires like piano playing, dancing, and scrapbooking/creating photo albums. When I took up scrapbooking, I did scrapbooking weekends and gathered friends to work on photos. The Seven IQ adventure of scrapbooking weekends and the Four EQ creativity of colors, titles, and text was complemented by my One penchant for organization and systems. No wonder I was so filled up by this hobby. It was a huge aha moment to lean into integration and feel more alive.

➤ When Ones engage their head, they moderate their gut preferences and judgments, leaning into joy and a spirit of adventure and collaboration. Where do you see IQ in yourself?

> ➤ When Ones engage their heart, they moderate their rightness and become open-minded, creative, and able to tolerate "good enough," rather than be upset at less than perfect. Where do you see EQ in yourself?
>
> ➤ What is it like for you to have IQ, EQ, and GQ?

HEALING CHILDHOOD HURTS: OPENING TO SERENITY

Children are wired for resilience, but residual childhood distress can creep into adult One relationships. One children can completely lose the message, "You are good." The default message you can learn is: "It's not okay to make a mistake." To cope, One children try to be perfect and do the right thing. These defenses protected and also mitigated against joyous connectedness and creativity. Do any of these messages resonate with you?

When these messages get triggered in adult interactions, then raw, ragged, unprocessed pain can erupt, sabotaging the FLOW of a One's goodness. Suddenly a shamed and critical four-year-old self inside you fixates on making the perfect decision. In this place, Ones get stuck on the edge of anger, judgment, and resentment. The Harmony Triad offers a way to be curious about trauma, defenses, childhood lies, and dismissed goodness that triggers a One's reactions today.

To Judge or Not to Judge

Stress can lead Ones into a Seven's compulsivity to overindulge where they overdo their need to control and be right. When things unfold against plan, they can pick up the Four energy of feeling utterly flawed and misunderstood. These readings offers insight on where Ones constrict and refuse to enter into joy.

"To what can I compare this generation? They are like children sitting in the marketplaces and calling out to others:

"'We played the pipe for you,
    and you did not dance;
we sang a dirge,
    and you did not mourn.'

"For John came neither eating nor drinking, and they say, 'He has a demon.' The Son of Man came eating and drinking, and they say, 'Here is a glutton and a drunkard, a friend of tax collectors and sinners.' But wisdom is proved right by her deeds." (Matthew 11:16-19)

1. John and Jesus were both judged because they didn't fit the cultural idea of how a holy person should look and act. When people don't meet your standards, how do you respond?

2. Where do you resist things like "dancing or mourning" because they don't conform to your idea of what is right?

▶▶▶ RECEIVING THE DISMISSED CHILDLIKE SELF

Receiving your dismissed child can heal and give Ones freedom to be serene and open again. Remember within every dutiful, reforming, stable One there is a deep, melancholic, insightful Four who wants to connect to others but does not sense that you are special enough. There can also be a little adventurous, distracted, and imaginative Seven who doesn't want to face discomfort and struggles while wanting more of what makes for a good life. To recognize where you dismissed your childlike self, pay attention to where you may have ignored feelings (EQ) and spontaneity (IQ).

Notice how this One's playful, happy Seven got her in trouble:

I vividly remember how in elementary school a few girls and I started messing around in the upper school bathroom. This is my first and only memory of misbehaving like this. We wadded up wet toilet paper and then tossed it at the ceiling so it stuck. Each of us must have thrown three to four toilet paper balls as we laughed our guts out. Then the custodian came in and caught us. Seriously, the one time I was having some silly and "unruly" fun, I was caught. To this day, it's very hard for me to relax or have crazy fun like that. I'm amazed that the one time I really broke the rules, I got caught.

3. What might it look like to withhold judgment and explore why others have a different opinion? How could entering into "dancing or mourning" balance your gut response to push back? How does this reading help you understand how to relate to those you differ with?

One person's faith allows them to eat anything, but another, whose faith is weak, eats only vegetables. The one who eats everything must not treat with contempt the one who does not, and the one who does not eat everything must not judge the one who does, for God has accepted them. (Romans 14:2-3)

You, then, why do you judge your brother or sister? Or why do you treat them with contempt? For we will all stand before God's judgment seat. (Romans 14:10)

For the kingdom of God is not a matter of eating and drinking, but of righteousness, peace and joy in the Holy Spirit, because anyone who serves Christ in this way is pleasing to God and receives human approval. (Romans 14:17-18)

1. What would it be like for the One in you to give up judgment and move to the Four, who gives grace and space to those who differ on "eating and drinking"?

2. The kingdom of God is not a set of rules but a place of "joy in the Holy Spirit." How would integrating a Seven's joy make the kingdom of God more evident in you?

3. Where has your judgment kept you from divine grace and joy?

Notice where this One feels his Four was shut down by his family:

When I was around seven or eight, my grandfather died. After the funeral service, we got in the car to go to the cemetery. Although my grandfather and I were not really close, I was overwhelmed by sadness and began to cry. My older brother and younger sister were fine; even my mother showed no emotion. My parents scolded me for crying and told me to stop it. I concluded it was not okay to feel deeply and express emotions. Their emotional stunted-ness made me distrust my feelings and see them as bad.

As you explore these questions, notice where you sense God's invitation to more deeply receive your dismissed child. Where do you shut down your IQ and EQ? Jot down any new insights and awareness. You are doing important and integrative work here.

> From the first story: an experience of being caught breaking the rules grew into a lifelong distrust of "crazy fun." Imagine what it is like to constantly toe the line and distrust joy. Where does this story resonate in you?

> From the second story: this One grew up in a family where his sensitivity was shamed. How does this affect his ability to be in the presence and FLOW of his God-given design?

> Inside the sensitive, perfecting One is a heart-full Four who wonders, "Will you abandon me?" and "Will I be loved or rejected?" Where do these messages show up in your life?

> Within the orderly, controlled One is a "life is a blast" Seven who fears missing out and wants to live without limits. Where do these characteristics show up in your life?

▶▶▶ JOURNALING YOUR DISMISSED CHILDLIKE SELF

As Ones receive your dismissed, childlike self, you may recognize where you dismissed EQ and IQ. Integrating and accessing your heart and head can help you relax your intensity and misery around life's imperfections. IQ and EQ help you discern how much re-forming energy is actually needed in this given moment. EQ opens you to warmth and

---

Prayer of Thomas à Kempis

Allow this prayer of Thomas à Kempis, which addresses the heart EQ, head IQ, and gut GQ energy of the Enneagram Triads, to become your prayer.

> *Grant me, O Lord, to know what I ought*
> *to know [IQ],*
> *To love what I ought to love [EQ],*
> *To praise what delights thee most,*
> *To value what is precious in thy sight,*
> *To hate what is offensive to thee [GQ].*
> *Do not suffer me to judge according to*
> *the sight of my eyes [GQ],*
> *Nor to pass sentence according to the*
> *hearing of the ears of ignorant men;*
> *But to discern [GQ] with a true judgment*
> *between things visible and spiritual,*
> *And above all, always to inquire what is*
> *the good pleasure of thy will.*

encouragement rather than critique. Integrating optimism (IQ) opens you to what could go right as you FLOW with love of God and neighbor.

Name and journal some of your hurts and courageously explore how you began to defend yourself with an inner reformer whose instinctive response is, "It would be better if . . ." Engage your IQ to monitor how much is yours to do. Ask your EQ, "How could less than perfect be good enough in this situation?" Feel free to choose among these questions and return to the other questions at another time.

➤ What is your story about finding the world harsh and critical? What happens when you excuse your tone and resentment because of past pain or current judgment of others?

➤ What default reactions and triggers of your childhood self still operate today? If you opened and accepted your imperfect self and imperfect others, what might happen?

➤ Ask God to help you recover your virtue of serenity. Open yourself to your childlike sensitivity and joy; as you do, others may open up to you and love you.

➤ Where has your sense of being okay *as you are* been repaired/healed or increased/solidified?

Critiquing Ones have an immediate default stance of "let my conscience be *your* guide." In your false self, you sit in the seat of judgment—on yourself and everyone else. The practice of admitting you might be wrong softens a

Healing Prayer

It is the unconditional and accepting love of God and others that offer Ones an alternative to your inner critic. Appreciation can heal your tone, help you take yourself less seriously, and turn your vice of anger into your virtue of serenity. In serenity, you can know what is yours to do and what you can let go. Reality really can be good enough.

This is a way to do healing prayer on your own. Relax into silence and solitude. Breathe deeply. Don't force it. Become present to God and yourself. Express your desire for ongoing healing. Ask God to bring to mind a past pain that is still being transmitted. Be still and wait.

When something comes to mind, follow this simple trail of healing prayer.

❖ *Imagine yourself and Jesus back in the memory. Get your bearings. Where is Jesus? Where are you?*

❖ *What are you feeling? (anxious, angry, stupid, foolish, unsafe, resentful, or something else)*

❖ *Do these feelings remind you of a time you had similar reactions? You can go with Jesus to that place and time or stay where you are.*

❖ *Continue to name what you feel in your experience. Ask Jesus if these feelings point to a lie you began to believe at that time. Give it a name.*

❖ *What is Jesus saying to you about this lie? Listen. Is there an image, word, or phrase that he speaks to you?*

❖ *Repeat the truth you have heard from Jesus about yourself gently and frequently. Let the truth be an antidote that lets the pain go into Jesus and sets you free.*

One's rigidity and makes engaging with others a positive, mutual experience (EQ). It might be helpful to read the chapter "Invitation to Admit I Might Be Wrong" in *Invitations from God* by Adele Ahlberg Calhoun.

This week when you feel your inner critic taking center stage and picking up a bullhorn to tell the world, open your heart to that person or situation. Keep track of times you willingly admit you might be wrong. Notice how you regulate your judgment and intensity by opening to ideas and opinions other than your own.

DISCERNMENT: DESOLATIONS AND CONSOLATIONS

Ignatius of Loyola taught that God's Guiding Spirit of wisdom moves in all three centers of intelligence—head, heart, and gut. When faced with a decision, Ignatius suggested noticing the consolations and desolations by asking: What does my heart feel? What does my mind think? What does my gut sense?

Consolations point Ones toward God's magnanimous goodness and grace. Consolations are evidence that a One is heading in the direction of EQ openness that uses IQ to recognize the GQ good in other options. Desolations of anger and resentment, which distort the FLOW of God's love, alert Ones that you have fallen away from the goodness and inner freedom that

doesn't need to perfect everyone and everything. (More information on Harmony Triad discernment is found in Soul Resource 5.)

Ones experience consolations such as easy goodness, sacred hope, gentle self-discipline, organized rest, beautiful depth, gracious discernment, insightful encouragement, realistic optimism, noble spirit, conscientious adventure, and empathetic righteousness. This is freedom.

Ones experience desolations such as anger, fear of imperfection, harsh inner criticism, rigid perfectionism, inflexible judgments, impatience, self-righteousness, self-condemnation, and serious criticism. These are signs that Ones are bound.

▶▶▶ PRESENT TO WHAT'S HAPPENING INSIDE

Both consolations and desolations point toward the purpose for which Ones were created. However, when Ones default to autopilot, your first response is to react rather than notice either consolations or desolations. In this story, a One becomes familiar with the terrain of his soul and notices how desolations and judgment can block his vision and alienate others. As consolations come into focus, he opens his heart to grace. Notice how the consolations and desolations of this One could direct him toward healing and the presence of God.

It is hard for me to draw close to people who don't meet my standards (desolation). I struggle to extend grace to colleagues who fail to fulfill expectations; volunteers who drop balls; and my spouse, who doesn't get all my perfectly laid out descriptions of how things should be. Of course, my grace deficit exists because I don't extend much grace to myself either. It is hard and no fun to be discontent with what is (desolation). Harmony Triads have helped me receive my inner critic as an invitation to grow in grace rather than beat myself up. My own struggles with never measuring up can actually help me empathize with and encourage others who struggle with self-judgment (consolation). I rejoice that people invite me to help them grow in their marriages, parenting, and ministry more than ever. Recognizing someone's core issues and offering practical help on how to experience more of God's transforming work in their lives is real consolation.

> ➤ How does your body constrict in desolation? Where do you carry your pain and frustration when things don't work as they "should"?

> ➤ Where does being wrong and having things less than perfect bring you desolation?

> ➤ When you are in desolation, pay attention to the Spirit's motions in your heart and head. Do you feel like a victim and alone in your desolation? How could checking in with your Seven IQ help you understand and offer hope to your desolation?

> *Prayer Practice for When You Feel Self-Critical*
>
> *Ones in particular don't want to be wrong, because it makes you feel like a bad person. So when you make a mistake, intentionally breathe into your disappointment and anger. Breathe in: "God, you are good." Breathe out: "God, I am good enough." Let this breath prayer open you to God and the moment. Something unexpected may happen if you receive the goodness in what is.*

▶▶▶ DESOLATION AND REACTION FORMATION

Ones have a default defense of reaction formation. Reaction formation means thinking or feeling one thing but expressing the opposite in order to stay "good" and in control. For example, if you feel you are being judged, you may work very hard to prove that judgment wrong. A One that engages with pornography may express puritanical feelings about sex to others. If you feel your emotions are bad, you may try to act really good. Reaction formation can arise from judgmental narratives like, "This just isn't right or fair!" or guilt narratives like, "I am not good enough." Stay with one or two of these questions and let the truth settle in.

Without judgment, notice where reaction formation shows up in you.

> ➤ Are there defenses besides reaction formation that block your discernment?

> ➤ How can the desolation of reaction formation lead you to greater awareness of God's devotion, forgiveness, and acceptance of you?

The Spirit's invitation to consolation often means engaging EQ that feels deeply with others and IQ that lightens up and even laughs at how you got something wrong. This ability to go deep and fly high allows you to move forward with holy joy and adventure. Today, notice when the Spirit invites you into the consolation of receiving reality with its highs and lows.

▶▶▶ CONSOLATIONS AND SERENITY

Ones are consoled as they follow God's Spirit out of reaction formation and open to grace that covers a multitude of mistakes, errors, and sins. When you know that "mercy triumphs over judgment" (James 2:13), you can be free to be who you are—warts and all. This freedom takes the stridency and brittleness out of your reforming energy and replaces it with a serenity that holds the complications of people who see things differently.

> ➤ Describe a situation in which you felt the Holy Spirit inviting you out of being the ultimate judge or critic and into serenity. What happened? What consolations came to you?

> ➤ When has serenity helped you stand in FLOW and enabled you to love God and others with your heart, soul, strength, and mind?

> I spent a lot of years trying to outrun or outsmart vulnerability [Four EQ] by making things certain and definite, black and white, good and bad [One GQ]. My inability to lean into the discomfort of vulnerability limited the fullness [Seven IQ] of those important experiences that are wrought with uncertainty: Love, belonging, trust, joy [Seven IQ], and creativity [Four EQ], to name a few.
>
> **BRÉNÉ BROWN**
> **(WITH OUR ADDITIONS)**

SPIRITUAL RHYTHMS FOR ONES

Attending to the motions of the soul on a daily basis helps Ones move from your old, false self of reactionary judgments and anger into an inner freedom that accepts and forgives. The Spirit's movement within enables you to integrate so your goodness creates joy.

These spiritual rhythms are all ways Ones can lean into spiritual and relational transformation. Not every practice will be God's invitation to you. Say yes to the practices that best capture your desire to be with God right now.

▶▶▶ PRACTICING PRESENCE: ONES

Re-read the FLOW definition in the Key Terms section. Notice the presence of Trinitarian harmony.

Father, Son, and Spirit belong and flow together.

Head, heart, and gut belong and flow together.

Faith, love, and hope belong and flow together.

Divine harmony calls Ones to be present so you can intentionally learn to receive things as they are, not as you presume they should be. Ones who are present to God and others with head, heart, and gut can integrate and hold dissonance and imperfection in yourself and others. Let the following meditative prayer move through your entire created being so it holds together. Staying with this prayer for a season can help Ones access their EQ and IQ, bringing access to their emotions and openness to a bigger version of reality.

Find a comfortable and awake position. Remember that the Spirit of God dwells within you and prays for you. Ask God to give you an open and receptive head, heart, and gut.

Gut Presence: Put yourself in the presence of the Spirit; notice what is happening in your body. Notice without judgment. Let your body tell you what it knows. How does your body react to the imperfections in life? Is there something your body knows and wants to do in this prayer? Where do you want to constrict, judge, and resist what's happening? Let your body tell you what it knows about that. Where is your body constricting around self-condemnation?

Heart Presence: Put yourself in the presence of Jesus. Breathe into your heart space. Feel your tenderness. Notice your heart's need to be accepted and loved. Breathe in and create even more space around your heart. Notice where you feel connected to or disconnected from people. Feel self-compassion for your desire to be valued by others. What in you needs joy, understanding, or a soothing touch? Open yourself to the reality that God is on your side. How does the truly loving Father God see you and speak to you?

Head Presence: Put yourself in the presence of your all-wise Creator. Move your head around on your shoulders. Feel its weight and presence. Breathe into your intellect. Observe your life in the body and think about your instinctive responses. What information does your body give you that you might be overlooking? What is it like to be open to new ideas and mental constructs? What is it like to bring information to your foregone conclusions of right and wrong? Welcome the ambiguity of not always knowing the answer and of everything not being clear-cut. Breathe into this space saying, "I can be open and be all right."

Pray into Your Harmony: Goodness Creates Joy

"Goodness creates joy" is a breath prayer that engages the life-giving intellect of a Seven that can hold things loosely, observe, consider possibilities, and lighten up about an issue before judging, as well as the life-giving heart of a Four with depth, soulfulness, connection, and warmth, allowing your heart to draw you closer instead of pushing others away.

Memorizing this prayer brings awareness in the moment about what is most true about you. You are more than your type. Breathe it in when you want to control, when you resist being told what to do, or when you constrict around being more right than others. Any time you get triggered and are tempted to forget who you are, breathe "goodness creates joy." Judgment, improving, and reforming can get you stuck in your gut. Open. FLOW.

> Therefore, as God's chosen people, holy and dearly loved, clothe yourselves with compassion, kindness, humility, gentleness and patience. Bear with each other and forgive one another if any of you has a grievance against someone. Forgive as the Lord forgave you. And over all these virtues put on love, which binds them all together in perfect unity.
> **COLOSSIANS 3:12-14**

Then call on all your God-given IQ, EQ, and GQ goodness.

FLOW Practice for Ones

In FLOW, Ones are **F**ree, **L**oving, **O**pen, and **W**ith. You stand in the presence of the three-in-one God and bring head, heart, and gut to your reforming. You also relate with the three Christian virtues of faith, hope, and love. When you constrict in misery at how many things need to be made better, breathe and ask the Spirit to give you inner freedom. Open your head, heart, and gut and stay with God in what is. Ask, "Is this good enough?" or "Is it my job to make this better?" Feel the freedom to say no as well as yes. At the end of the day, log what happened when you were not in FLOW. What happened when you were in FLOW? Celebrate when God's goodness flowed through you to others. Confess when it didn't. Begin again tomorrow.

Practice Confession

Vulnerability and transparency about who you are before God and others is part of transformation and connection. Confess your:

▶ *Vices of anger, judgment, and resentment:* ask God and a trusted spiritual friend to help you make the journey to grace and serenity.

▶ *Condemnations and corrections:* "Why do they do that? Here, let me show you how to do it." Ask God to help you release your compulsive monitoring of others and yourself.

▶ *Guilt:* "I've failed again." Ask God for grace to see when "good enough is good enough."

▶ *Insecurity:* having to be right, fear of making mistakes.

▶ *Self-righteous rationalizations:* "I know best." "I refuse to budge." "I did nothing wrong."

▶ *Blame:* "It's their fault."

Receive words of assurance: "Therefore, there is now no condemnation for those who are in Christ Jesus" (Romans 8:1).

Breath Prayers

Notice your magnificent breath. Feel the oxygen fill your lungs and lift your chest. Follow your breath in and down. Take time to notice what is happening in your heart. Feel the strength of your created life as you breathe in: "You have formed my inward parts; I am perfectly and wonderfully made . . . may my soul know that very well." Spend a few minutes with this breath prayer. Follow your breath to liberty—you don't have to be the judge of the whole earth.

Keep breathing into your body. Breathing in from the soles of your feet, fill your belly with breath, and continue breathing to the crown of your head. Feel your experience. Breathe into your head, your heart, and your gut. Without judgment, notice whatever comes up. If memories come, welcome them with your joyful, deep goodness. Stay with them. Take action to stay inside and hold yourself in a loving way. Below are more breath prayers.

❖ *Inhale: "Made in God's image."*
  Exhale: "I am not the judge."

❖ *Inhale: "God, you are good."*
  Exhale: "God, I am good enough."

❖ *Inhale: "Goodness,"*
  exhale: "creates joy!"

Practice Admitting You Might Be Wrong

Instead of speaking authoritatively and conclusively about things, practice starting your comments with, "I might not see all there is around this issue; this is what I offer" or "I could be wrong or off-base." Using phrases like this removes some of your inherent intensity, opens you to other views, and often allows your perspective (potentially right) to be heard by others more easily.

Practice Play

Ones tend to be serious about everything. Welcome the playful spirit of the Seven, which can lighten your compulsion to do it right.

▶ Make a list of things that bring you pleasure. Schedule them and actually do them!

▶ Hang out with people who make you happy and help you laugh at yourself.

▶ In meetings, don't stifle the laughter of others to keep your agenda moving. Let go and let the joy carry you.

▶ Ask the Spirit to give you joy as you engage in your natural reforming efforts.

Practice Gratitude

This important discipline counters your false self tendency of only seeing the bad and what needs changing.

▶ Ask God to give you eyes to see all the good around you and in you. Name these good things by thanking God for them.

▶ Gratitude realigns your heart (EQ), bringing a sense of connectedness to your experiences and allowing for wider perspective of what is actually there (IQ).

Practice Grace Giving

Your ability to discern good and bad enables you to see the gifts in others. Naming the good of others offers them grace and freedom. The desire and intention to give grace loosens your propensity to judge.

Practice Detachment

When you think you know best or when you are so attached to your idea that you can't let go, it is time to pray: "God, your will: nothing more, nothing less, and nothing else." This prayer loosens your gut constriction around your agenda and creates a space for holy detachment.

Blessing for the Beloved One

As we close this section, take time to breathe in this blessing and create space in your soul.

> *May the three-in-one God bless this grace-filled journey home to your true self.*
>
> *May God the Father teach you the joy of variety and spontaneity.*
>
> *May the heart of Jesus console you and relieve you of guilt for what isn't yet perfected.*
>
> *May the Holy Spirit ground you in the goodness of God and God alone.*
>
> *May the Sacred Goodness of the Trinity lead you on your road while on this journey, upholding you and loving you.*

Empathy for ONES

Every child has a need to receive affirmation from their caretakers. Some Ones may have had critical and judgmental caregivers who expected perfection and undermined confidence. Sensitive One children internalized these messages and did their best to be good, obedient, and right, but ended up feeling angry, resentful, and misunderstood. Here you can explore your responses to the Ones in your life and how you might grow in empathy and see them as God does.

Empathy is a true self response that harmonizes and breaks down the we/they divide. But this can be challenging when it comes to loving Ones, given their critical nature and steaming anger. Even with that, we may come to rely on their stability, organization, and discernment. Understanding how Ones became focused on getting things right can open compassionate and empathetic interactions with them. Here, a One describes her journey to integration.

I was a child in the middle of many siblings with bigger voices, problems, and needs, which meant my parents needed me to be good. Mistakes and failures brought critique and punishment that was swift and harsh. Expressing anger only made things worse. There was never an encouraging word. I don't know when I internalized that voice of criticism. It has not served me well. I am overly serious. And I resent it! The Enneagram was a lifeline; it put me in touch with the anger I had denied. The Harmony Triads helped me intentionally lean into something more than my default guilt and touchiness about criticism. My Seven IQ reminds me to lighten up, life doesn't have to be so heavy and serious. My Four EQ puts me in touch with emotions; I own up to what I feel. I go deep with people and admit there is more than *one* way of seeing things. Integrating IQ, EQ, and GQ has saved my marriage and life.

1. As you consider the One story, notice:
   - What are you thinking about this One?
   - What are you feeling about this One?
   - What is your gut instinct about this One?

2. When have you had your behavior critiqued or mistake punished? What was that like for you?

3. Have you ever constricted while trying to be perfect only to be corrected by someone? What was that like for you?

4. Why do you think Ones struggle with being serious and resentful?

UNDERSTANDING THE DEFENSE MECHANISM OF REACTION FORMATION

Ones don't want to think, feel, or do things they think are bad, so they compensate by exaggerating exactly the opposite tendency in themselves. This is called reaction formation. This One discovered how his defense mechanism works.

When I find a deficiency in myself or receive criticism, the impact is painful. My inner critic is horrified and humiliated that my failures and imperfections are exposed. Rather than admit my faults, I immediately double down on trying to prove how I am the opposite of these imperfections. Rather than own up, I blame and/or comment on the "bad" behavior of others so no one will suspect those things go on in me. I thought I was really good until the Enneagram named my defense as reaction formation. I was stunned to see how often I avoided transformation by pretending to be better than I was. My false self often eluded truth by exerting a really controlled response that only slightly covered up the anger and resentment that boiled inside. As grace broke through my self effort, I began to come to God with all my flaws, which was the first step in developing healthy patterns of relating.

1. What connections or resistances are you feeling for this One?

2. Try to imagine living with this One's inner critic. Can you recognize the distress of looking for acceptance but finding only greater pressure to appear flawless?

3. How can you encourage Ones that imperfections don't change their beloved-ness?

4. How might you join the Holy Spirit in praying for a re-forming, principled One in your life?

RELATING TO A ONE

We find grace to see things from a One's point of view when we remember that under a One's rigid exterior is a sensitive individual trying to silence their inner critic.

- Appreciate their high standards, steadiness, helpfulness, and hard work. Assure them of their worth.

- Encouragement gets better results from Ones than criticism. Tell them you would welcome their encouragement—they can be good at this.

- Ones love for people to apologize. Admit your mistakes.

- Remember that Ones pick up the slightest negative remarks. You will have better luck registering complaints at a time when they seem open and unstressed. Prepare them by saying, "I want to talk with you about something, and I need you to remember that I respect you and/or love you."

- Ones can dish out teasing but have a hard time not taking your teasing seriously.

- Their perfectionism is about improving things—give them room to help you improve things.

The following list summarizes key characteristics of Ones. Consider your responses to these qualities.

- *Authentic, true self:* Good

- *Compulsive, false self:* Angry

- *Virtue leading back to true self:* Serenity, grace

- *Personality style:* Reformer, perfecter

- *Work style:* Quality performer

- *Leadership/action style:* Organizer, stabilizer, clarifier

- *Relationships:* Moral

- *Core motivation:* Rightness, control

- *Negative fixation:* Anger

- *Narrative:* "I can never get this right. I am bad."

- *Communication:* What's right and correct

- *One with a Nine wing:* Likely to be more peaceful, relaxed

- *One with a Two wing:* More caring, compassionate, concerned for others

- *Basic fear:* Being imperfect/defective

- *Basic desire:* To be good, moral

- *Drive:* To be right, strive higher and improve everything, live up to ideals; to be so good no one can criticize

Based on the description above:

1. How does it feel to be a One? What descriptors give clues on how to relate to a One?

2. Is there a better way to say what is true of Ones?

3. One's reforming energy can wind them up tight. What is it like to meet their energy with your gut and some easy goodness?

4. Ones want to be appreciated for seeing how to make things better. How can you express your appreciation for a One and encourage them to integrate their EQ and IQ?

THE HEART TRIAD
Twos, Threes, and Fours

PART II

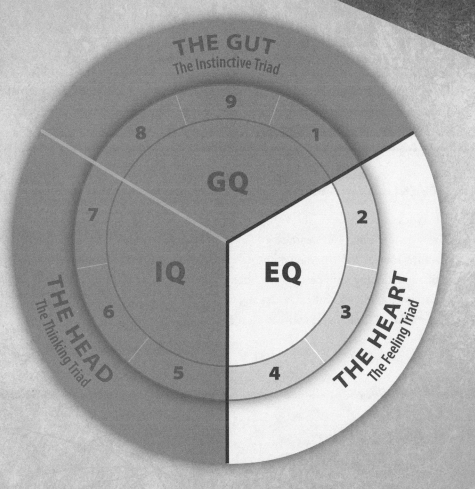

THE GUT
The Instinctive Triad

9

8   1

GQ

7   2

IQ   EQ

3

6

THE HEAD
The Thinking Triad

THE HEART
The Feeling Triad

5   4

THE HEART TRIAD HAS EMOTIONAL AWARENESS
OR HEART INTELLIGENCE (EQ)

Twos, Threes, and Fours perceive or filter the world through the emotional temperature, needs, and responses of others. This triad is energized by the outer world of relationships and nurtures connections. The natural, personal energy of Twos, Threes, and Fours is attractive and leans toward empathy and engagement. Twos reflect God's love. Threes reflect God's effectiveness. Fours reflect God's creativity. The virtue of the Two is humility. The virtue of the Three is veracity. The virtue of the Four is equanimity.

EQ

Your heart has its own neural system. There are more neurons sending information from your heart region (EQ) to your brain than vice versa. People with healthy EQ can authentically care and do good things without needing a response from others. Their love, industry, and creativity are given freely without strings. They embody the sacrificial care and love of Jesus. They resonate with the words of Jesus: "Greater love has no one than this: to lay down one's life for one's friends" (John 15:13).

HEART DEFENSIVE POSTURE

The Heart Triad is a needy triad because Twos, Threes, and Fours live for response from others. When they don't get the responses they seek, they can feel incompetent, inadequate, and disconnected. These feelings lead to inner distress and their dominant fixation of shame and anxiety. To lessen their sense of shame and anxiety, heart people *do* things to gain approval, prove their value, and increase connection.

EXPERIENCING THE SACRED

Heart types often connect with God through relationships, imagery, and symbols that impress the presence and nearness of God on them. Sacred texts, beautiful poetry, architecture, music, and art connect the neediness of this sensitive triad to the God who can fill their longings and desires. The book of Psalms names the human condition with all its feelings, laments, and praise. It validates the felt experience of the Heart Triad and connects Twos, Threes, and Fours to God and others.

TWOS

Love Contemplates Then Decides

I've got to show the world, world's got to see.
See all the love, love that's in me.

CAT STEVENS

I am a friendly,
self-sacrificing person.
I love to see what a person needs
and then be the one to give it to them. I am
very intuitive and sensitive to others. I have a strong
desire to be loved and appreciated for what I do. I
would like to do more for people than I do and will
go above and beyond the call of duty. I naturally give of myself. Being busy with the care
of others and tending to their needs can
make me unaware of my own needs. I am
not good at saying no. I don't want to
disappoint and I put more energy into
loving others than loving myself. Some
people may think I am clingy or codependent or possessive. It saddens me if
people think I'm trying to control them
through my caring. I like people to see me as
cheerful, self-sufficient, warm-hearted, and sacrificing. I work very hard to connect in a heartfelt
way. I am nurturing and empathetic but sometimes
when I am hurt I become "martyr-like" and say things
like, "after all I've done for you!" When I am
offended, I can get vindictive or
take revenge.

WHO I AM AND WHO I AM NOT

Twos bear the image of God as love. Your life resonates with Matthew 25:35: "For I was hungry and you gave me something to eat, I was thirsty and you gave me something to drink, I was a stranger and you invited me in."

Love and care are inevitably part of a Two's story. Stories about who we are and who we are not shape what we do, who we become, and where we get stuck. Twos often have a narrative about being helpful, encouraging, and loving. You skip over the chapters of your life about giving to get or needing a response. This section gives you awareness of some words that shape the narrative of a Two.

▶▶▶ **BELOVED TWOS**

Spend some time with the words below that describe who Twos are and are not. Circle the characteristics that resonate with your journey. Star words that express your gifts. Underline words that describe parts of your personality that are unusable by God in their present form. Put a checkmark beside characteristics that you *celebrate*.

Twos Descriptive Words List

I AM		I AM NOT	
helpful	thoughtful	selfish	thoughtless
needed	considerate	needy	inconsiderate
indispensable	responsive	useless	unresponsive
generous	ready	petty	unconcerned
caring	feeling	uncaring	cold
supportive	intuitive	destructive	insensitive
nurturing	observant	violent	callous
loving	attentive	hateful	inattentive
lovable	serving	angry	stingy
peaceful	self-sacrificing	aggressive	self-centered
caretaking	altruistic	neglectful	self-absorbed
empathetic	warm	uncaring	unwelcoming
sympathetic	hospitable	heartless	alone
sensitive	friendly	indifferent	

➤ Which words reflect the image of God in you?

➤ Which words are you most attached to? Addicted to? Compulsive about?

➤ Which words do you resist and judge the most?

➤ If you opened up to the words you resist without judgment, how might your life and relationships shift?

➤ Journal about the words that reflect how God looks after you.

► ► ► **GETTING TO KNOW TWOS**

This Two shares the story of how both nature and nurture nudged her toward loving connection. While opportunities to care for a brother may seem difficult for some, this Two flourished and delighted in them.

> My Two energy showed up in childhood. I had loving parents, and we lived in a friendly, homogeneous neighborhood where children were cherished. My environment was a petri dish of Two energy. It made me into a friendly, warm-hearted child who engaged easily in conversations with young and old. My youngest brother was developmentally disabled, and I enjoyed opportunities to care for him. His condition helped me develop a nurturing side. Looking back, I recognize a little giver who was empathetic, sincere, generous, warm, and always looking to connect.

➤ What does this Two childhood story bring up in you?

➤ What is your memory of your first Two experience?

➤ What is it like for you to feel that you are needed and helpful to others? What happens in your heart space?

TRUE SELF AND FALSE SELF: THE LOVING PERSON

Who we are or are not comes with expression and energy. The attitudes, behaviors, and motivations of beloved Twos convey a loving and serving presence. Emerging from union with God, a Two's true self can give sacrificially without needing a response. A Two's false self is the compulsive, deeply entrenched, old nature that constricts around how many people need and love you. It is the psychological or ego self that is a complex mixture of nature, nurture, needs, and free will.

This section will help you begin to recognize compulsive and impulsive false self reactions as well as true self FLOW that loves God, others, and self.

True Self Twos: Sacred Love

Twos are fashioned to reflect God's loving nurture. Embodying divine love resonates with you. You make warm-hearted, empathetic, self-sacrificing friends. Healthy Twos relate easily, nurture generously, and love unconditionally. Naturally attentive to the needs and desires of others, you show strong care and sense how much help is needed. True self Twos respect your needs as well as the needs of others. You are able to discern what is yours to do and not do in the world. You give appropriately and honor your

Breath Prayer

In silence and solitude, ask God to help you see yourself clearly. Begin with breathing. Breathe in: "Made in God's image," and then breathe out: "I reflect love." Spend a few minutes with this breath prayer. Feel the goodness and freedom of being made in God's image; feel the liberty of being a reflection of love rather than the Source of Love. Breathe this prayer in and out throughout the day.

own limits. When Twos are present to God, self, and others, you meet needs in response to the Spirit's prompting and without expectation of a response or pat on the back. Transforming Twos reveal that God humbly came in person through Jesus because God adores us.

False Self Twos: Constrict in Pride, People Pleasing, and Fear of Being Unloved

Compulsive, false self Twos are proud of your loving and giving and how it makes you indispensable to others. Addicted to your own feats of loving makes you feel proud that no one else loves as selflessly as you do. Pride is your vice, and it pushes past appropriate boundaries and blinds Twos to where your giving comes with a hook. Pride can also blind you to how clingy, possessive, and martyr-like you are if people don't respond as you want. Un-centered Twos want returns on good deeds: notes of appreciation, dinners in your honor, and influence in others' lives. You keep track if others don't reciprocate. Dependent on others' approval, false self Twos can become insecure and vindictive.

▶▶▶ TRUE OR FALSE SELF

As you think about your true and false self, consider the following questions. Notice what comes up for you; notice without judgment. What questions particularly invite you to jot down or journal responses?

➤ How do true self Two characteristics show up in your relationships?

➤ Where do false self Two qualities show up in your relationships? How does pride show up? ("I must prove I have worth!") How does shame show up? ("I am not enough!") When you feel distressed by disconnection, what do you do to lower your anxiety?

Giving to Get

It can be hard to see where care for others is rooted in selfish motives. In this reading, Jesus addresses the false self that gives to get. Consider where you might give hospitality and care with a hook that expects to be invited back.

Then Jesus said to his host, "When you give a luncheon or dinner, do not invite your friends, your brothers or sisters, your relatives, or your rich neighbors; if you do, they may invite you back and so you will be repaid. But when you give a banquet, invite the poor, the crippled, the lame, the blind, and you will be blessed. Although they cannot repay you, you will be repaid at the resurrection of the righteous." (Luke 14:12-14)

1. What comes up in you as you read Jesus' words?

2. St. Vincent de Paul cautioned his brothers not to expect gratitude for giving service and love with these words: "It is only for your love alone that the poor will forgive you the bread you give them." When have your motives for serving included being noticed, thanked, repaid, or honored for your charity?

3. How can you befriend, encourage, and give to someone who cannot pay you back or advance you in some way?

> ➤ What makes you constrict and shut down your heart affections? What is a cue to open yourself to others?

> ➤ How do you feel the difference between centered, true self energy and edgy, false self energy?

HARMONY: LOVE CONTEMPLATES THEN DECIDES

Twos are often identified as the loving number, but you are much more than just one number! You bear the image and harmony of a three-in-one God. When beloved Twos integrate your IQ and GQ, you harmonize, and your love flows with the wisdom of the Five and the agency of the Eight. This section creates awareness of how FLOW is the unique gift of the Harmony Triads.

In harmony and FLOW, a Two's supportive care ponders what is actually helpful to others with the IQ of a Five and generates self-reliance rather than codependency in others with the GQ of an Eight.

►►► MORE THAN YOUR TYPE

This story describes a Two, Five, and Eight journey to integration. This beloved Two is doing good work around the importance of boundaries. He is learning to discern when to use his gut to say no rather than yes. He also learns that using his head to detach from people-pleasing gives him freedom. Notice how integrating Five IQ and Eight GQ gives this overly involved heart Two the ability to choose what is and is not his to do.

> I was the baby of the family and my mother's favorite. She relied on me for intimacy, conversation, and companionship. There were four years between myself and my next oldest sibling, so everyone was away at college when I began high school—everyone except my mother and my ninety-three-year-old grandmother. The lack of strong male leadership during those years led me to resent my mother's strong Eight behavior of meddling and interference. I took on the Two helper role, adapted to avoid conflict, and tried to please. I would also escape into my Five "cave" to protect myself. Beginning to understand my undeveloped Eight and unacknowledged Five explains so much. The Two, Five, and Eight Harmony Triad explains why I used to respond instantly when someone pressed me for intimacy. I see why I let my boundaries go so others would respond to me with affection. I am finally finding a path to transformation.

> ➤ When you are distressed by feeling disconnected, how do you ignore boundaries and limits? How could a more observant response actually make you a better connector?

> ➤ How do you power into your gut when you don't feel appreciated? What would it look like to redirect your hurt at disconnection in a contemplative way?

> ➤ Imagine tempering caretaking energy with confident GQ energy as well as IQ energy that ponders the motives behind your need for connection. What do you see?

▶▶▶ IQ, GQ, EQ

This Two describes his journey to integration. Attending to his caring and unselfish energy led this Two to take decisive Eight GQ action in choosing his career. Strong GQ confidence developed his passion for Five IQ learning. Notice how accessing his Harmony Triad has brought passion, boundaries, and wisdom to his relational warmth.

> During high school, I developed a passion for golf, and for many years hoped to become a professional golfer. I was drawn to golf because it was an individual sport. Results were totally up to me. I now understand that this draw to individualism was the Five in me. At the same time, I had a hang up about pursuing professional golf because it seemed like a selfish existence with no place for serving others. This hesitation led me to walk away from golf and pursue academics and IQ instead. Academic success grew Eight self-confidence energy. It also led to judgments and lack of vulnerability in relationships. When I became a teacher, my GQ gave me strong, resourceful, decisive energy. My EQ also brought a sense of empathy, warmth, and love for students and friends.

Watch Me Serve

This reading describes how over-serving and wanting to make an impression can actually get in the way of connection and presence. Notice how Jesus cares that both Mary and Martha have the inner freedom to choose what is better.

> As Jesus and his disciples were on their way, he came to a village where a woman named Martha opened her home to him. She had a sister called Mary, who sat at the Lord's feet listening to what he said. But Martha was distracted by all the preparations that had to be made. She came to him and asked, "Lord, don't you care that my sister has left me to do the work by myself? Tell her to help me!"
>
> "Martha, Martha," the Lord answered, "you are worried and upset about many things, but few things are needed—or indeed only one. Mary has chosen what is better, and it will not be taken away from her." (Luke 10:38-42)

1. When does serving insulate you from authentically being with others?

2. Martha started out wanting to be hospitable and ended up frustrated with her guests for not appreciating what she is doing. She orders Jesus, "Tell her (Mary) to help me!" Where do you move to Eight intensity and lash out when others don't seem to need you? How does pride in serving make your serving all about you?

3. How do Jesus' words invite you to be mindful and present to choosing what is better rather than attempting to get others to respond to your exaggerated need for validation?

> ➤ When Twos engage their head, they step back and moderate their distress at not being appreciated. Where do you see IQ in yourself?

> ➤ When Twos engage their gut, they step up to take on conflict and hard relational issues. Where do you see GQ in yourself?

> ➤ What is it like for you to have IQ, GQ, and EQ?

HEALING CHILDHOOD HURTS: OPENING TO HUMILITY

Children are wired for resilience. Still, residual childhood baggage and messages can leak into adult Two relationships. Two children can lose the message, "You are wanted." The default message you can learn is, "It's not okay to have your own needs." To cope, Two children give, please, and try to become indispensable. These defenses mitigate against limits and self-awareness. Do any of these messages resonate with you?

When these messages get triggered in adult interactions, then raw, ragged, unprocessed pain can erupt, sabotaging the FLOW of a Two's love. Suddenly a needy four-year-old inside you begins to call the shots and want attention. Defaulting to the false self, you get stuck on the edge of pride, possessiveness, and insecurity.

The Harmony Triad offers a way for Twos to be curious about the trauma, defenses, childhood lies, and dismissed needs that shape your relationships today.

Prayer of Ignatius of Loyola

Allow this prayer of Ignatius of Loyola, which addresses the heart, head, and gut energy of the Enneagram Triads, to become your prayer. This week, pray the mind, heart, and strength of the Trinity into your life and interactions.

> *Take, Lord, and receive all of my liberty,*
> *my memory, my understanding [IQ],*
> *and my entire will,*
> *All I have I call my own.*

> *You have given all to me.*
> *To you, Lord, I return it.*

> *Everything is yours; do with it what*
> *you will [GQ].*
> *Give me only your love [EQ] and*
> *your grace,*
> *that is enough for me.*

▶▶▶ RECEIVING THE DISMISSED CHILDLIKE SELF

Receiving your dismissed child can heal and give beloved Twos freedom to be humble, insightful, and decisive. Remember, within every warm, compassionate, and helpful Two there is an independent, domineering, controlling Eight who believes that vulnerability and sensitivity are marks of weakness. There is also a dissembling, detached, and private Five who is afraid they will be sucked dry by all the needs around them. To recognize where you dismissed your childlike self and your needs, pay attention to where you may have ignored your GQ and IQ.

This Two shares his story of growing up in a world where compassionate pursuits were discouraged and un-nurtured. Pay attention to how he integrates his IQ, EQ, and GQ.

My grandfather and my dad owned businesses; it was how men provided. My brothers followed suit. My parents' experience of the Depression also made them value financial security. My siblings and parents had a hard time understanding me. They were afraid my connecting, giving side wasn't tough enough to make money. My father would say, "I love you, but I don't get what makes you tick." The insinuation was clear to me: "What if I married, had kids, and couldn't provide the kind of opportunities I had been given? Maybe I should be a priest!?" Hoping to keep me strong and entrepreneurial, my parents gave kudos to any Eight GQ accomplishments. My Two EQ and Five IQ traits were dismissed and/or ignored. It has been teachers, friends, spiritual mentors, and especially my wife who have helped me heal, embrace my Two self, and integrate my Five and Eight.

As you read the questions below, notice where you sense God's invitation to more deeply receive your dismissed child. Write down any new insights and awareness. You are doing important and integrative work here.

➤ This Two described his family as not fully understanding how he ticked. What is it like to have a narrative like this shape you? How does this story resonate in you?

➤ Within the gregarious, sensitive Two is a "hide in the cave" Five who fears, "I won't have enough energy for this." Where does this message show up in your life?

➤ Underneath the gentle-hearted Two is a take-control, in-charge Eight who wonders, "Can we please stop coddling and get on with it?" Notice when your inner child reacts like this.

➤ Where do you dismiss your head (IQ) and your gut (GQ)?

▶▶▶ JOURNALING YOUR DISMISSED CHILDLIKE SELF

Integrating and accessing your IQ and GQ can make you aware of what needs to happen so you take care of you and not everyone else. Getting reacquainted with GQ gives you strength to hold boundaries and take your own desires seriously. Integrating IQ brings perspective to your relational distress. Checking out what your body feels and your head perceives gives you more than feelings to work with on your path to harmony.

Name and journal some of your hurts and tenderly explore when you began to defend yourself by comparing the way you love to the way others love. Engage your IQ and make time to ponder and monitor the GQ strength of your responses. Feel free to choose among the questions and return to other questions at another time.

➤ What is your story about finding your caring feelings and needs dismissed? Where do you continue to dismiss needs or desires because of past trauma and wanting to please? What default reactions and triggers of your childhood self still operate today?

> ➤ When did you begin to feel proud of how you loved and feel critical of others' lack of care? When has loving been a way you manipulated others? Courageously explore when you began to give yourself away in order to feel worthy.

> ➤ Ask God to help you return to your virtue of humility. Open to the childlikeness that helps you love others without agenda and for the sheer pleasure of it.

> ➤ Where has the importance of your presence been repaired/healed or increased/solidified?

Helpful Twos have a default posture of "all you need is love" or "you will miss me when I am gone." In your false self, you can get stuck in martyr mode. God's invitation is to break free from pride and hardheartedness toward people who don't seem to need you. The spiritual practice of forgiving puts Twos in a place to receive others as they are, rather than as you want them to be. It may be helpful for you to read the "Invitation to Forgive" and "Invitation to Pray" chapters in *Invitations from God* by Adele Ahlberg Calhoun.

When you feel your heart hardening and a bit of snap and meanness enters your voice, open your heart. The person is most likely not wanting to hurt you. Speak up and tell them you are hurt. Regardless of their response, ask God for grace to forgive them for not responding as you would like. Forgiveness is different than reconciliation.

Healing Prayer

When Twos process your wounds in the presence of God's unconditional love and those who love you, it is easier to love and value yourself. When that happens, you move from being needy and over-giving in relationships to loving with appropriate generosity and altruism. Your vice of pride is transformed into your virtue of humility.

This is a way to do healing prayer on your own. Relax into silence and solitude. Breathe deeply. Don't force it. Become present to God and yourself. Ask God to show you a past pain in your life that is still being transmitted. Be still and wait. When something comes to mind, follow this simple trail of healing prayer.

- ❖ *Imagine yourself and Jesus back in the memory. Get your bearings. Where is Jesus? Where are you?*

- ❖ *What are you feeling? (anxious, ashamed, unappreciated, needy, unworthy, or something else)*

- ❖ *Do these feelings remind you of a time you had similar reactions? You can go with Jesus to that place and time or stay where you are.*

- ❖ *Continue to name what you feel in your experience. Ask Jesus if these feelings point to a lie you began to believe at that time. Give it a name.*

- ❖ *What is Jesus saying to you about this lie? Listen. Is there an image, word, or phrase that he speaks to you? Let Jesus' words replace lies with truth about who you are.*

- ❖ *Repeat the truth you have heard about yourself from Jesus gently and frequently. Let the truth be an antidote that lets the pain go into Jesus and sets you free.*

Forgiveness sets you free from bitterness and martyrdom. This week, keep track of the times you soften your heart as it begins to harden, and ask for the strength (GQ) to voice your hurt and lean toward God's forgiving heart.

DISCERNMENT: CONSOLATIONS AND DESOLATIONS

Ignatius of Loyola taught that God's Guiding Spirit of wisdom moves in all three centers of intelligence—head, heart, and gut. When faced with a decision, Ignatius suggested noticing the consolations and desolations by asking: What does my heart feel? What does my mind think? What does my gut sense?

Consolations point Twos toward God's presence and a love that doesn't give to get. Consolations are evidence that a Two is heading in the direction of EQ love that can IQ ponder what is best and then act with GQ strength. Desolations of disconnection and shame, which distort the FLOW of God's love, alert Twos that you have fallen into your false self and are in need of God's grace to return to the inner freedom that doesn't give to get. (More information on Harmony Triad discernment is found in Soul Resource 5.)

Twos experience consolations such as love without a hook, sensitive power, compassionate confidence, warm direction, sympathetic detachment, altruistic courage, responsive thoughtfulness, holy vulnerability, and attentive wisdom. This is freedom.

Twos experience desolations such as pride, manipulation, clinginess, and preoccupation with approval. The desolations that make a Two calculating, possessive, overly sensitive, insecure, prideful, martyr-like, and codependent leave you bound.

▶▶▶ PRESENT TO WHAT'S HAPPENING INSIDE

Both consolations and desolations point toward the purpose for which Twos were created. This Two is studying the map of her soul. She notices signposts of desolation and consolation and how she knows herself through the words of others. When Twos default to the autopilot of finding approval through what others mirror back to you, you give to point of depletion to raise your self-esteem and in the process lose yourself. Notice how the consolations and desolations of this Two could direct them toward healing and the presence of God.

A while back, a spiritual friend told me that my mantra had become: "If you knew me like I know me, you'd reject me like I reject me." I carry a deep wound of not feeling loved (desolation). My friend's thought penetrated my heart (desolation), and I knew her words were true (consolation). I began to intentionally ask myself, "What do you want?" I thought about how I loved others, and I began to show that loving kindness toward myself. I noticed my own exhaustion and needs. I told God about them. And I asked for courage to know how to speak of these things to my spiritual friend. This hard work feels so restorative (consolation).

> Where does "not feeling loved" distress you and bring desolation?

> When you are in desolation, pay attention to the Spirit's motions in your head and gut. Do you get mad and push against your desolation? How could checking in with your IQ help you understand the desolation of feeling responsible for everyone?

▶▶▶ DESOLATION AND REPRESSION

Insecure and needy Twos have a default defense of repression. Repression suppresses unacceptable feelings and converts you into using a more acceptable form of emotional energy. For Twos, repression might happen when you ignore your needs and focus on how someone else needs you. Repression develops an "I am indispensable" narrative that mitigates against self-awareness as well as support and love. Without judgment, notice where you repress the truth about what you need and want. Stay with one or two questions and let the truth settle in.

> When have you lied, given gifts, or used flattery to get others to like you? How does Eight anger and meanness show up? When does pride manifest in martyrdom: "Look at all I have done for you!" Where does pride manifest in, "I don't need anything"?

> How does your body constrict and tighten up when people don't seem to like you? Where do you carry this distress and frustration?

> How does loving in your own strength close you off from consolations and keep you from standing in the FLOW of God's love?

> Are there defenses besides repression that block your discernment?

> *Prayer Practice for When You Feel Under-Appreciated*
>
> *Twos in particular wonder how people can be so unloving and ungrateful. When you feel distress at lack of appreciation, intentionally breathe deeply into that void. Breathe in: "God, you love me." Breathe out: "I am wanted." Let this breath prayer open you to God and the moment. Something unexpected might happen if you receive people as they are and wait for God to show up.*

▶▶▶ CONSOLATIONS AND HUMILITY

The Spirit's invitation to consolation often means the thinking or pondering IQ recognizes that giving feels more important than receiving. Humility allows others to give. Humility can receive. It can step back to discern where help is actually wanted in another's experience of desolation. It can contemplate the need for help in one's own desolation. Your wise IQ and dynamic GQ help you move with thought-through giving. Notice when the Spirit invites you into the consolation of caring—not as you want to give, but as others want to receive.

Twos are consoled as you follow God's Spirit out of pride into a humility that owns personal limits and needs. Humility allows Twos to recognize how being drained, exhausted, and running on empty affects everyone (including yourself) negatively. Humility also opens a way for Twos to see yourself through God's eyes and care. You don't need to be everything to everyone. Divine love can flow through your human limitations as well as the limitations of others.

> ➤ Describe a situation in which you felt the Holy Spirit inviting you to let go of your image of yourself as the measure of what it looks like to love and care for others. What happened? What consolations came to you?

> ➤ When has humility helped you stand in the FLOW of God's love for others? What does it look like for you to love yourself or let others love you with heart, soul, strength, and mind?

SPIRITUAL RHYTHMS FOR TWOS

Therefore, I urge you, brothers and sisters, in view of God's mercy, to offer your bodies as a living sacrifice, holy and pleasing to God—this is your true and proper worship. Do not conform to the pattern of this world, but be transformed by the renewing of your mind. Then you will be able to test and approve what God's will is—his good, pleasing, and perfect will. (Romans 12:1-2)

Twos are quick to offer your heart. Paul urges us to offer our bodies as an act of worship that actually renews old default patterns of the mind. Intentionally offering your body to God reminds Twos to care for the body you offer to God. Offering your body also moves you to act selflessly and with insight about how action for others depletes or energizes you. Grounded in your body, Twos can hold boundaries and say no. Offering your bodies can renew a Two's neural pathways. Then you can discern what God's will is for you.

Regularly attending to the Holy Spirit's motions of the soul helps beloved Twos recognize when your care is rooted in inner freedom rather than codependence or needing to be needed. The Spirit gives Twos a sense of your beloved-ness so you can integrate a love that is rooted in contemplation and non-manipulative decisiveness.

These spiritual rhythms are all ways Twos can lean into God's invitations to transformation and mind renewal. Not every practice will be the one for you. Say yes to the practices that best capture your desire to be with God right now.

▶▶▶ PRACTICING PRESENCE: TWOS

Re-read the FLOW definition in the Key Terms section. Notice the presence of Trinitarian harmony.

Father, Son, and Spirit belong and flow together.

Head, heart, and gut belong and flow together.

Faith, love, and hope belong and flow together.

Divine harmony calls Twos to be present to the truth that you already belong. You don't need to do something to prove you are worthy of love and belonging. Twos who are present to God and others with head, heart, and gut can integrate this heart belonging into your entire created being. Let the following meditative prayer hold your head observations, heart feelings, and gut resilience together. Staying with this prayer for a season can help Twos access their GQ and IQ so you don't feel every relational issue is about your inadequacy. IQ, EQ, and GQ bring stability to your emotions, insecurities, and needs.

Find a comfortable and awake position. Remember that the Spirit of God dwells within you and prays for you. Ask God to give you an open and receptive head, heart, and gut.

Gut Presence: Put yourself in the presence of the Spirit. Breathe into your gut space. Notice what is happening in your body. Notice without judgment. Let your body tell you what it knows. Is there something your body wants to do in this prayer? Do that. Experience your ability to care—give thanks for your strong welcoming nature. Can you notice where your body constricts and deflects love? When do you give your attention to others before observing what your body tells you about limits, tiredness, and needs?

Heart Presence: Put yourself in the presence of Jesus. Breathe into your heart space. Feel your tenderness. Notice your heart's need to be held and cherished. Breathe in and create even more space around your heart. Notice your own needs. Invite self-compassion. What in you needs care, a kind word, or a soothing touch? Name these places before the Good Shepherd. How does the Good Shepherd respond to you?

Head Presence: Put yourself in the presence of the Wise Creator. Move your head around on your shoulders. Feel its weight and tightness. Breathe into your intellect. Observe your life in the body. What does your head tell you? What is it like to trust questions and perspectives rather than your heart's intuition? Is there a place where your heart moves you to, "Do first, think later"? Ask your head to show you what it would be like to, "Think first, do later."

Pray into Your Harmony:
Love Contemplates Then Decides

"Love contemplates then decides" is a breath prayer that helps you engage the life-giving intellect of Five that can hold things loosely, observe, detach, and learn more about an issue before responding, as well as the life-giving strength of Eight that is confident action, fairness, leadership, and direct communication.

Memorizing this prayer brings awareness to what is most true about you to real-life situations. You are more than your type. Breathe this prayer in preparation for the board meeting, a challenging conversation, or a stressful day. Anytime you feel triggered and are tempted to constrict and tighten around your need for affection and approval, open up and breathe "love contemplates then decides." You don't need to stay stuck in your emotions. Open to the FLOW of divine love. Then call on all your God-given loving care to ponder and act.

> I love you the more [Two EQ] in that I believe you had liked me for my own sake [Eight GQ] and for nothing else [Five IQ].
>
> **JOHN KEATS (WITH OUR ADDITIONS)**

FLOW Practice for Twos

In FLOW, beloved Twos are **F**ree, **L**oving, **O**pen, and **W**ith. You stand in the presence of the three-in-one God and integrate head, heart, and gut in your loving. You also relate with the three Christian virtues of faith, hope, and love. When you notice that you are constricting and stuck in giving to get, when you tighten around your need to be needed, or when you take care of everyone except you, this is the moment to breathe and ask the Spirit to give you inner freedom to be with what is. Open your head and gut and ask, "What is being asked of me, and do I have the time and energy to do it?" Feel the freedom to say no as well as yes. At the end of the day, log what happened when you were not in FLOW. What happened when you were in FLOW? Celebrate when God's love for others flowed through you. Confess when it didn't. Begin again tomorrow.

Practice Confession

Tell your Creator about the real neediness and sin in you. Confess your:

- ▶ *Vice of pride:* this makes your way of loving the benchmark for everyone else. Ask God and a trusted accountability partner to help you make the journey to greater humility.

- ▶ *Anxiety and distress:* feelings you have around disconnection and lack of recognition.

- ▶ *Meanness and martyr-like behavior:* when others don't respond as you want.

- ▶ *Shame:* feeling unworthy of loving and belonging.

- ▶ *Giving to get:* doing things for others in order to get them to like you or do something for you.

- ▶ *Courting attention:* trying to gain the favor of certain important people.

Receive God's assurance: "You are forgiven and worthy of love and belonging."

Breath Prayers

Notice your magnificent breath. Feel the oxygen fill your lungs and lift your chest. Follow your breath in and down. Take time to notice what is happening in your heart. Feel the strength of your created life as you breathe in: "You have formed my inward parts; I am lovingly and wonderfully made . . . may my soul know that very well." Spend a few minutes with this breath prayer. Follow your breath to liberty—you don't have to be the all-loving Creator.

Keep breathing into your body. Breathing in from the soles of your feet, fill your belly with breath, and continue breathing to the crown of your head. Feel your experience. Breathe into your head, your heart, and your gut. Without judgment, notice whatever comes up. If memories come, welcome them with your wise, loving strength. Stay with them. Take action to stay inside and hold yourself in a loving way. Use the breath prayers below when they fit the situation you are in.

- ❖ *Inhale: "Made in God's image." Exhale: "I reflect love."*

- ❖ *Inhale: "God, you love me." Exhale: "I am wanted."*

- ❖ *Inhale: "Love contemplates," exhale: "then decides."*

Practice Self-Care

Self-care honors God through nurturing and protecting your body, mind, and heart with your needs and desires.

- ▶ Jesus says, "Love your neighbor as yourself" (Mark 12:31). Think of ways you love others. How could you love yourself like you love others?

- ▶ Walk, run, work out—do what makes your body feel good.

- ▶ Make a list of boundaries in order to give space for yourself.

- ▶ Let others love you. Receive their love. Life isn't about you paying them back.

- ▶ Be sure to rest adequately.

- ▶ Don't offer spontaneous yeses. Say no to invitations to help when they don't fit your present life situation. Less can be more.

- ▶ Explore and experiment with some hobbies or interests that would give you joy.

- ▶ Fill your own inner tank with some alone time that is all about you.

Practice Intercessory Prayer

Convert your concern for others into prayer for them.

- ▶ In silence, hold a person's name in the presence of God. Listen to how the Spirit of God might pray for this person. Let the Spirit's prayer direct how you pray.

- ▶ When you see people, let your first response be a short prayer for them.

- ▶ In public settings, ask God to meet the needs of the people in the room.

- ▶ When you feel inclined to overdo your care for someone, pray for them instead. This is doing something for them.

Practice Compassion

The Trinitarian God has compassion on human beings. God the Father is on our side. The Holy Spirit inhabits us. Jesus reaches toward us with mercy and friendship. Twos know how to give God's extravagant care in practical ways.

- ▶ Who in your neighborhood, school, or workplace needs encouragement? A meal? An advocate as they go to the doctor? Help them.

- ▶ When you are tempted to criticize someone for not helping out as you do, show them understanding.

- ▶ Volunteer some of your time where people don't know you and where they might not say thank you.

- ▶ Show patience and kindness to the people in your family who aren't as sensitive as you want them to be toward you.

Practice Hospitality

Hospitality creates a safe open space where people can experience their own beloved-ness. Paul says, "Welcome one another as Christ has welcomed you" (Romans 15:7 ESV).

- ▶ What is your experience of God welcoming you? Of others welcoming you?

- ▶ Hospitality is qualitatively different from entertaining. It is an experience of loving guests as though they were family. When you have guests, how will you make them comfortable enough to curl up on your couch and take their shoes off?

- ▶ Reach out to a stranger, or even an enemy, with hospitality.

- ▶ Invite people beyond your friendship circle to dinner.

▶ Bring the hospitality of God with you wherever you go. Be open, receptive, accepting, and kind.

Practice the Prayer of Detachment

Draw on your harmony Five when you are too attached to helping and being needed in a specific way. Pray: "God, your will; nothing more, nothing less, and nothing else." This prayer connects you to the prayer of Jesus: "Father . . . yet not my will, but yours be done" (Luke 22:42). This prayer can loosen your constriction and tightness around expectations of others. It detaches and creates space for something new.

Blessing for the Beloved Two

As we close this section, take time to breathe in this blessing and create space in your soul.

The Lord bless this humble journey home to your true self.

May God the Father direct you with insight as you contemplate how to love freely.

May the heart of Jesus infuse and shape your heart's desires.

May the Holy Spirit ground you with strength and agency as you care for difficult people.

May the sacred love of the Trinity lead you on your road while on this journey, guiding you and cherishing you.

Empathy for TWOS

Friendship is not a reward for our discriminating and good taste in finding one another out. It is the instrument by which God reveals to each of us the beauties of others.

C. S. LEWIS

Every child should be able to know their needs matter. Twos may have had caregivers who didn't see or respond to their needs. To survive, they suppressed their desires and feelings and focused on the needs and approval of others. Here you can explore your default responses to Twos you know and how you might grow in empathy and seeing them as God does.

Empathy is a true self response that harmonizes and breaks down the we/they divide. For instance, we may find Twos clingy, needy, over-caring, and hypersensitive. Or we may think Twos are the best friends anyone can ever have. Understanding how Twos became over-carers can open compassionate and empathetic interactions with them.

This Two describes his journey. See if you can enter into the story and engage your understanding heart.

As a child, I needed to protect and guard myself. I silenced my Two emotions and needs because they could be used against me. Like an Eight, I would not be weak or vulnerable. When threatened, I became confrontational to protect myself. My pretend-to-be-

strong defense unconsciously drove my life and my relationships. Wanting connection but silencing my emotions and toughening up has left me with much soul work. Silence, solitude, breath prayer, and the Harmony Triads help me receive my tender Two self as well as my larger than life GQ self. I am a gifted student who trusts my IQ to take me where I want to go. Yet I see that I need vulnerability, not just ideas, if I want to really connect and have friends.

1. As you consider this Two story, notice:
   - What are you thinking about this Two?
   - What are you feeling about this Two?
   - What is your gut instinct about this Two?

2. When have you had your own emotions and needs dismissed? What was it like for you?

3. If you ever focused on how well you love someone and then were hurt because they didn't love you back, what was that like for you?

UNDERSTANDING THE DEFENSE MECHANISM OF REPRESSION

This Two describes her journey to integration and empathy. Notice how you are thinking, feeling, and reacting to this Two.

When my father died, I shut off the deep, loving Two EQ side of me. Period! I knew that I needed to love more fully and deeply, but that part of me just seemed lost. It felt like every time I reached out to love others, they didn't want my love. The vulnerability was excruciating. I wondered if anyone would ever love me. Sometimes

I worried that I might be too needy. So I shut down my needs and attended to others. The Harmony Triads gave me two great gifts I didn't know existed. I now recognize that God created me to be a whole person; God put IQ and GQ within me. These energies give me perspective on my needs as well as the needs of others. I am learning to love in less needy ways. I am integrating and coming alive to myself and all that is possible.

1. This Two repressed her gifting to love. What connections and resistances are you feeling with this Two?

2. Get inside a Two's story. Where do you recognize the needy child's distress that a lack of connection and having needs makes them unlovable?

3. How could you demonstrate God's approval of and love for a Two?

4. How might you join the Holy Spirit in praying for a Two you know?

RELATING TO A TWO

We find grace to see things from a beloved Two's point of view when we remember that under the Two's generous exterior is a tender child who believed his or her needs didn't matter.

- Twos consistently volunteer, and their default answer is yes. They say, "It's no problem!" even when it may be. Ask about their limits and needs by asking, "Do you really have the bandwidth to do this?"

- Twos want you to share your life with them. It makes them feel needed. If they deflect questions by turning the discussion back to you, say, "I'll answer your question if you will answer it too."

- Twos are distressed and take it personally when they feel connections break. Let them know that disagreements and conflicts won't break your relationship. Be gentle if you refuse their help.

- Twos lose energy when they aren't appreciated. Lavish praise, kindness, and shout-outs for all they do.

- Twos can find silence frustrating as it doesn't lead to connection. When planning meetings and events, give them time to interact, and they will enjoy it more.

- Twos like it when you match some of their loving energy.

The following list summarizes key characteristics of Twos. Consider your responses to these characteristics in yourself.

- *Authentic, true self:* Loving
- *Compulsive, false self:* Prideful
- *Virtue leading back to true self:* Humility
- *Personality style:* Caring

- *Work style:* Helper, server
- *Leadership/action style:* Pleaser
- *Relationships:* Helpful
- *Core motivation:* Approval, affection
- *Negative fixation:* Shame, fear of humiliation
- *Narrative:* "I am not enough. I must prove that I am."
- *Communication:* What's helpful, compassionate
- *Two with a One wing:* Task-oriented, idealistic, judgmental
- *Two with a Three wing:* Gregarious, competitive, image-conscious
- *Basic fear:* Being rejected, unwanted
- *Basic desire:* To be loved
- *Drive:* To love and be loved, to express feelings for others, to be needed and respond to human need, to be appreciated for their giving

Based on the description above:

1. How does it feel to be a Two? Which descriptors give clues on how to relate to a Two?

2. Is there a better way to say what is true of Twos?

3. Twos are connectors and like to feel the love. What is it like to receive the feelings and care of a Two with your own heart compassion?

4. How can you encourage the Twos you know to stand up for themselves and ask for what they need? Your encouragement can help them integrate IQ and GQ.

THREES

Effective Loyalty Harmonizes

If other people are putting in 40-hour workweeks and you're putting in 100-hour workweeks, then even if you're doing the same thing, you know that you will achieve in four months what it takes them a year to achieve.

ELON MUSK

I am a productive achiever who wants to make things succeed. I like things to work efficiently. Greasing the wheels to make stuff happen is second nature. I like to shine and look competent and fruitful. My image matters. I want people to think I am wonderful and accomplished. I can take my identity from what I do and achieve. Sometimes I think my value comes from doing and not being. Life for me is often a series of tasks, goals, and accomplishments that I do at a high rate of speed. I want to avoid failure! I like to lead and am a great motivator and team player. I set aside my emotions or needs to get a job done. I like to be on top and am irritated with incompetent people and those who slow the process down. Slowing the pace feels unproductive and like we are failing. Under pressure I will cut corners and push the process even if it means being deceitful and superficial.

WHO I AM AND WHO I AM NOT

Threes bear the image of the effective God. Your life resonates with: "God said, 'Let there be light,' and there was light" (Genesis 1:3).

Efficiency and productivity are inevitably part of Three stories. You rush past chapters of your life on failure, workaholism, or vulnerability. This section offers awareness of stories that shape a Three.

▶▶▶ BELOVED THREES

Spend some time with the words below that describe who Threes are and are not. Circle the characteristics that resonate with your journey. Star words that express your gifts. Underline words that describe parts of your personality that are unusable by God in their present form. Put a checkmark beside characteristics that trigger you.

Threes Descriptive Words List

I AM		I AM NOT	
successful	leader	failure	follower
productive	winner	inactive	flop
connected	networker	alone	drifter
competent	savvy	incompetent	naïve
capable	slick	incapable	sticky, tacky
accomplished	organized	indolent	disorganized
organized	attractive	disorganized	unattractive
get things done	looking good	time waster	slob
fast	confident	lethargic	diffident
promoter	self-assured	wait and see	loser
brilliant	sociable	mediocre	shy
bottom line	hard worker	bogged down	lazy

> ➤ Which words reflect the image of God in you?

> ➤ Which words are you most attached to? Addicted to? Compulsive about?

> ➤ Which words do you resist and judge the most?

> ➤ If you opened up to the words you resist without judgment, how might your life and relationships shift?

> ➤ Journal about the words that reflect how God's loving care looks after you.

▶▶▶ GETTING TO KNOW THREES

This Three reflects on how she became a competitive overachiever. Notice how producing and pushing through shape her narrative.

My husband and I were young church planters. We pushed, dreamed, strategized, schemed, leaned into justice work, and counseled until the wee hours of the morning. I overworked and went without sleep, and I was proud of it. "Late to bed, early to rise, work like hell, and advertise" was the anthem of my life. Ten years later at age forty, I was diagnosed with multiple sclerosis (MS). I convinced myself the diagnosis was a badge of honor! I'd joke, "Maybe I worked so hard that I wore off my myelin sheath," or "I'd rather burn out than fizzle out!" When the neurologist said managing MS included rest, I laughed and said, "I usually push through things, and it all works out."

Workaholism came with my family of origin. I was born into an Italian Catholic mob (not "The Mob," even though some wondered). My five older siblings loved and welcomed me into their developmentally bigger, smarter, faster, and more talented lives. From the get go, I tried to prove myself and compete on their terms. I listened to their music (Crosby, Stills, Nash & Young; Jethro Tull; Joni Mitchell), I understood their humor (The Firesign Theatre, George Carlin), and protested their war (Vietnam). But no matter how well I did or how much affection and approval I received, I felt like I was less than them. Wanting to be ten years older made for poor choices in middle school and high school: smoking pot, drinking, and an occasional hallucinogenic.

Oh, and my parents. Mother was a model—gorgeous and charming. My dad marched with Dr. King and sat on the Detroit area archbishop's council for race relations. He chaired boards, won awards, and gave generously to the community. My admiration and love for my family formed my need to shine, produce, impress important people, and change the world.

> What does this Three story bring up in you?

> What is your memory of your first Three experience?

> What is it like to feel the need to achieve?

> What is it like for you to know who you truly are in your heart?

Breath Prayer

In silence and solitude, ask God to help you see yourself clearly. Begin with breathing.

Breathe in: "Made in God's image," and then breathe out: "I am not a persona." Spend the day with this breath prayer. Feel the goodness of being made in God's image; feel the inner freedom that comes when you step into what is true about you and let go of your shiny image.

TRUE SELF AND FALSE SELF: THE EFFECTIVE PERSON

Who we are or are not comes with expression and energy. The attitudes, behaviors, and motivations of beloved Threes convey driven presence. Your true self emerges from union with God. It is not built on achievements, performance, or roles. Your false self is compulsive and deeply entrenched in the old nature or ego self, which is constructed on a complex mixture of nature, nurture, achievements, image building, and free will. This section will help you recognize compulsive and impulsive false self reactions to impress, as well as make you aware of when you FLOW with God's loving productivity.

True Self Threes: Sacred Confidence

Threes are designed to reflect God's motivated, connected, and effective energy. Your presence says, "I am here and able!" Transforming Threes motivate others and help them shine. You are adaptable, authentic, achievement-oriented, self-assured, magnetic, ambitious, and competent. Action-oriented Threes don't just produce and manufacture product. You reproduce from your intimacy with God. You lean into servant leadership and can set an example of how to relax your pace and agenda. True self Threes stop working and rest! You embody sacred confidence and are everything you seem to be. When you are present to God, you seek divine inspiration and reveal divine efficacy that never cuts corners or overlooks people.

False Self Threes: Constrict in Deception, Vanity, and Workaholism

Compulsive, false self Threes are driven by image, performance, and your hot compulsions to compete and overwork. You unplug from deeper feelings, ignore limits, and fake connection to important people. An un-harmonized Three says, "Watch me do this with competency and pizzazz!" To impress others and earn praise, you construct a persona that constricts and tightens around tasks, image, and achievements. Ashamed of failure, you set your ethical compass on success and deceive both yourself and others about who you are. You will ignore your limits, take on more than you can do, and then fake it till you make it or "spin it to win it." This twisting of reality leads to your signature sin of deceit. Threes get distressed when you can't lead, set the pace, and "have the right people on the bus." You will cut corners and do whatever it takes to win and "get 'er done." You can become a human *doing* rather than a human *being*.

▶▶▶ TRUE OR FALSE SELF

As you think about your true and false self, consider the following questions. Notice what comes up for you; notice without judgment. What questions particularly invite you to jot down or journal responses?

➤ How do true self Three characteristics show up in your relationships?

➤ Where do false self Three qualities show up in your relationships with others? How does shame show up? ("I am not enough.") When distress shows up saying, "I must prove I have worth!" or "I can't fail!," what do you do to lower your anxiety?

➤ What makes you constrict your heart and perform for approval? What is a cue to relax self-deception and open to truth?

➤ How do you feel the difference between centered, true self presence and edgy, false self presence?

HARMONY: EFFECTIVE LOYALTY HARMONIZES

Threes are often identified as the effective achiever, but you are much more than just one number! You bear the image and harmony of a three-in-one God. When beloved Threes integrate your IQ and GQ, you harmonize. Your effectiveness flows with the loyalty of the Six and the peacefulness of the Nine. This section creates awareness of how FLOW is the unique gift of the Harmony Triads.

In harmony and FLOW, a Three's effective *doing* is working for the truth and good of all (Six IQ) and is self-forgetful and mediating (Nine GQ).

▶▶▶ MORE THAN YOUR TYPE

This beloved Three is learning how sacred confidence helps him detach from the addiction to prove his worth and always be on. Balancing his deceiving, performing heart with his head and gut enables him to embrace the truth-seeking of a Six and patient-moving Nine energy. Integrating head and gut slows him down and brings discernment to his hectic life. Notice how monitoring his frenetic energy with IQ and GQ makes both his relationships and projects go better.

Drive for Success

The drive to be successful can blind us to what is most important in life. In this reading, Jesus addresses the false self that sets its sights on landing on top. Consider where you might push others or Jesus to "do for me whatever I ask."

Then James and John, the sons of Zebedee, came to him. "Teacher," they said, "we want you to do for us whatever we ask."

"What do you want me to do for you?" he asked.

They replied, "Let one of us sit at your right and the other at your left in your glory."

"You don't know what you are asking," Jesus said. "Can you drink the cup I drink or be baptized with the baptism I am baptized with?"

"We can," they answered.

Jesus said to them, "You will drink the cup I drink and be baptized with the baptism I am baptized with, but to sit at my right or left is not for me to grant. These places belong to those for whom they have been prepared." (Mark 10:35-40)

1. Where have you worked a room to be in the best seat? Where do you jockey to connect to people in positions of power?

2. How are you with letting things unfold without pushing your way?

3. Where can you let go of the need to be seen, shine, and produce without needing to win or gain recognition?

I made Bob Hope's words my own: "You never get tired unless you stop and take time for it." I didn't rest because I didn't want someone to get ahead of me. I didn't waste time on projects where I couldn't win. "Not enough" was a default narrative that motivated me to prove myself at every turn. I invested in a successful image and learned to be whatever looked good. Unconsciously, I connected exclusively with people who could advance my addiction to success. Learning the Harmony Triads made me aware of my Six IQ, which cares about faithfulness to God, others, and myself. I now allow Six questions to bring truth into my relationships and agendas. My Six also helps me follow and let go of my drive to be out front. My gut Nine says there is a time to end work each day! There is a time to release my agenda and enter the peace and presence of my family. The practices of a faithful Six and a restful Nine help me remember who I really am.

> What in the above story resonates with you?

> When and where do you ignore limits and truth? How could being authentic about limits and truth increase connection and help you focus on what and who matters most?

> How do you ignore the time it takes to think about the common good and just push your work agenda? How might loyalty and rest shape a productivity that benefits others as well as the kingdom of God?

> Imagine yourself tempering your energy for achievement with the energy of loyalty (Six IQ) and peace (Nine GQ). Does the idea that you are more than your type excite you? Scare you? Make you anxious?

Need to Be the Best

This narrative highlights parental favoritism, sibling rivalry, and the need to be the most important and blessed. Jacob, the younger twin, feels overlooked by his father and does his level best to steal his father's blessing from his brother Esau. However, achieving the blessing through deceit puts his life in danger. Where do you find yourself in Jacob's story?

Rebekah said to her son Jacob, "Look, I overheard your father say to your brother Esau, 'Bring me some game and prepare me some tasty food to eat, so that I may give you my blessing in the presence of the LORD before I die.' Now, my son, listen carefully and do what I tell you: Go out to the flock and bring me two choice young goats, so I can prepare some tasty food for your father, just the way he likes it. Then take it to your father to eat, so that he may give you his blessing before he dies."

Jacob said to Rebekah his mother, "But my brother Esau is a hairy man while I have smooth skin. What if my father touches me? I would appear to be tricking him and would bring down a curse on myself rather than a blessing."

►►► IQ, EQ, GQ

This Three lets go of the need to perform and intentionally makes space for others by leaning into his IQ and GQ to integrate. Notice how he pays attention to his body and the ground when he walks. How is he learning to be curious and ask open-ended questions rather than stay in type and fix things?

> I've had a Four mentor for ten years. Yet when I meet with him, I still go into list-making, performance, and prep mode. What can I say or do to assure him I know what I am talking about? What issues and wins do I highlight? Though he's given me opportunities he hasn't offered to others, I still feel I am not enough and I wonder who I am to him. Could it be my mentor reminds me of my Four mom, who was so special that I didn't hold a candle to her? I am learning to wake up to and let go of my automatic, performing self and my list-making distress. When I step into my mentor's office, I intentionally let go of my performing self, pay attention to my breath, and practice self-effacing (GQ). I try to be curious (IQ) and really listen, rather than think of what to say while he's talking. When I am tempted to impress, I remember that I will miss the moment if I am performing. I return to my breath and keep practicing presence. It's a new way of being. Welcoming my GQ and IQ helps me slow down and like myself.

> ➤ When Threes engage their head, they step back and consider people, not just tasks. Where do you see IQ in yourself?

> ➤ When Threes engage their gut, they let the inner hustler chill and relax. Where do you see GQ in yourself?

> ➤ What is it like for you to have IQ, EQ, and GQ?

His mother said to him, "My son, let the curse fall on me. Just do what I say; go and get them for me."
So he went and got them and brought them to his mother, and she prepared some tasty food, just the way his father liked it. Then Rebekah took the best clothes of Esau her older son, which she had in the house, and put them on her younger son Jacob. She also covered his hands and the smooth part of his neck with the goatskins. Then she handed to her son Jacob the tasty food and the bread she had made.
He went to his father and said, "My father."
"Yes, my son," he answered. "Who is it?"
Jacob said to his father, "I am Esau your firstborn. I have done as you told me. Please sit up and eat some of my game, so that you may give me your blessing." (Genesis 27:6-19)

Fourteen years after this episode of deceiving his father and stealing the blessing from his brother, Jacob has an all-night wrestling match with an angel. In that place, Jacob finally receives the blessing that is true.

1. When have you feared who you are is not enough?

2. When have you used deception to get something from someone? When do you take matters into your own hands and play God?

3. How are you with slowing down and letting truth (rather than your strategies) open the way for you?

HEALING CHILDHOOD HURTS: OPENING TO TRUTH

Children are wired for resilience. Still, residual childhood baggage and messages can leak into adult Three relationships. Three children can lose the message, "You are loved for yourself." The default message you can learn is, "Your own feelings and identity are not enough." Three children learn to cope by constructing an image (identification). Competition is a way you protect. This mitigates against loyalty and rest.

When these messages get triggered in adult interactions, then raw, ragged, and unprocessed pain can erupt, sabotaging the FLOW of a Three's efficacy. Suddenly a needy, four-year-old inside you feels deeply distressed that efforts and accomplishments go unappreciated. Defaulting to the false self, you compete harder to prove your worth. Competition moves you from your center to your edge of workaholism, vainglory (false glory), and deception. The Harmony Triad offers a way for Threes to be curious about the trauma, defenses, and childhood lies about not being worthy that shape your relationships today.

Prayer of Ignatius of Loyola

Allow this prayer of Ignatius of Loyola, which addresses the heart, head, and gut energy of the Enneagram Triads, to become your prayer. This week, pray the mind, heart, and strength of the Trinity into your life and interactions.

> *Father, I dedicate this new day to you;*
> *   as I go about my work [EQ],*
> *   I ask you to bless those with whom I*
> *   come in contact [EQ].*
>
> *Lord, I pray for all men and women*
> *   who work to earn their living;*
> *   give them satisfaction in what*
> *   they do [GQ].*
>
> *Spirit of God,*
> *   comfort the unemployed and their*
> *   families;*
> *   they are your children and my brothers*
> *   and sisters [IQ].*
> *   I ask you to help them find work soon.*

▶▶▶ RECEIVING THE DISMISSED CHILDLIKE SELF

Receiving your dismissed child can heal and give Threes freedom to be truthful and authentic again. Remember, within the confident, high-energy, and charismatic Three there is a fearful, self-doubting, untrusting Six who believes in an unsafe world in which you must prepare for the worst and be on guard. There is also a little Nine who wants to stay out of conflict, avoid the limelight, and procrastinate about what is hard. To recognize where you dismissed your childlike self and your needs, pay attention to where you may have ignored your GQ and IQ.

This Three notices where her desire for peace and rest was dismissed. Be curious about how trusting Six-like thoughts could have shaped her truth.

Our family legacy is filled with generations of alcohol and substance abuse, mental illness, suicide, divorce, murder . . . all of the biggies. My grandfather was an evil, sick, and twisted human being who abused his children and wife verbally, sexually, and physically.

The trauma of my childhood made me distrustful and afraid of a hostile world like the Six. I held the family secrets and played into the deceit of the Three. I made competing my world. Gymnastics nurtured my performing Three; by age seven, I was dreaming of the Olympics. My goal was to push through pain and win the Perfect Ten! When my family fell apart, the gym became my home and my escape. The more I achieved, the more attention I received. I would go to the gym before and after school even though I was emotionally, physically, and mentally spent. The achiever in me never stopped working to be wanted, valued, and seen as excellent. Winning led me to dismiss the rest and peace of my Nine.

As you read these questions, notice where you sense God's invitation to more deeply receive your dismissed child. Write down any new insights and awareness. You are doing important and integrative work here.

> Growing up under extreme duress and uncertainty about her value led this Three to define her life as a competition. How does this affect her ability to be present and FLOW with her God-given design?

> Within the driven, vainglorious Three is a numbed out, "hide under the covers" Nine who is passive-aggressive about what is required of her. Take a slow and silent walk or lay down and allow your body to remember where these messages show up in your life.

> Within the driven, deceived Three is the questioning Six who asks, "Am I right? Will I be safe?" When does your inner child ask or dismiss these questions?

> How do you dismiss your head IQ and gut GQ?

▶▶▶ JOURNALING YOUR DISMISSED CHILDLIKE SELF

Integrating and accessing your IQ and GQ can make you aware of what needs to happen so you can heal and find freedom to be authentic and less driven by image and work. Getting reacquainted with GQ gives strength to hold boundaries, say no, and act on your own desires. Integrating IQ brings perspective to your relational distress. Checking out what your body senses and your head perceives offers ways to integrate and find harmony in a way that isn't just about winning.

Name and journal some of your hurts and tenderly explore when you began to defend yourself by comparing yourself and your worth to that of others. Engage your IQ and make time to ponder and monitor the GQ strength of your responses. Truth from your IQ and EQ can relax the constricting need for relentless affirmation and approval. Feel free to choose among these questions and return to other questions at another time. This is hard work. Take your time. Journal.

> What is your story about needing to impress and be successful? What triggers your malformed belief that you are a failure and will be rejected? What childlike defenses still operate today?

> Where do you overwork or deceive because of shame or past trauma?

➤ What is causing distress in your heart right now? What is that about? If you relaxed to nurture yourself and trusted things to work on their own, what might happen?

➤ Where has your trust been repaired/healed or increased/solidified?

Immediate and never-fail Threes have a default stance of, "Make it happen." In your false self you find following another's lead risky, frustrating, inefficient, and a waste of your own talent. God's invitation to follow provides a huge opportunity to heal, let go of vainglory, and ask, "Who am I and who is God when I'm not leading?" It may be helpful to explore the chapter "Invitation to Follow" in *Invitations from God* by Adele Ahlberg Calhoun.

When you get frustrated by following and want to take the lead, open your heart. A leader needs followers. You need people to engage and support you. What can grow in you if you let go of needing to be at the helm and relax into following? This week, keep track of the times you open your heart to another's leadership. Consider how your presence can encourage others and set yourself free.

DISCERNMENT: DESOLATIONS AND CONSOLATIONS

Ignatius of Loyola taught that God's Guiding Spirit of wisdom moves in all three centers of intelligence—head, heart, and gut. When faced with a decision, Ignatius suggested noticing your consolations and desolations by asking:

Healing Prayer

When beloved Threes process your wounds in the presence of a restful God who knows and unconditionally receives you, it is easier to slow down and do inner work that helps you be a human being and not just a human doing. To know the truth of who you are when you aren't achieving and when no one is looking, Threes need to intentionally embrace silence and solitude. In God's restful care, Threes can find inner freedom to FLOW with true self effectiveness that makes a lasting impact. Your vice of vainglory is transformed into your virtue of truth.

This is a way to do healing prayer on your own. Relax into silence and solitude. Breathe deeply. Don't force it. Become present to God and yourself. Ask God to bring to mind a past sorrow that is still being transmitted. Be still and wait. When something comes to mind, follow this simple trail of healing prayer.

❖ *Imagine yourself and Jesus back in the memory. Get your bearings. Where is Jesus? Where are you?*

❖ *What are you feeling? (anxious, ashamed, unappreciated, needy, or something else)*

❖ *Do these feelings remind you of a time you had similar reactions? You can go with Jesus to that place and time or stay where you are.*

❖ *Continue to name what you feel in your experience. Ask Jesus if these feelings point to a lie you began to believe at that time. Give it a name.*

❖ *What is Jesus saying to you about this lie? Listen. Is there an image, word, or phrase that he speaks to you?*

❖ *Repeat the truth you have heard from Jesus about yourself gently and frequently. Let the truth be an antidote that lets the pain go into Jesus and sets you free.*

What does my heart feel? What does my mind think? What does my gut sense?

Ignatius suggested that consolations point Threes toward God's presence and an effectiveness that can rest and be loyal to people and tasks. Consolations are evidence that a Three is heading in the right direction when you slow down and register the IQ implications and the GQ pragmatic bottom line of a decision and how it affects people. Desolations of anxiety, shame, and vainglory help Threes notice when you have fallen into overperforming to look successful and thus miss bringing harmonic results. (More information on Harmony Triad discernment is found in Soul Resource 5.)

Threes experience consolations such as harmonized relationships, peaceful optimism, unconditional value, humble competence, servant leadership, empowering presence, and contemplative action. This is your freedom.

Threes experience desolations such as vainglorious competition, workaholism, deceit, image management, fear of incompetence, and worthless dread. When Threes fear being a failure, you self-promote to be admired. This is bondage.

▶▶▶ PRESENT TO WHAT'S HAPPENING INSIDE

Consolations and desolations can both point toward the purpose for which Threes were created. Here we focus on consolations and desolations particular to Threes. This Three studies the map of his soul and notices signposts of desolation in sadness, failure, and addiction to producing. He recognizes how deceit blocks discernment and how efficiency and persona use and rush past people. Notice how the consolations and desolations of this Three direct him toward healing and the presence of God.

I find myself ruminating on the first step from Alcoholics Anonymous: "We admit we are powerless over alcohol and that our lives have become unmanageable." While I'm not an alcoholic, I am addicted to producing. The defense mechanism of identification got me my job. My inner hustler makes me an effective salesperson. Still, when life becomes unmanageable, I feel like a miserable failure (desolation). I currently have a project deadline I'll miss because I am overcommitted to my avocational work (desolation). My default response is to throw my head back, push the pedal to the metal, and fake it until I make it (desolation). I continually ignore signs of sadness and fatigue, and I give impatient and condescending responses to coworkers and family. I'm worried that I am losing myself and my heart's desire for genuine connection (desolation). When pressed, I default to, "Tell the people what they want" and, "If it sizzles, it sells." When I'm aware of this, it's a cue to slow down. I breathe and allow myself to wonder, "What kind of energy is needed now?" (consolation). I want balance. But practicing presence is scary and *very* inefficient; still, I am learning that presence regulates my distressed heart (consolation).

➤ Where does "unmanageable" make you uncomfortable and bring desolation?

➤ When you are in desolation, pay attention to the Spirit's motions in your head and gut. Do you start spinning to try to turn your desolation into consolation? How could checking in with your IQ help you understand and respond to your desolation?

▶▶▶ DESOLATIONS AND IDENTIFICATION

Unaware, forward-moving, achieve-at-all-cost Threes have a default defense of identification. Identification is taking on a role so entirely that *you* lose relationship with who *you* really are. Identification blends the attributes and characteristics of another person or project into your personality. Identification happens when Threes over-identify with your successes and reject connection to anything or anyone that looks like failure. Without judgment, notice where you repress the truth about yourself. Stay with one or two questions. You can come back to the others as truth settles in.

> When have you lied, spun failure into success, or exaggerated to get others to like you? When do you pull away or push people to conform to your agenda so you look good? When has approval and affirmation dismissed loyal IQ questions and peaceful GQ response?

> How does your body constrict and tighten up in desolation? Where do you carry your distress and frustration when people don't respond to you?

> How does achieving in ego and false self rather than in partnership with God's effective FLOW close you off from consolations?

> Are there defenses besides identification that constrict your discernment?

> *Prayer Practice When Stressed Out by Too Much to Do*
>
> *Threes in particular don't like to slow down. It feels inefficient to let go of an agenda and practice presence—presence to self, God, and others. When you find yourself in distress about timelines, deadlines, and bottom lines, breathe in: "God's plans." Breathe out: "Not my agenda." Let this breath prayer open you to God and the moment.*

▶▶▶ CONSOLATIONS AND TRUTH

The Spirit's invitation to consolation often means engaging IQ that takes time to question what loyalty would do. Faithful IQ and chill GQ help Threes move with a team-building pace. Today, notice where the Spirit invites you out of desolation and into the consolations that draw you closer to God and others.

Threes are consoled as they follow God's Holy Spirit out of identification and image management to their virtue of authenticity and truth. Truth challenges Threes to have a sane self-estimate. In consolation, Threes can discern when your dynamism is about you (vainglory) and when it is focused on bringing out the glory of others.

> Describe a situation in which you felt the Spirit inviting you out of deception and spinning into truth. What happened? What consolations came to you?

> When has truth helped you stand in FLOW that effectively serves and loves God with your heart, soul, strength, and mind?

SPIRITUAL RHYTHMS FOR THREES

You were taught, with regard to your former way of life, to put off your old self, which is being corrupted by its deceitful desires; to be made new in the attitude of your minds; and to put on the new self, created to be like God in true righteousness and holiness. (Ephesians 4:22-24)

Threes are quick to offer *doing*. You can also deceitfully spin your *doing* to make it look marvelously successful when it's not. "Deceitful desires" corrupt the true self. Paul indicates that transformation happens when we intentionally put on the true, truthful self. Doing this affects the attitudes Threes have toward success and failure, and toward image and what "true righteousness" look likes. As Threes partner with the Holy Spirit

for transformation, you replace the old false self ego *doing* with true self rhythms that create new neural pathways and ways of responding.

Attending to the motions of the soul on a daily basis helps Threes move from addiction to *doing* and needing a response to the inner freedom to tell the truth about your limits, failures, and need to be seen. The Spirit's movement within helps Threes integrate so your effective loyalty harmonizes.

These spiritual rhythms are all ways Threes can lean into God's invitations to transformation and mind renewal. Not every practice will be God's invitation to you. Say yes to the practices that best capture your desire to be with God right now.

▶▶▶ PRACTICING PRESENCE: THREES

Re-read the FLOW definition in the Key Terms section. Notice the presence of Trinitarian harmony.

Father, Son, and Spirit belong and flow together.

Head, heart, and gut belong and flow together.

Faith, love, and hope belong and flow together.

Divine harmony calls Threes to awareness that what you are doing is not who you are. Threes who integrate IQ, GQ, and EQ bring authentic presence to God and others. The following meditative prayer brings balance and measure to a Three's drive. Staying with this prayer for a season opens Threes to receive your true self.

Find a comfortable and awake position. Remember that the Spirit of God dwells within you and prays for you. Ask God to give you an open and receptive head, gut, and heart.

Gut Presence: Put yourself in the presence of the Spirit. Notice what is happening in your body. Notice without judgment. Let your body tell you what it knows. Is there something your body wants to do in this prayer? Do that. Experience your ability to lead and accomplish. Give thanks for your effective nature. Can you notice where your body constricts and deflects truth by coming on strong? Observe what your body tells you about limits, waiting, and incompetence.

Heart Presence: Put yourself in the presence of Jesus. Breathe into your heart space. Feel your vulnerability and heart-need to achieve and be appreciated. Breathe in and create even more space around your heart. Notice your drive and ability. What is it like to be with your heart rather than fake a feeling? Invite self-compassion. What in you needs to power down and be "like a weaned child with its mother" (Psalm 131:2)? Where do you need an encouraging word or an appreciative touch? Name these places in the loving presence of Jesus. How does Jesus respond to you?

Head Presence: Put yourself in the presence of your Heavenly Father. Move your head around on your shoulders. Feel its fear and insight. Breathe into your intellect. Observe your mental life. What does your IQ tell you? What is it like to trust IQ questions and perspectives rather than your normal "move in and get it done" heart instinct? Where does your heart move you to put tasks before people? Ask your head to show you what it would be like to see people first and then do.

Pray into Your Harmony: Effective Loyalty Harmonizes

"Effective loyalty harmonizes" is a breath prayer to help you engage the life-giving instincts of a Nine such as peace, harmony, and self-forgetfulness; as well as the life-giving intellect of a Six that questions and considers the common good before enacting.

Memorizing this prayer brings awareness to what is most true about you to real-life situations. You are more than your type. Breathe this prayer in preparation for the meeting, a deadline, landing a deal, and leading the charge. Any time you get triggered and are tempted to forget who you are, open up and breathe "effective loyalty harmonizes." You don't need to get tight and constricted around productivity and image. Open to and call on all your God-given effectiveness.

FLOW Practice for Threes

In FLOW, you are **F**ree, **L**oving, **O**pen, and **W**ith. In FLOW, Threes stand in the presence of the three-in-one God and integrate head, gut, and heart in your achieving. Your relating flows with the Christian virtues of faith, hope, and love. When you notice that you are stuck in achieving and constricting around your success, this is the moment to breathe and ask the Spirit to give you inner freedom to open your head and gut and to be with God and what is. Ask, "Where is my hyper-speed limiting what I see?" or "How much energy do I need in this moment?" At the end of the day, pause and take a deeper look. Log what happened when you welcomed FLOW. What happened when you were not in FLOW? Celebrate how God's efficacy flows through and confess when it doesn't. Begin again tomorrow.

> Young people say, What good can one person do? What is the sense [GQ] of our small effort? They cannot see that we must lay one brick at a time, take one step at a time; we can be responsible [IQ] only for the one action of the present moment. But we can beg for an increase of love in our hearts that will vitalize and transform all our individual actions [EQ], and know that God will take them and multiply them, as Jesus multiplied the loaves and fishes.
>
> **DOROTHY DAY,**
> ***LOAVES AND FISHES***
> **(WITH OUR ADDITIONS)**

Practice Confession

Letting go of a successful image is part of transformation and connection. Confess your:

▶ *Vice of deceit:* lying, spinning your accomplishments, exaggerating to be seen in a better light, not telling the whole truth. Ask God and a friend to help you make the journey to rest and truth.

▶ *Workaholism:* when you confuse your vocational roles with your identity.

▶ *Anxiety:* about what people think of you.

▶ *Guilt:* over pretending to be someone you are not or manufacturing an image.

▶ *Cutting corners:* to get results and outcomes faster.

▶ *Frustration:* with not having a lead role.

▶ *Devaluing:* decrying those who aren't successful and those who don't have your EQ.

Receive these words of assurance: "Before the God who makes all things work, you rest in the finished work of the cross."

Practice Honesty/Truth About Who You Are

Feel your heart's desire for authenticity and true connection.

▶ Threes create reality out of their words. Pay attention to where you spin, exaggerate, and lie to make an impression. What is happening inside you?

▶ When you sense you want to embroider truth, ask for grace to let truth speak. Notice what happens when you speak truth.

▶ What is the truth about your ability to trust IQ Six people and learn from GQ Nine people who have potential energy rather than kinetic energy like you?

▶ When you hear yourself exaggerate, back up and say, "I get carried away with my stories. Let me backtrack and make sure this is accurate."

Breath Prayers

Notice your magnificent breath. Feel the oxygen fill your lungs and lift your chest. Follow your breath in and down. Take time to notice what is happening in your heart. Feel the productivity of your created life as you breathe in: "You have formed my inward parts; I am effectively and wonderfully made . . . may my soul know that very well." Spend a few minutes with this breath prayer. Follow your breath to the liberty of not having to be the Creator who accomplishes all things.

Keep breathing into your body. Breathing in from the soles of your feet, fill your belly with breath, and continue breathing to the crown of your head. Feel your experience. Breathe into your head, your heart, and your gut. Without judgment, notice whatever comes up. If memories come, welcome them with your effective, winsome breath. Stay with them. Take action to stay inside and hold yourself in a loving way. Use the breath prayers below when they fit the situation you are in.

❖ *Inhale: "Made in God's image."*
   Exhale: "I am not a persona."

❖ *Inhale: "Do all things,"*
   exhale: "through Christ, with Christ, in Christ."

❖ *Inhale: "God, your plans,"*
   exhale: "not mine."

Practice Secrecy

Secrecy is a practice of anonymity. Giving and serving anonymously addresses the disordered need for visibility and attention in Threes.

- ▶ When you feel the urge to tell everyone your latest accomplishment, self-mute. Let the truth that God sees you and what you have done fill the inner void.

- ▶ Minimize your accomplishments. Don't name drop. What goes on in you?

- ▶ When someone asks to introduce you, limit the number of things you have done and choose the three or four that matter most to you. Does this feel like enough? Talk to God about this.

Practice the Presence of Your Own Feelings

Threes read the feelings of others and identify with emotions inherent in the roles they play. To discover what is happening in you, breathe into your heart space. Listen to the rhythm of your heart. Let the steady thud, thud, thud of your heart slow you down.

- ▶ Silence, solitude, and slowing down can help you get in touch with your own feelings.

- ▶ Name your feelings about success and winning. Do you carry these feelings somewhere in your body? What are the feelings telling you?

- ▶ Before you rush on, ask your feelings, "Do I understand what you are trying to tell me?"

- ▶ Do these feelings hold an invitation from God? If you can hear the invitation, you have practiced their presence. Listen to what God wants to say to you.

Practice Slowing and Patience

Your gift of effective impact is kinder and gentler when it is tempered with patience. In biblical words, "love suffers long" (1 Corinthians 13:4 NKJV). Patience goes the distance peaceably; it honors tasks *and* people by slowing to give presence.

- ▶ When you move too quickly and when you are too attached to moving the ball down the field, you miss things! Call a time-out so you can pay attention. Suffer the long story; patiently hear out the questions and fears of others.

- ▶ Be curious and ask God, "Who wants to help me?" or "How can I bring harmony rather than hurry?" or "What kind of example am I presenting of work/life balance?"

Blessing for the Beloved Three

As we close this section, take time to breathe in this blessing and create space in your soul.

May the holy, three-in-one God bless this honest journey home to your true self.

May God the Creator direct you with curiosity as you faithfully question your next steps.

May the heart of Jesus permeate and awaken your own heart's desire.

May the Holy Spirit ground you in the slow work of becoming authentic.

May the sacred truth of the Trinity lead you on your road, upholding you and loving you.

Empathy for THREES

Every child has a need to be approved of by their caregivers. Threes may have had caregivers who undermined their inherent value and tied attention to how they performed. So Threes drove hard to create a worthy image that would bring them approval. Here you can explore your responses to Threes and how you might grow in empathy, seeing them as God does.

Empathy is a true self response that harmonizes and breaks down the we/they divide. You may resist a Three's disingenuous, over-polished, look-at-me persona. Or you may be drawn to a Three's charm, vitality, and leadership. Understanding how a Three became competitive and duplicitous can open compassionate and empathetic interactions with them.

This Three is working to integrate the trauma and shame that led her to dismiss her emotions, keep secrets, and become a human *doing*. Let your IQ, GQ, and EQ direct you toward understanding and compassion as you read.

When I was six months old, my grandmother attempted suicide while babysitting me. It was horrific. She drank Sevin (a pesticide), and then changed her mind and called 911. Three grueling days later, she passed. Mom never discussed it. My parents had no clue how to cope, so they faked that they were okay—like a Three does. This incident triggered Mom's nervous breakdown nine years later.

I first started dismissing my little Six around the time of her breakdown. When fear popped up, I shut down and stuffed it. I did the same with my emotions because I feared feeling the pain of what was going on at home and school. Classmates made hurtful comments about me turning out like my mom. To cope, I became a success-oriented, achievement-addicted human *doing*.

It was working with my dismissed inner child that brought healing. God took me to a memory where I saw that my shame cycle was rooted in an experience with my father. Processing this memory with God had a profound and freeing impact. Every day I pray to grow my Six trust and my Nine yield, so I can have true Three sacred confidence. My IQ, EQ, GQ mantra is: trust, yield, sacred confidence. This prayer squashes old lies such as, "It's not okay to fail." My prayer frees me to let my real, true self shine.

Read through the questions. Choose to answer the ones that capture your attention. These questions can be most useful to you when you are working with a Three.

1. As you consider the story, notice:
   - What are you thinking about this Three?
   - What are you feeling about this Three?
   - What is your gut instinct about this Three?

2. When have you pushed pain and feelings away through performing and achieving? Where has shame and vainglory wrecked your empathy?

3. Can you find a disconnected, cautious Six child hiding behind the image conscientious, anxious Three?

4. Get inside a Three's story with its shame and need for approval. How does their lack of integrating IQ and GQ mitigate against truth, presence, slowing down, and caring for others?

UNDERSTANDING THE DEFENSE MECHANISM OF IDENTIFICATION

Another Three reveals how she defended herself through identification.

> In my family, achievements and making your mark mattered. Doing well was not enough to get praise; I had to do better than others. I had to live up to the motto hanging over our fireplace: "ever upward!" To prove my worth, I spun my successes, ran for class offices, lettered in sports, and attended three Ivy League schools. I totally identified with being *the* winner. I hid anxiety about being unimportant behind a charming, driven persona that brought me admiration and approval. I was so identified with my image that it took time and failure for me to want to know the real me.

1. This Three identified with successes and achievements. What connections or resistances do you have with this Three?

2. How can you encourage a Three to live into limits and the goodness of their created being?

3. How might you join the Holy Spirit in praying for a Three you know?

RELATING TO A THREE

We find grace to see things from a Three's point of view when we remember that under the lightning speed of a Three is a tender, anxious child who is still producing to be loved.

- When Threes take on more than is possible, ask, "How are you doing?" or "Can you share the load?"

- A Three's inner supervisor wakes up saying, "Start the to-do list and expand your network!" Instead of *carpe diem* (seize the day), suggest *salve diem* (greet the day).

- Encourage Threes to listen to their feelings. Ask open-ended questions about their desires, busyness, and goals.

- Be curious and interested in their breathtaking capacity and energy; celebrate their achievements. Threes like support; they pick up on your spoken and unspoken resistance.

- Threes are preoccupied with the future. When they miss things you say, they are thinking of what's next.

- Threes don't want to be slowed down by negativity or lack of enthusiasm. Lean into what is good about their plans and be discerning about criticism.

The following list summarizes key characteristics of our beloved Threes. Consider your responses to these characteristics.

- *Authentic, true self:* Effective, achiever

- *Compulsive, false self:* Deceitful

- *Virtue back to true self:* Truth

- *Personality:* Efficacious

- *Work style:* Producer, networker

- *Leadership/action style:* Motivator

- *Thinking style:* Effective

- *Relational style:* Task-oriented, producer

- *Core motivation:* Approval, affection

- *Negative fixation:* Shame, fear of humiliation

- *Narrative:* "I am not enough; I must show I have worth."

- *Communication:* Energetically, assertively

- *Three with a Two wing:* More collaborative, friendly, concerned for others

- *Three with a Four wing:* More creative, responsive, deep

- *Basic fear:* Of being worthless

- *Basic desire:* To feel valuable and worthwhile

- *Drive:* Want to be affirmed, have success, be admired

Based on the description above:

1. How does it feel to be a Three? What descriptors give clues about how to relate to Threes?

2. Is there a better way to say what is true of Threes?

3. What is it like to receive the industry of a Three with your own heart compassion?

4. How can you encourage the Threes you know to slow down, rest, and experience the goodness of their created being? Encourage them when they use IQ and GQ.

FOURS
Creativity Joyfully Renews

The most beautiful people we have known are those who have known defeat, known suffering, known struggle, known loss, and have found their way out of the depths. These persons have an appreciation, a sensitivity, and an understanding of life that fills them with compassion, gentleness, and a deep loving concern. Beautiful people do not just happen.

ELISABETH KÜBLER-ROSS

I am a sensitive person with cavernous feelings and a vibrant, creative imagination. I feel complicated and different from other people. When people don't understand or connect with me, I feel melancholy or depression. I seek depth, meaning, and authenticity of feeling and expression. Beauty, love, sorrow, and longing resonate within me. Looking at a piece of art, a sunset, or listening to music can be a religious experience for me. I love aesthetics and can change my clothing or environment over and over again to reflect what I feel inside. Some people see me as being overly dramatic, but I see life in the sixth dimension. I yearn for deep relationships. I persistently pursue emotional connectedness and feel distressed when people leave me. It often feels like something is missing from my life. Something different or more would make my life fulfilling. I will keep seeking to attain it. I can be envious of the gifts and abilities of others—if I had what they had, I would be truly unique. I am introspective, creative, intuitive, and in touch with the hidden depths and emotions of life.

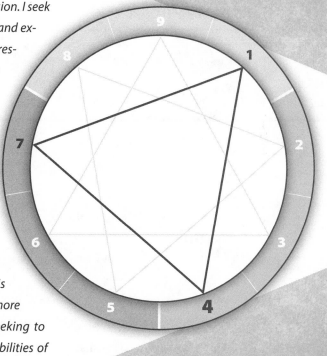

WHO I AM AND WHO I AM NOT

Fours bear the image of the deeply unique and unrepeatable Creator who "has made everything beautiful in its time. He has also set eternity in the human heart; yet no one can fathom what God has done from beginning to end" (Ecclesiastes 3:11).

Originality and search for meaning are inevitably part of a Four's story. Stories about who we are and who we are not shape what we do, who we become, and where we get stuck. Fours often have a narrative about longings and what's missing from your life. You yearn to create, go deep, belong, and do it all in a way no one has ever seen. This section offers awareness of stories that shape a Four.

▶▶▶ **BELOVED FOURS**

Spend some time with the words below that describe who Fours are and are not. Circle the characteristics that shaped your narrative about you. Star words that express your gifts. Underline words that describe parts of your personality that are unusable by God in their present form. Put a checkmark beside characteristics that you *celebrate*.

Fours Descriptive Words List

I AM		I AM NOT	
original	classy	copy	tasteless
different	stylish	dull	off the rack
creative	flamboyant	unimaginative	common
special	intuitive	typical	obtuse; linear
extraordinary	empathetic	ordinary	insensitive
remarkable	imaginative	mundane	literal
unique	individualist	banal	groupie
exciting	refined	boring	rough
unpredictable	sophisticated	routine	boorish
lonely	tasteful	gregarious	tacky
elite	deep	trendy	superficial

➤ Which words reflect the image of God in you?

➤ Which words are you most attached to? Addicted to? Compulsive about?

➤ Which words do you resist and judge the most?

➤ If you opened up to the words you resist without judgment, how might your life and relationships shift?

➤ Journal about the words that reflect how God looks after you.

►►► GETTING TO KNOW FOURS

This beloved Four shares how her default narrative became "my specialness is unwelcome." Notice how she felt unworthy and not unique enough to make the friends she wanted and what helped her begin to embrace her uniqueness.

> Growing up, messages about creativity and individuality were quite mixed. Being the only daughter after three sons made me special. However, my brothers did not appreciate my specialness. To this day they call me "princess" without much affection. Being "special" meant I got my own room. But it also meant that when I was ten and wanted to earn money mowing the lawn like my brothers, my dad said, "It's not a girl's job." My jobs were the unpaid ones of cleaning the bathroom and setting the table. I argued about the injustice of all this and finally was paid $2.50 per lawn mowing. But there was no equity around the unpaid housework. I'd still rather mow the lawn than mop the floor.

> Despite being "special," I grew up with (and still have) anxiety about being invisible. My brothers didn't want their little sister tagging along! I also had trouble making friends with the girls who really interested me. I envied them, suffered low self-esteem, and experienced many Four longings. I was lonely, melancholy, and full of strong emotions that I didn't express until I was a young adult. I felt most alive when I was in nature. Outdoors, I experienced an okay-ness and a vibrancy about myself. In nature, I felt connected to God, and my mystic soul could soar. During teenage years I began to express my enormous feelings in poetry and later photography. My husband wasn't intimidated that I was a better photographer than he was. He received the depth of my poetry as well as my flamboyant clothing or speech. When I became a teacher, I used my dramatic flair to invite kids to own their creativity.

> ### Breath Prayer
>
> *In silence and solitude, ask God to help you see yourself clearly. Begin with breathing. Breathe in: "Made in God's image," then breathe out: "Nothing is ordinary." Spend a few minutes with this breath prayer. Feel the goodness and freedom of being made in God's image; feel the liberty that comes from seeing the extraordinary in yourself and all things. Breathe this prayer in and out throughout the day.*

➤ What does this Four childhood story bring up in you?

➤ What is your memory of your first Four experiences?

➤ What is it like for you to feel that your depth and unique gifting enrich the lives of others? What happens in your heart space?

TRUE SELF AND FALSE SELF: THE ORIGINAL PERSON

Who we are or are not comes with expression and energy. The attitudes, behaviors, and motivations of beloved Fours convey creative heart presence. True self Fours are content with who you are and engage others from a place of union with God. False self Fours compulsively construct a unique image that is deeply entrenched in the ego old nature self with its mix of nature, nurture, relationships, trauma, and free will. This section will help you begin to recognize compulsive and impulsive false self reactions, as well as true self FLOW that loves God, others, and self.

True Self Fours: Holy Creativity

Fours are designed to reflect holy origin. You embody the originality of the Divine Creator who designs the glories and mysteries of all that is. Fours are authentic, self-revealing, vulnerable, intuitive, and personal. You resonate with the paradoxes of life: beauty and tragedy, joy and grief, elation and despair. Integrated Fours hold reality with compassion rather than drama. You are grounded, stable, and deeply present to and in solidarity with God and others. You can relax, and you can find and celebrate the extraordinary in hard times, others, and yourself. Your equanimity of soul and emotional depth create without angst and lead others into places of vulnerability and compassion. You offer us your virtue of equanimity.

False Self Fours: Constricted in Envy, Narcissism, and What's Missing

Un-resourced Fours can have "cavernous" feelings that make you feel defective, abandoned, ordinary, and distressed. Over-identifying with past sufferings, you get stuck on the dark edges of your personality where you lose perspective and presence to God and others. When Fours fall away from presence, you can fixate on bohemian, aristocratic, or eccentric personas. Focusing on what is missing, distant, and dreamed, you disconnect from others, escape into fantasy scenarios, and/or indulge in thoughts of your own worthlessness. Fantasy narratives that are nurtured can become more real than what is. False self Fours are unaware of how you can become hypersensitive, narcissistic, and contemptuous of the ordinary. Wanting to be "extra"-ordinary, you envy qualities in others to make up for what is missing and ordinary in yourself. Envy is the Four's vice.

▶▶▶ TRUE OR FALSE SELF

As you think about your true and false self, consider the following questions. Notice what comes up for you; notice without judgment. What questions particularly invite you to jot down or journal responses?

➤ How do true self Four characteristics show up in your relationships?

➤ Where do false self Four qualities show up in your relationships with others? How does distress about being ordinary affect you? When does shame make you feel unworthy of love and belonging? How do you express your unique self-worth?

➤ What makes you constrict in envy and feelings of not being enough? What is a cue to open and embrace your beloved and unique self?

➤ How do you feel the difference between centered, true self energy and edgy, false self energy?

HARMONY: CREATIVITY JOYFULLY RENEWS

Fours are often identified as the original number, but you are much more than just one number! You bear the image and harmony of the three-in-one God. When beloved Fours integrate your head and gut, you harmonize and your creativity flows with the joy of the Seven and the renewing energy of the One. This section creates awareness of how FLOW is the unique gift of the Harmony Triads.

In harmony and FLOW, a Four's beautiful creativity responds with the free-spirited enthusiasm of a Seven IQ and the stable, persevering discernment of a One GQ.

▶▶▶ MORE THAN YOUR TYPE

Beloved Fours can be compulsive about needing to make a lasting impression through artistic expression so others won't abandon them. This story describes a Four who is learning to release her intensity, unusual self-presentation, and need to be special. As she embraces her sacred origin, she releases her penchant for drama and integrates the Seven's

Why Obsess?

It is easy for Fours to focus on having unique and beautiful gifts, clothes, experiences, and relationships. In this reading, Jesus addresses the anxious false self that worries about stuff that doesn't last. Consider where you might place your trust in your unique presentation rather than in the Creator who already sees your unique beloved-ness.

"Therefore I tell you, do not worry about your life, what you will eat or drink; or about your body, what you will wear. Is not life more than food, and the body more than clothes? Look at the birds of the air; they do not sow or reap or store away in barns, and yet your heavenly Father feeds them. Are you not much more valuable than they? Can any one of you by worrying add a single hour to your life?

"And why do you worry about clothes? See how the flowers of the field grow. They do not labor or spin. Yet I tell you that not even Solomon in all his splendor was dressed like one of these. If that is how God clothes the grass of the field, which is here today and tomorrow is thrown into the fire, will he not much more clothe you—you of little faith?" (Matthew 6:25-30)

1. How are you affected by style, trends, and beautiful design? When do you look to these things to compensate for what you feel is missing in you?

2. How does it feel to have Jesus tell you not to worry about your life, clothes, or food? What is it like for you to risk on what Jesus says?

3. Jesus finds evidence of God's care in the beauty of nature. Where do you sense God's presence and care as you are in nature?

joy and the One's stability. Notice how integrating IQ and GQ keeps her from relying solely on her heart-need to be unique and opens her to lightness of being.

> I have often wanted to feel special to others. But special was not valued when I grew up. Order, obedience, and conformity were what mattered. To measure up to all the "oughts," I took myself very seriously. Being lighthearted, making creative messes, expressing my own desires, and improvising on my chores was not welcome. It just produced criticism and withdrawal of connection. I'd walk around on eggshells hoping to reconnect. It didn't help. Sometimes my mom wouldn't speak to me for a couple of days. This taught me to be dutiful like a One and dismiss my playful Seven. It wasn't until college that I began to explore and express my spontaneous Seven energy. I also took part in sit-ins and protested the war, accessing One reforming energy. I climbed mountains, sunbathed in the nude, wore outlandish clothes, watched film noir, and visited Europe using adventuring Seven energy. I had never felt more alive. I still feel the pull of seriousness. And I am deeply distressed when someone disconnects and turns me out of their heart. Seven habits of gratitude and intentionally embracing joy balance me. My One grounds me so I get things done.

➤ When are you overly serious and dramatic about depth or being special? How could reframing events with the levity of Seven IQ provide perspective on what really matters?

Your True Name

Disconnection and isolation make Fours distressed and anxious that you are not enough. To ease your anxiety about being left, you can construct an amalgamation of identities that separates you from what is truest about yourself. In this reading, Jesus heals a man who has lost his truest self. Notice how Jesus integrates and grounds him in the stability of One GQ and the hope of Seven IQ. Integrating gut and head and heart brings sanity, freedom, and creativity.

> They went across the lake to the region of the Gerasenes. When Jesus got out of the boat, a man with an impure spirit came from the tombs to meet him. This man lived in the tombs, and no one could bind him anymore, not even with a chain. For he had often been chained hand and foot, but he tore the chains apart and broke the irons on his feet. No one was strong enough to subdue him. Night and day among the tombs and in the hills he would cry out and cut himself with stones.
>
> When he saw Jesus from a distance, he ran and fell on his knees in front of him. He shouted at the top of his voice, "What do you want with me, Jesus, Son of the Most High God? In God's name don't torture me!" For Jesus had said to him, "Come out of this man, you impure spirit!"
>
> Then Jesus asked him, "What is your name?"
>
> "My name is Legion," he replied, "for we are many." And he begged Jesus again and again not to send them out of the area.

> ➤ How do you respond when someone disconnects from you? What might happen if you let some of the angst and despair go and receive the grounded-ness of the One's GQ? Remember that light and love are greater than dark and distress.

> ➤ Imagine yourself tempering your compulsivity for the unique and original with open-ness to grounded optimism. What do you see?

▶▶▶ IQ, GQ, EQ

This Four describes her Four, Seven, and One journey to integration. Out of unpredict-ability and lack of connection, she develops GQ fortitude and IQ perspective about her feelings. How does this story help you recognize IQ, GQ, and EQ responses in your life?

My mom was flamboyant and crazy, and she was always bringing home another man. Her disinterest and lack of predictability meant my brother and I raised ourselves. I longed to be special to my mom—to anyone, actually. To get her attention, I tried to figure out what was missing in me. If I figured that out, she might not abandon us. But it didn't matter what I did; I always felt that her presence said: "You bore me. You aren't interesting or college material." To escape my internal darkness, I chased romance and fantasized about being adored and rescued by a knight in shining armor. When my knight came, our marriage was

A large herd of pigs was feeding on the nearby hillside. The demons begged Jesus, "Send us among the pigs; allow us to go into them." He gave them permission, and the impure spirits came out and went into the pigs. The herd, about two thousand in number, rushed down the steep bank into the lake and were drowned.

Those tending the pigs ran off and reported this in the town and countryside, and the people went out to see what had happened. When they came to Jesus, they saw the man who had been possessed by the legion of demons, sitting there, dressed and in his right mind; and they were afraid. Those who had seen it told the people what had happened to the demon-possessed man—and told about the pigs as well. Then the people began to plead with Jesus to leave their region.

As Jesus was getting into the boat, the man who had been demon-possessed begged to go with him. Jesus did not let him, but said, "Go home to your own people and tell them how much the Lord has done for you, and how he has had mercy on you." So the man went away and began to tell in the Decapolis how much Jesus had done for him. And all the people were amazed. (Mark 5:1-20)

1. Jesus is clear that this man's name is not "Legion." Fours often have a sense of cobbling together a "legion" of selves to compensate for the desolation of your ordinariness. How do you compensate for desolation about your ordinariness and disconnection?

2. What is it like to have Jesus be present to you in all your scattered-ness?

3. What is it like to have him invite you into your true name?

disastrous. . . . In desperation, we went to a counselor. There I learned that my emotions weren't who I was. My feelings were like weather that came and went. I was stunned that my feelings were not my identity. I didn't need to be a victim to lies or past hurts. I discovered I was uniquely made in God's image. I began to believe I was intelligent and got promotions at work. I could author my life and choices. I know now that integrating my GQ agency and IQ competence gave me ways to channel overwhelming emotions. My head and my gut helped me transform emotional drama into emotional equilibrium.

➤ When Fours engage their IQ, they moderate their heart and reframe what distresses them. They look at the light and not just the darkness. Where do you see IQ in yourself?

➤ When Fours engage their gut, they moderate their heart and become conscientious, realistic, and hard working. Where do you see GQ in yourself?

➤ What is it like for you to have IQ, GQ, and EQ?

HEALING CHILDHOOD HURTS: OPENING TO EQUANIMITY

Children are wired for resilience. Still, residual childhood baggage and messages can leak into adult Four relationships. Dramatic Four children longed to feel special. Being invisible brought distress, so you dove deep into your achy longings to be more than what you were. Four children can lose the message, "You are seen for who you are." The default message you can learn is, "It's not okay to be too different or free spirited." To cope, Four children retreated deep inside feelings and hurts. These defenses mitigated against spontaneity and grounded-ness.

When these messages get triggered in adult interactions, then raw, ragged, unprocessed pain can erupt, sabotaging the FLOW of a Four's love. Suddenly an anxious four-year-old inside you gets stuck on the edge of needing to be special.

The Harmony Triad offers a way for Fours to be curious about the trauma, defenses, childhood lies, and dismissed needs that shape your relationships today so you can step into your virtue of equanimity. Equanimity calmly holds the paradoxes and mystery of deeply troubling things.

Prayer of Teilhard de Chardin

Allow this prayer of Teilhard de Chardin, which integrates heart, head, and gut, to become your prayer.

God, at his most vitally active and most incarnate, is not remote from us, wholly apart from the sphere of the tangible; on the contrary, at every moment, he awaits us in the activity, the work to be done, which every moment brings. He is, in a sense, at the point of my pen, my pick, my paintbrush, my needle—and my heart [EQ] and my thought [IQ]. It is by carrying to its natural completion the stroke, the line, the stitch I am working on that I shall lay hold on [GQ] that ultimate end toward which my will at its deepest levels tends.

▶▶▶ RECEIVING THE DISMISSED CHILDLIKE SELF

Receiving your dismissed child can heal and give Fours freedom to be unashamedly unique. Remember, within every creative, deep, and fringy Four there is an experience-oriented Seven inner child who longs for adventure and goes for the gusto. There is also a little One who is self-critical, judgmental, and resentful. To recognize where you dismissed your authentic childlike self, pay attention to where you may have ignored your head, gut, and heart.

This beloved Four shares her story of how she knuckled down, retreated, and shut down her creative heart because no one appreciated it. Notice her feelings and how she stifled her Seven IQ and Four EQ and tried to be practical like a One.

> As a child, I ached and longed for beauty and artistic expression. But artistic endeavors made messes and cost money, and my mother was obsessed with keeping things neat. My father had an artistic bent, and I remember him squirting dabs of richly colored paints from their tubes and applying them with the palette knife to the canvas. I dreamed of being invited to paint alongside him. But he never included me, and I never dared ask. In high school, I finally bought some watercolor paper and cheap watercolors. But I felt guilty about spending money on something unnecessary. I still struggle with spending money on creative endeavors that don't pragmatically benefit others. It seems wasteful. One exception to the creative shutdown when I was growing up was my wardrobe. My mother was thrilled to have a daughter, and she splurged some on my wardrobe. Still, those shopping trips often ended with the caution from her: "Now, don't tell your father how much we spent." I now recognize how often I had to stifle my Seven's joy and free-spirited spontaneity. I was so desperate for affection and tenderness I tried to be perfectly practical like a One.

As you read the questions below, notice where you sense God's invitation to more deeply receive your dismissed child. Write down any new insights and awareness. You are doing important and integrative work here.

➤ This Four grew up in a world where her desires and longings went unnoticed. How does this affect her ability to FLOW with her God-given design?

➤ Within this Four is a judgmental One who feels guilty spending money on something unnecessary. Where does this message sabotage your life? How do you dismiss your gut?

➤ Fours often carry within them an adventure-driven Seven with a thousand dreams, strategies, and plans. When are your plans visionary, and where are they an escape from routine, duty, and ordinary life? How do you dismiss your head?

▶▶▶ JOURNALING YOUR DISMISSED CHILDLIKE SELF

Integrating your heart with your IQ capacity to lighten up and your GQ stable agency gives you harmony. Equanimity comes as Four depths are integrated with delight and conviction. Name and journal some of your Seven frivolous, fun-loving side. Name things you wanted to express and never did. Explore when you resorted to living vicariously through fantasies that made you unique and important. Work on a few questions and return to other questions at another time.

> What is your story about feeling you didn't belong in your world? What default reactions and triggers of your childhood self still operate today?

> Where do you dismiss your uniqueness, joy, and grounded-ness because of shame or past trauma?

> Where has your need to have approval for your specialness been repaired/healed or increased/solidified?

Ask God to help you open to your virtue of childlike equanimity that makes you less dramatic and aloof and connects you with others. Oversensitive, creative Fours can have a default stance that is overly serious. It can be hard for Fours to recall your life without drama and desolation. God's invitation is to remember your experiences within God's larger story. The spiritual practice of remembering reframes a Four's experiences in a redemptive context that brings equanimity as well as pathos. It may be helpful for you to read the chapter "Invitation to Remember" in *Invitations from God* by Adele Ahlberg Calhoun.

When you filter your experiences through dramatic introspection and what's missing, open your heart to how and where these human experiences and feelings turn up in Scripture or the life of Jesus. For instance,

Healing Prayer

When Fours process your wounds in solidarity with Jesus, "a man of sorrows, and acquainted with grief" (Isaiah 53:3 ESV), you come into the presence of the God who can hold your pain. The over-dramatizing of distress is transformed into the ability to bear and hold sorrow as well as all the bright emotions in authentic and redemptive ways. When this happens, your vice of envy is transformed into your virtue of equanimity.

To do healing prayer on your own, relax into silence and solitude. Breathe deeply. Don't force it. Become present to God and yourself. Ask God to show your desire for ongoing healing. Ask God to bring to mind a past sorrow that is still being transmitted. Be still and wait. When something comes to mind, follow this simple trail of healing prayer.

❖ *Imagine yourself and Jesus back in the memory. Get your bearings. Where is Jesus? Where are you?*

❖ *What are you feeling? (anxious, abandoned, invisible, ordinary, or something else)*

❖ *Do these feelings remind you of a time you had similar reactions? You can go with Jesus to that place and time or stay where you are.*

❖ *Continue to name what you feel in your experience. Ask Jesus if these feelings point to a lie you began to believe at that time. Give it a name.*

❖ *What is Jesus saying to you about this lie? Listen. Is there an image, word, or phrase that he speaks to you?*

❖ *Repeat the truth you have heard from Jesus about yourself gently and frequently. Let the truth be an antidote that lets the pain go into Jesus and sets you free.*

the Psalms resound with the depths of human experience. And if you feel abandoned, imagine standing in solidarity with Jesus as Judas betrays him. This week, keep track of the times you open your heart as it begins to constrict around a painful experience. What happens?

DISCERNMENT: DESOLATIONS AND CONSOLATIONS

Ignatius of Loyola taught that God's Spirit moves in all three centers of intelligence—head, heart, and gut. When faced with a decision, Ignatius suggested noticing the consolations and desolations by asking: What does my heart feel? What does my mind think? What does my gut sense?

Consolations point beloved Fours toward the reality that God created you as unique and beloved. Consolations are evidence that a Four is heading in the direction of GQ truth, IQ levity, and EQ creativity. Desolations of being ordinary and unworthy distort the FLOW of God's creativity and love, and alert Fours that you have fallen into your false self and need grace to return to your original beauty. (More information on Harmony Triad discernment is found in Soul Resource 5.)

Fours experience consolations such as sacred mystery, transforming imagination, holy sensitivity, vulnerable reformation, ordered romance, creative goodness, renewing action, grounded adventure, equanimity, and beauty. These characteristics express real freedom.

Fours experience desolations and distress around insignificance, self-absorption, ordinariness, abandonment, self-loathing, moodiness, depression, envy, something's missing, not being enough, artistic sublimation, and longing for a rescuer. These characteristics express real bondage.

▶▶▶ PRESENT TO WHAT'S HAPPENING INSIDE

Both consolations and desolations point toward the purpose for which Fours were created. This Four studies the map of his soul and notices signposts of desolation in his messy, defended life. He recognizes how introjection can cloud judgment and lead to darkness. Notice how the consolations and desolations of this Four could direct him out of narcissism toward the presence of God.

> I founded a company that I am in the midst of taking public. But I am really anxious about making my innovations public (desolation). I like to be interviewed and quoted (consolation). But I can torture myself with thinking about how people will use my original ideas, creative hard work, and intellectual property without ever giving me credit (desolation). I flip between feeling I am making a huge contribution to my field and feeling anxious that I will be dismissed and become invisible (consolation and desolation). Things look good for the future of my company, but I wonder how it will go. Sometimes I constrict around sharing my ideas with investors and/or default to withdrawal and resentment about not being recognized for my unique contributions.

> ➤ What causes you to feel desolation around work, relationships, and creative projects?

> ➤ How could engaging a Seven's lightness of being and/or a One's conscientiousness bring perspective to this Four's desolation?

▶▶▶ DESOLATIONS AND INTROJECTION

To compensate for deep-seated feelings of ordinariness, Fours construct complicated defense structures involving unique presentation, eccentric personas, artistic sublimation, and introjection. Introjection assumes that all the dull, ugly, and common things they see in others are really in them. Fours channel their personal distress into poetry, drama, drawing, painting, art, and music. Sublimating feelings in artistic expression helps Fours cope with desolation.

> ➤ How do you introject bad qualities into yourself and/or incorporate the characteristics of persons you admire or envy into your own psyche and presentation?

> ➤ How does your body constrict in introjection and desolation? Where do you carry your pain and aloofness at not being special in the eyes of others?

Prayer Practice

Fours in particular don't like the ordinary or boring. It feels flat and life draining. So when things seem boring, breathe deeply into the mundane. Breathe in: "Beautiful Creator." Breathe out: "I am grateful for the present moment." Let the prayer ground you in presence.

> ➤ The Spirit's invitation to consolation often means engaging your IQ and GQ so you can reframe feelings of desolation and introjection with the reality of your beloved-ness. Today notice where the Spirit invites you out of desolation and into consolation—even consolation in the middle of desolation.

> ➤ Are there defenses besides introjection that block your discernment?

▶▶▶ CONSOLATIONS AND EQUANIMITY

The Spirit's invitation to consolation often means engaging your IQ spirit of adventurous joy and holding it together with the world's EQ sorrow. Consolations happen as you combine this IQ and EQ with GQ stability that makes meaning from the breadth of reality.

Fours are consoled as you follow the Holy Spirit out of your exaggerated feelings and distress at not being unique enough into the FLOW of creativity that serves others. In FLOW, Fours can enter dark places of human suffering with equanimity and not be overwhelmed.

> ➤ Describe a situation in which you felt the Holy Spirit inviting you out of introjection and into equanimity. What happened? What consolations came to you?

> ➤ When has equanimity helped you stand in FLOW that loves God with your heart, soul, strength, and mind?

SPIRITUAL RHYTHMS FOR FOURS

Now the Lord is the Spirit, and where the Spirit of the Lord is, there is freedom. And we all, who with unveiled faces contemplate the Lord's glory, are being transformed into his image with ever-increasing glory, which comes from the Lord, who is the Spirit. (2 Corinthians 3:17-18)

Fours long for freedom—freedom to authentically know and be known. This Scripture text indicates that freedom and transformation come as we contemplate something and someone besides ourselves and our feelings. The following spiritual rhythms invite Fours to intentionally step into FLOW that practices love of God, neighbor, and self. Say yes to the practices that best capture your desire to reflect the divine with ever-increasing glory.

▶▶▶ PRACTICING PRESENCE: FOURS

Re-read the FLOW definition in the Key Terms section. Notice the presence of Trinitarian harmony.

Father, Son, and Spirit belong and flow together.

Head, heart, and gut belong and flow together.

Faith, love, and hope belong and flow together.

Divine harmony calls Fours to be present so your creativity is not just about you but an offering for the joy and benefit of others. Fours who are present to God, others, and self with your head, heart, and gut grow your capacity to hold feelings with objectivity and openness. Let the following meditative prayer move through your entire created being so it holds you together. Staying with this prayer for a season can help Fours access your IQ and GQ, bringing stability and lightness to your emotions and needs.

Find a comfortable and awake position. Remember that the Spirit of God dwells within you and prays for you. Ask God to give you an open and receptive head, heart, and gut.

Gut Presence: Put yourself in the presence of the Holy Spirit. Breathe into your body and gut. Notice what is happening. Notice without judgment. How does your body react to not being special? Is there something your body wants to do in this prayer? Do that. Experience your grounded feelings. Give thanks for your grounded depth. Where do you withdraw or catastrophize when you lose connection? Let your body tell you what it knows about that. What is it like to receive your unique body or the body of another as enough?

Heart Presence: Put yourself in the presence of Jesus. Breathe into your heart space. Feel your unique creativity. Notice your heart's need to be special. Breathe in and create even more space around your heart. Notice where you feel connected and disconnected. Tap into your deep feelings and love of beauty. Ask for grace to receive yourself as Jesus' beloved son or daughter. Where are you filled with sorrow or anxiety? Hand these places to Jesus. How does the Healer respond to you?

Head Presence: Put yourself in the presence of your Creator. Move your head around on your shoulders. Feel its weight and tightness. Breathe into your magnificent mind—the mind of Christ. Observe your life in the body. What does your head tell you? What questions would you like to ask your heart space? What does it mean to trust joy as well as suffering? Consider how planning, joy, and spontaneity can lead you into freedom and transformation. What is it like to inform and reframe your feelings with head perspective?

Pray into Your Harmony: Creativity Joyfully Renews

"Creativity joyfully renews" is a breath prayer that helps you embrace the life-giving instincts of One GQ such as objectivity, stability, and self-discipline, as well as the Seven IQ of optimism, joy, play, and spontaneity.

> Be original [EQ]. That's my best advice. You're going to find that there is something you do well [One GQ], and try to do it with as much originality as you can, and don't skimp on the words [Seven IQ]. Work on the words [One GQ].
>
> **BOB SEGER**
> **(WITH OUR ADDITIONS)**

Memorizing this prayer brings awareness of what is most true about you into real-life situations. You are more than your type. Breathe this prayer when you are triggered with anxiety or shame about who you are. Breathe, "creativity joyfully renews." Let go of the constriction around needing to be special and unique; open your heart to God and others. Then call on all your God-given creativity.

FLOW Practice for Fours

In FLOW, Fours are **F**ree, **L**oving, **O**pen, and **W**ith. You stand in the presence of the three-in-one God and integrate head, gut, and heart in generous creativity. You also relate with the three Christian virtues of faith, hope, and love. When you notice that you are constricting around a need to be noticed for unique contributions, breathe and ask for inner freedom to open to God's delight in your unique being and stay with what is. Ask your gut, "How are feelings blocking a larger perspective?" Ask

your head, "Where am I suppressing joy with a default melancholy?" Then step into the FLOW of God's creativity and welcome the ability to bring beauty out of hardship. At the end of the day, log what happened when you were not in FLOW. What happened when you were in FLOW? Celebrate when God's creative beauty flowed through you. Confess when it didn't. Begin again tomorrow.

Practice Confession

Vulnerability and transparency about who you are before God and others is part of transformation and connection. Confess your:

- ▶ *Vice of envy:* and where it wounds you and others. Ask God and a soul friend to help you make the journey to equanimity and freedom.

- ▶ *Angst/shame:* about inadequacy, having a fatal flaw, and not being enough

- ▶ *Addiction:* to needing to be special and beloved more than others

- ▶ *Introjection:* along with self-accusations and self-hatred

- ▶ *Resistances:* to ordinary and mundane

Receive Jesus' assurance: "Before the God who creates and re-creates, you are uniquely mine."

Practice Gratitude

Thankfulness lifts a Four's heavy heart. It helps you see there is goodness even in dark times.

▶ Keep a daily gratitude journal and record your reasons for gratitude.

▶ Watch your gratitudes accumulate by filling a glass with marbles, beans, or stones that signify something for which you are thankful.

▶ Five times a day, practice saying thank you to others. Tell them why you are grateful.

Practice the Presence of the Ordinary

Let go of having to exaggerate or dramatize experience or feelings in order to enjoy.

▶ Notice how ordinary, daily things are often "extra"-ordinary. Share your insights with a soul friend.

▶ Release your judgments about what is dull and ugly. Look more deeply. What graces, lessons, and beauty can you find in these things?

▶ Imagine how God sees the things that you find dull or boring. Pray about these things as you think God would.

Practice Visio Divina

Fours often find nature a "thin place" where they encounter God. *Visio divina* (literally, holy seeing) seeks God in the beauty of created things.

▶ "The heavens declare the glory of God" (Psalm 19:1). Take time to look at the sky and let it speak to you of the Creator. What do the heavens say to you? What do you want to say to God?

▶ Jesus says, "Look at the birds of the air" (Matthew 6:26). Birds, lilies, bread, and wine all express truth about God's care.

Breath Prayers

Notice your magnificent breath. Feel the oxygen fill your lungs and lift your chest. Follow your breath in and down. Take time to notice what is happening in your heart. Feel the beauty of your created life as you breathe in: "You have formed my inward parts; I am creatively and wonderfully made . . . may my soul know that very well." Spend a few minutes with this breath prayer. Follow your breath to liberty—you don't have to be the all-original Creator.

Keep breathing into your body. Breathing in from the soles of your feet, fill your belly with breath, and continue breathing to the crown of your head. Feel your experience. Breathe into your head, your gut, and your heart. Without judgment, notice whatever comes up. If memories come, welcome them with your creative, feeling being. Stay with them. Take action to hold yourself in a loving way. Use the breath prayers below when they fit the situation you are in.

❖ *Inhale: "Made in God's image."*
   Exhale: "There is no ordinary."

❖ *Inhale: "Beautiful Creator,"*
   exhale: "I am grateful to be present."

❖ *Inhale: "Creativity,"*
   exhale: "joyfully renews."

Spend some time in creation this week. Take a walk or run. Pay attention. What is God saying to you?

▶ Find a painting or photograph that means something to you. Ask God to give you eyes to see. What do you think God wants you to see? Talk to God about this.

Practice Praying with a Cross

Fours resonate with those who suffer. Both of the images of Jesus nailed to the cross and the empty cross give Fours a place to put the pain you feel for yourself and others.

▶ Hold a crucifix. Notice the wounds of Jesus. Push your burdens and the sufferings of the world into his wounds. There is no terrible thing that Jesus cannot bear. What does Jesus say to you from this cross? Talk to him about your pain.

▶ Hold an empty cross. The empty cross is evidence that Jesus has turned the worst day in history into the day of salvation, forgiveness, and freedom. What does Jesus say to you from this cross? Listen and respond.

▶ Carry a crucifix or cross with you in your pocket. Let it remind you of how to hold suffering in solidarity with God's own sorrow.

Practice Integrating EQ, IQ, GQ

Notice when you trust your heartfelt EQ feelings more than IQ and GQ. When you want to engage a creative impulse that makes beauty and brings depth, persevere with One tenacity and Seven delight.

Blessing for the Beloved Four

As we close this section, take time to breathe in this blessing and create space in your soul.

May the Holy Three bless your journey home to your truly unique self.

May God the Father direct you with joy and give you holy perspective.

May the heart of Jesus invite you into solidarity with him in sufferings.

May the Holy Spirit ground you in hope in all your connections and creativity.

May the sacred equanimity of the Trinity lead you on your road, upholding you and loving you.

Empathy for FOURS

Be vulnerable, my dear; it's okay.
You are so beautiful in all your softness, in all your pain.

ANONYMOUS

Every child needs to be affirmed for their unique beloved-ness. Early on, beloved Fours may have had caregivers who rewarded conformity rather than uniqueness. This made them feel different from the rest of their family. Since that difference wasn't welcomed, they often felt abandoned and alone. To survive, they suppressed intense feelings and authentic desires. Here you can explore your responses to Fours and how you might grow in empathy and seeing them as God does.

Empathy is a true self response that harmonizes and breaks down the we/they divide. For instance, we may find Fours narcissistic, aloof, and intense. Or we may think Fours are some of the most creative and interesting people we know. Understanding how the envy, drama, and sense of what's missing developed in a Four can create compassion and receptivity in our interactions with them.

Below a Four describes her journey. Notice your feeling, thinking, and reacting to this Four.

My early memories of heartbreak, darkness, and pain used to overwhelm me with melancholy. Valleys and huge feelings were my normal. I suppose they still are, but I am trying to traverse the landscape in my story with equanimity. My Three achieving wing and principled One father pushed me to work. Life was serious, and there was no time to play like a Seven. My Three

and One got things done, and my Seven just went missing. Thank God there is transformation. I'm a young mom, and Harmony Triads help me integrate the positive, playful side of Seven so my kids don't learn to dismiss joy (as I did growing up). Letting go of seriousness can land me in a Seven-ish lack of boundaries and an appetite for everything extraordinary. When Four melancholy and distress overwhelm me, I need Seven presence to lighten up and One presence to ground me and help me shoulder responsibilities. Gut One energy helps me reframe challenging situations so I don't get stuck in melancholy.

1. As you consider the Four story, notice:
   - What are you feeling about this Four?
   - What are you thinking about this Four?
   - What is your gut instinct about this Four?

2. When have melancholy, seriousness, heartbreak, abandonment, or overwork disconnected you from empathy?

3. When do you see the playful, spontaneous Seven child or steady, reforming One child hiding within the serious Four?

4. How does a heart-anxiety that Fours feel about being abandoned mitigate against the connection and attention they seek?

UNDERSTANDING THE DEFENSE MECHANISM OF INTROJECTION

Fours don't project; they introject and magnify foibles, weaknesses, and mistakes in themselves. This Four remembers the pain of disconnection. Do you see how the defense mechanism of introjection shows up here?

I remember being a joyful, free, and social child. I expressed that joy and desire to connect by frequently getting out of my chair at school. My teacher warned me that if I got up again, she would tie me to my chair while the class went to recess. I got up to get a black crayon, and the boy next to me told on me! The teacher hauled me to the front of the class and did just as she'd said. Shame, abandonment, distress, and anxiety poured over me. I internalized the pain of being literally bound, trapped, and overpowered. I felt being tied to the chair was proof that I was unworthy of love and belonging. Conformity rather than freedom mattered most. I did not remember getting untied until a time of healing prayer in my early adult years. Jesus came into my prayer, untied me, held me, and comforted me.

1. What connections and resistances are you feeling with this Four?

2. In this Four's story, with its sense of "something is wrong with me," can you recognize the creative spirit that felt shame when expressing authentic feelings and behaviors?

3. How could you demonstrate God's approval of a Four's uniqueness?

4. How might you join the Holy Spirit in praying for a Four you know?

RELATING TO A FOUR

We find grace to see things from a Four's point of view when we remember that under the overdone affect and sensitivity of a Four is a child who felt they didn't belong and couldn't be themselves.

- Appreciate their perceptivity, depth, and ability to hold paradox.

- Disconnection brings deep distress; initiate connection and stay connected.

- Accept that what feels like "drama" to you is their absolute reality. Ask, "What is this like for you? What do you need or want from me?"

- Welcome their resonance to pain and beauty without trying to fix it.

- Ask if they are willing to share their creative efforts with you; they find it risky.

- When they despair because something is missing from their work or life, be their grounded support.

- Recognize how rules, policies, and red tape can stifle their enthusiasm and creativity.

- Don't expect them to fall into line like everyone else. Give them space to get on board in their own way. They are not against you.

- Fours are uncomfortable with "either/or" thinking. Accept their comfort with gray.

The following list summarizes key characteristics of our beloved Fours. Consider your responses to these characteristics.

- *Authentic, true self:* Creative

- *Compulsive, false self:* Envious
- *Virtue leading back to true self:* Equanimity
- *Personality style:* Creator
- *Work style:* Expressionist
- *Leadership/action style:* Personalist or expressionist
- *Relationships:* Approach-withdrawal
- *Core motivation:* Originality
- *Negative fixation:* Distress, shame
- *Narrative:* "I'm not worthy of love and belonging."
- *Communication:* Dramatic
- *Four with a Three wing:* More efficient, active, enterprising
- *Four with a Five wing:* More logical, detached, analytical
- *Basic fear:* Insignificance, invisibility
- *Basic desire:* Uniqueness, significance
- *Drive:* Connection and isolation, express feelings and moods, create feelings and connection in others

Based on the description above:

1. How does it feel to be a Four? Which descriptors give you clues about how to relate to a Four?

2. Is there a better way to say what is true of Fours?

3. Fours want people to appreciate their unique characteristics. What is it like for you to give this gift to a Four?

4. Fours are anxious when there is no connection. How can you reassure them?

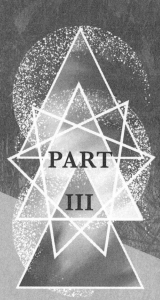

PART III

THE HEAD TRIAD

Fives, Sixes, and Sevens

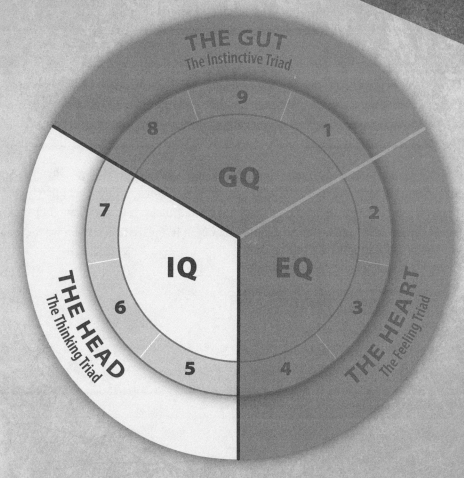

THE HEAD TRIAD HAS COGNITIVE AWARENESS
OR THINKING INTELLIGENCE (IQ)

Fives, Sixes, and Sevens perceive or filter the world through their mental faculties. Their little grey cells constantly generate ideas, plans, and rationales. The inner life of the mind gives them energy and inspiration. The perspective of the Five, practicality of the Six, and vision of the Seven all reflect the God whose "understanding no one can fathom" (Isaiah 40:28). The virtue of the Five is detachment. The virtue of the Six is courage. The virtue of the Seven is sobriety.

IQ

The safety and security of our world often ride on the shoulders of head people who know how to gather, analyze, and compute information into plans, strategies, and action. Healthy IQ people know how much information is needed in any given moment. They often embody the proverb: "The beginning of wisdom is this: Get wisdom. / Though it cost all you have, get understanding" (Proverbs 4:7).

HEAD DEFENSIVE POSTURE

The Head Triad struggles with a variety of fears. Under stress, fears become the dominant fixation. So to feel safe, they overdo protective strategies, escapes, and beliefs. Their over-thinking, over-planning, withdrawing from pain, and gathering of data can sabotage action and decision making.

EXPERIENCING THE SACRED

Head intelligence people often nourish their souls by learning new things. They enjoy books, ideas, study, questions, teaching, experiences, and conversations that open them to the wonder and reason of new things. As head people integrate their GQ and EQ, they recognize that a "safe" place is more than an answer. It is a place inside them where the Spirit of God dwells.

FIVES

Wisdom Lovingly Directs

Any fool can know; the point is to understand.
ALBERT EINSTEIN

I am a quiet,
cerebral observer. I
seek knowledge and observe
life at a distance. I value my space and
privacy and want to be safe and in control of my
feelings. I don't like to share my feelings. It's easier for
me to figure them out when I am alone. I avoid
crowds. Rude, loud, or demanding people who
express strong feelings exhaust me. I don't
have a strong need to be with people. I do
not like to be in the middle of things. I
would rather sit back and analyze
what's happening. I also enjoy thinking
about an experience later when I'm not
in the thick of it. At my best I am calm,
perceptive, curious, and insightful. I
sometimes feel socially awkward. I think
my intellect can compensate for some of
that, so I gather lots of information. People
sometimes find me withholding and arrogant.
When I am stressed, I tend to hoard my energy and
myself. I also can get agitated and think that someone
has either moved my things or disturbed my
work. My mental life is very active,
and my emotional life is
very private.

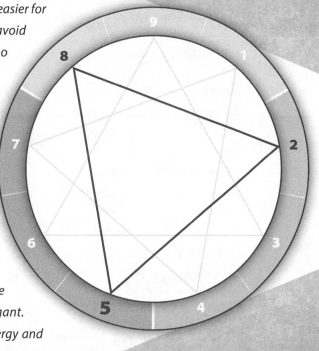

WHO I AM AND WHO I AM NOT

Fives bear the image of God as wise. Your life resonates with:

"Who has known the mind of the Lord
   so as to instruct him?"
But we have the mind of Christ.
   (1 Corinthians 2:16)

Wisdom is inevitably part of your story. Stories about who we are and who we are not shape what we do and don't do, who we become, and where we stall out. Fives often have a story that includes learning, understanding, observation, and being alone. You skip over chapters of your life on engaging with others or generously sharing what you know. This section invites awareness of influences that shape a Five.

▶▶▶ **BELOVED FIVES**

Spend some time with the words below that describe who Fives are and are not. Circle the characteristics that resonate with your journey. Star words that express your gifts. Underline words that describe parts of your personality that are unusable by God in their present form. Put a checkmark beside characteristics that you *celebrate*.

Fives Descriptive Words List

I AM		I AM NOT	
wise	analyzer	foolish	trivializing
perceptive	undemonstrative	naive	flaky
astute	contained	stupid	feeling
witty	contemplative	dull	effusive
aware	mystic	oblivious	in action
observant	studious	gullible	simplistic
curious	reserved	unaware	unreflective
good listener	serious	in action	flamboyant
thorough	pedantic	intrusive	silly
whole picture		unprepared	entertaining
synthesizing		myopic	

➤ Which words reflect the image of God in you?

➤ Which words are you most attached to? Addicted to? Compulsive about?

➤ Which words do you resist and judge the most?

➤ If you opened up to the words you resist without judgment, how might your life and relationships shift?

➤ Journal about the words that reflect how God understands and sees you.

▶▶▶ GETTING TO KNOW FIVES

These Fives remember how their journeys began. Notice where they found pleasure and how they escaped or filled the void they felt inside themselves.

> One of my earliest memories is of identifying the words in a book. Reading books for pleasure helped me escape the uncertain atmosphere at home. My mother was more quiet and task driven than relational. Incomplete education and lack of confidence made her clean and cook and direct rather than connect and educate. I learned more about relationships from books than from people, and I was probably more socially awkward than I remember. I was a good student who enjoyed classmates. I had one good friend, but I was never comfortable in a group.

Another Five story:

> At an early age I learned not to draw attention to myself. As the Japanese say, "The nail that sticks out gets hammered down." The unspoken message was to not have feelings, and if you do, block them. Better to not stick out or need recognition. Be the invisible hands that serve and help behind the scenes. I coped by withdrawing into my books. Knowledge seemed to fill the inner emptiness within. The Enneagram helped me recognize my feelings and make a conscious choice about when to put them aside and when not to. In conflict, putting aside my feelings brings calm. But I make a mental note to go back and process my feelings so I understand myself. Processing comes with a price. I am usually exhausted for several days afterward. It has been a life-long struggle to come out of hiding.

These beloved Fives felt unsafe navigating the world of conflict, feelings, and relationships so they withdrew into their heads. The escape and safety of books and information protected them and shaped their self-understanding.

> ➤ What do these stories bring up in you?

> ➤ What is your memory of your first Five experience?

> ➤ What is it like for you to know something is true in your head?

Breath Prayer

In silence and solitude, ask God to help you see yourself clearly. Begin with breathing. Breathe in: "Made in God's image," and then breathe out: "I can show up." Spend a few minutes with this breath prayer. Feel the goodness and freedom of being made in God's image; feel the liberty of not needing to know it all. Breathe this prayer in and out throughout the day.

TRUE SELF AND FALSE SELF: THE WISE PERSON

Who we are or are not comes with expression and energy. The attitudes, behaviors, and motivations of beloved Fives convey wise energy. Your true self emerges from union with God. It is built on being beloved of God rather than on the information you know and your intelligence.

A Five's false self is the compulsive, deeply entrenched, old nature, ego self that constricts around fear and scarcity. This section will help you begin to recognize compulsive and impulsive false self reactions as well as true self FLOW that loves God, others, and self.

True Self Fives: Sacred Wisdom

Fives are designed to embody God's wisdom. You are objective, curious, innovative, and focused. You want to wade into complexities and engage "the little grey cells." A true self Five is in touch with sacred knowing. Your IQ comes laced with empathy EQ and decisive action GQ that serves others. Transforming Fives come out of hiding, make contact, and do what scares you. You touch the pulse of the moment with your knowledge and share! When you are present to God, you detach from your addiction to safety and belong to more than yourself. Healthy Fives are visionary and team players. You can move from the withdrawing edges of your personality to engagement and connection. The Christian tradition describes wise presence like this: "The wisdom that comes from heaven is first of all pure; then peace-loving, considerate, submissive, full of mercy and good fruit, impartial and sincere" (James 3:17). Fives reveal that true wisdom knows how to relax, generously teach, and give presence, energy, and love to others.

False Self Fives: Constrict in Withdrawal and Avarice

To avoid looking foolish or incompetent, false self Fives over-identify with knowledge and intelligence. You pontificate, prognosticate, and otherwise hold forth. This disordered attachment to information moves you from presence and up into your head, where you disconnect from uncomfortable feelings and body awareness. When Fives aren't in presence, you operate from a scarcity mentality and isolate yourself, defaulting to your vice of avarice. Avarice withdraws from emotional outlays and hoards time and energy. Avarice overdoes privacy and boundaries, and it constricts around stinginess. False self Fives default to protection and are wary of anything scary or draining. To solve problems and potential threats, you move to your edge, gather more data, lecture, stonewall, and argue.

▶▶▶ TRUE OR FALSE SELF

Consider the following questions about your true and false self. Notice what comes up for you—notice without judgment. What questions particularly invite you to jot down or journal responses?

➤ How do true self Five characteristics show up in your relationships?

➤ Where do false self Five qualities show up in your relationships with others? When and why are you stingy and withholding? Where do you isolate and retreat into your head so you don't have to share your feelings? How does avarice show up? ("I don't know or have enough!") How does fear show up? ("I will look foolish!")

➤ Where do you constrict against generously giving yourself to others? What is a cue to relax your boundaries and privacy?

➤ How do you feel the difference between centered, true self presence and edgy, false self detachment? How do you pull back or freeze others out when you don't have enough energy?

HARMONY: WISDOM LOVINGLY DIRECTS

Fives are often identified as the wise number, but you are much more than just one number! You bear the image and harmony of a three-in-one God. When beloved Fives integrate your heart and gut intelligence, you harmonize, and your wisdom flows with Eight agency and Two care. This section creates awareness of how FLOW is the unique gift of the Harmony Triads.

In harmony and FLOW, a beloved Five's gift of understanding doesn't stay locked up in your heads. It flows with warm engagement of others (Two EQ) and decisiveness and leadership (Eight GQ).

►►► MORE THAN YOUR TYPE

The story below describes a Five, Eight, and Two journey to integration. This Five is remembering how his story led him to integrate so he could be present to more than his thoughts. Integration that embraces the action orientation of an Eight and the connecting

Running Out of Energy

In this text, Jesus' followers have run out of energy for the people and task in front of them. They have a scarcity mentality like a Five about food and dealing with needs, so they want to withdraw. Where do you parcel out your energy because you are afraid you won't have enough?

> When Jesus landed and saw a large crowd, he had compassion on them and healed their sick.
>
> As evening approached, the disciples came to him and said, "This is a remote place, and it's already getting late. Send the crowds away, so they can go to the villages and buy themselves some food."
>
> Jesus replied, "They do not need to go away. You give them something to eat."
>
> "We have here only five loaves of bread and two fish," they answered.
>
> "Bring them here to me," he said. And he directed the people to sit down on the grass. Taking the five loaves and the two fish and looking up to heaven, he gave thanks and broke the loaves. Then he gave them to the disciples, and the disciples gave them to the people. They all ate and were satisfied, and the disciples picked up twelve basketfuls of broken pieces that were left over. The number of those who ate was about five thousand men, besides women and children. (Matthew 14:14-21)

1. Contrast Jesus' and the disciples' responses to the crowd and the scarcity of provisions. Which is more like you?

2. What is your response to exhaustion? To scarce emotional and physical resources? When do you want to withdraw and hoard time and resources?

3. What is it like for you to be present to people with whatever you have?

heart of a Two helps Fives moderate your overthinking reactions and gives you room to express empathy, strength, and connection.

> As a child, I dismissed my Eight gut and Two heart. In junior high, I discovered I was smart, and this brought attention! Other students would seek me out to tutor and help with their schoolwork. It was then my Two and Eight energy showed up. I enjoyed helping others, and having something to offer enabled me to begin moving out of my unhealthy, withdrawn, and introverted Five. I leaned toward my Eight agency and became class president, an all-state gymnast, the concert choir soloist, and an honor-roll student. My Two energy also helped me connect and give guidance. Still, much of my energy went to holding off my empty heart. Hollow inside, I tried to fill myself with non-stop affirmation for my intellect. No accolade was too much, but neither was any accolade enough. The hunger to be some-one remained. Integrating my IQ and EQ helped me learn how to be present to myself and others so I could be relational and not just heady.

> ➤ When you feel unsafe, how do you ignore tenderness and vulnerability? How could a warm-hearted response actually lower your anxiety and help you connect?

> ➤ How do you retreat from acting on your ideas and dismiss your gut energy?

> ➤ Imagine increasing your wisdom by showing up with strong, engaged presence that notices the emotional climate in an interchange. What do you see?

►►► GQ, EQ, IQ

This Five describes his journey to integration. Pay attention to how often using his heart and gut intelligence brought harmony and enjoyment into his life.

> Growing up, I got good grades and read voraciously but I kept my thoughts and opinions to myself. At home, validation came from agreement with parents, not free speech. If I ventured a counter opinion, I was made to feel stupid and unacceptable. This made me isolate and withdraw, which didn't give me practice in relationships. I depended on my head to get me through. I joined a winning debate team—but found it difficult to engage in conversations that weren't issue driven. I could win arguments but not friends, par-ticularly women friends. For many years, I only trusted my head. My head could protect me. I dismissed emotions as fickle and gut instincts as untrustworthy. In college, I stum-bled on to an Enneagram book that gave me a language for who I was. I began to go to my Eight (GQ) and risked saying vulnerable things out loud. I tried to get out of my head and act on my thoughts. I also began to pay attention to any feeling (EQ) I *thought* I had. I journaled to try to understand it. I also asked myself, "What is all your learning for? How can you use what you know for justice and community?" As I began to lean into feelings and actions, I connected more. It was much later that I realized I was working with the Harmony Triad. I was using gut strength and heart feelings to engage. And when I risked that, I felt alive and enjoyed people. I have a long way to go. But I know I need my heart EQ and gut GQ to live a full life.

> ➤ When Fives engage their gut, they moderate their head and become decisive. Where do you see GQ in yourself?

> ➤ When Fives engage their heart, they moderate their head and become engaged, caring, and compassionate. Where do you see EQ in yourself?

> ➤ What is it like for you to have GQ, EQ, and IQ?

HEALING CHILDHOOD HURTS: OPENING TO DETACHMENT

Children are wired for resilience. Still, residual childhood baggage and messages can leak into adult Five relationships. Five children can lose the message that it's okay to be comfortable in the world. The default message you can learn is, "You will be embarrassed and look foolish if you are emotional and bold." To cope, Five children withdrew, detached, and went into your head. These defenses mitigate against engagement and action. Do any of these messages resonate with you?

When these messages get triggered in adult interactions, then raw, ragged, unprocessed pain can erupt, sabotaging the FLOW of a Five's

Response to Perceived Foolishness

Beloved Fives can get stuck on your edge when things don't seem rational to you. In this reading a woman expresses her love toward Jesus in an extravagant and perhaps "wasteful" way. Notice how those present rebuked her for not doing the obviously prudent and wise thing. How does Jesus interpret the woman's gift?

While he was in Bethany, reclining at the table in the home of Simon the Leper, a woman came with an alabaster jar of very expensive perfume, made of pure nard. She broke the jar and poured the perfume on his head.

Some of those present were saying indignantly to one another, "Why this waste of perfume? It could have been sold for more than a year's wages and the money given to the poor." And they rebuked her harshly.

"Leave her alone," said Jesus. "Why are you bothering her? She has done a beautiful thing to me. The poor you will always have with you, and you can help them any time you want. But you will not always have me. She did what she could. She poured perfume on my body beforehand to prepare for my burial. (Mark 14:3-8)

1. What is Simon's attitude to the extravagant and emotional gift? What is your attitude to extravagant and emotional gifts?

2. What makes you indignant? When do you treat people harshly?

3. What would it be like for you to contemplate people's motives and efforts through Jesus' eyes? When could it be wise to say, "They did what they could"?

wisdom. Suddenly a fearful four-year-old inside you gets afraid to make important decisions. Defaulting to the false self, Fives lose your center and isolate so you won't look foolish or have too little information and energy. The Harmony Triad offers a way for Fives to be curious about how the trauma, defenses, childhood lies, and default withdrawal shape your relationships today. Fives must learn to distinguish between your virtue and vice of detachment. Detachment is a virtue when it brings perspective for the sake of others. Detachment is a vice when it withdraws, isolates, and thinks processing past pain is stupid. Proper detachment does not unhook from loving God, others, and self with all your head, heart and gut.

▶▶▶ RECEIVING THE DISMISSED CHILDLIKE SELF

Receiving your dismissed child can heal and give Fives freedom to engage and make decisions. Remember within every passive, reticent, and unavailable Five is an intense, assertive, and dismissive Eight who is driven to get what you want. There is also a tender, sensitive, inner Two who worries that you are not worthy of love and belonging. To recognize where you dismissed your fearful, childlike self, pay attention to where you may have ignored your GQ and EQ.

This reticent Five shares his story of growing up in a world where it wasn't safe to express feelings. Can you find the tender, loving, heart-full Two inner child who couldn't trust his vulnerability to others? Be curious about how engaging like an Eight gave him courage and shaped his story.

> Growing up, I wasn't allowed to have feelings. Consequently my automatic default was to block my feelings. I struggled as a young adult to recover and pay attention to those feelings. Now, I am intentional about when to be attentive to feelings and people and when to put feelings aside in order to attend to difficult situations. I make a mental note when I do this, reminding myself to go back later and process those feelings. This enables me to be decisive, strong, and calm in a storm of conflict. People make remarks about my ability to detach from all the drama and emotions when dealing with difficult people and situations. This ability is costly; I am usually exhausted for several days afterward as I

Prayer of Ignatius of Loyola

Allow this prayer of Ignatius of Loyola, which addresses the heart, head, and gut motivations of the Enneagram Triads, to become your prayer. This week, pray the mind, heart, and strength of the Trinity into your life and interactions.

> *Eternal Word, only begotten Son of God,*
> *Teach me true generosity [IQ].*
> *Teach me to serve you as you deserve,*
> *To give without counting the cost,*
> *To fight heedless of wounds [GQ],*
> *To labor without seeking rest,*
> *To sacrifice myself without thought of*
>   *any reward [EQ],*
> *Save the knowledge [IQ] that I have*
>   *done your will.*

work to pick up my feelings. I have to be intentional and come out of hiding to make my wisdom practical.

As you read these questions notice where you sense God's invitation to more deeply receive your dismissed child. Write down any new insights and awareness. Be courageous; this is important and integrative work.

> This Five practices being attentive and present to feelings and people. What are the costs and rewards of this engagement?

> When you face a difficult relational situation, how do you lean into or dismiss your heart intelligence?

> Where does the introverted Five draw upon the "take charge" Eight GQ that takes action to accomplish something significant? How do you access or dismiss your gut?

▶▶▶ JOURNALING YOUR DISMISSED CHILDLIKE SELF

As Fives receive your dismissed, childlike self, you may recognize when you began to turn away from your GQ and EQ for fear of being sucked dry by the needs of people around you. Getting reacquainted with your gut strength helps beloved Fives voice ideas and stand up for justice. It also makes you aware of how the insensitive, domineering Eight can show up when you feel threatened. Integrating EQ brings wise vulnerability to relational distress, as well as a capacity to hold the needs of others without fear. To recognize where you dismissed your childlike self and your fears, pay attention to where you may have ignored your GQ and EQ.

Name and journal some of your reservations about showing up and connecting. Explore when chaos and lack of order made you want to isolate. Engage your EQ; notice when you felt unsafe to care and feel. This is hard work. Take your time.

> What created your feeling of being uncomfortable in the world? Where do you dismiss your agency because of fear or past trauma?

> What default reactions and triggers of your childhood self still operate today?

> Ask God to help you reclaim your virtue of detachment for the sake of others (rather than for privacy and isolation). Intentionally release self-protection and open to childlike engagement. Notice what happens.

> Where has your trust been broken/repaired/healed or increased/solidified?

Fives like privacy and withdraw to conserve energy. Being generous and present with time and space can feel very overwhelming and unsafe. The spiritual practices of generosity and practicing the presence of people offer Fives an intentional way to engage and experience who you are and what God can supply when it is beyond what you think and have. It may be helpful for you to read the chapter "Invitation to Practice the Presence of People" in *Invitations from God* by Adele Ahlberg Calhoun.

This week, practice being generous with yourself and what you know. When you begin to measure the energy it takes to show up, consider what you might miss if you withdraw. How might engaging be exhilarating and open you to more wisdom? Keep track of the times you practice the presence of people and lean toward God's generous heart in your interactions.

DISCERNMENT: DESOLATIONS AND CONSOLATIONS

Ignatius of Loyola taught that God's Guiding Spirit of wisdom moves in all three centers of intelligence—head, heart, and gut. When faced with a decision, Ignatius suggested noticing the consolations and desolations by asking: What does my heart feel? What does my mind think? What does my gut sense? (More information on Harmony Triad discernment is found in Soul Resource 5.)

Consolations point Fives toward presence to God and others. Consolations are evidence that Fives are heading in the direction of IQ wisdom that flows with EQ love and GQ agency. Desolations can deplete Fives. But desolations also alert Fives to your need of balance and ways of allocating energy that don't move you away from God and others.

Fives experience consolations such as divine wisdom, calm, loving detachment, generous objectivity, humble competence, focused justice, transforming perspective, insightful nurture, smart service, and insightful care. This is freedom.

Fives experience desolations such as negativity, cynicism, withholding, withdrawing, detachment, isolation, avarice, greed, intellectual hubris, and fear of appearing ignorant. These desolations leave you bound.

Healing Prayer

When Fives process your wounds in the presence of God's wisdom and protection, you feel safe to risk offering your considerable gifting to others. Healing moves isolating Fives toward loving action. Your vice of avarice and hoarding of energy and self is transformed into your virtue of right detachment.

This is a way to do healing prayer on your own. Relax into silence and solitude. Breathe deeply. Don't force it. Become present to God and yourself. Ask God to show your desire for ongoing healing. Ask God to bring to mind a past sorrow that is still being transmitted. Be still and wait. When something comes to mind, follow this simple trail of healing prayer.

- ❖ *Imagine yourself and Jesus back in the memory. Get your bearings. Where is Jesus? Where are you?*

- ❖ *What are you feeling? (anxious, overwhelmed, exhausted, afraid, stupid, foolish, unsafe, sucked dry, or something else)*

- ❖ *Do these feelings remind you of a time you had similar reactions? You can go with Jesus to that place and time or stay where you are.*

- ❖ *Continue to name what you feel in your experience. Ask Jesus if these feelings point to a lie you began to believe at that time. Give it a name.*

- ❖ *What is Jesus saying to you about this lie? Listen. Is there an image, word, or phrase that he speaks to you?*

- ❖ *Repeat the truth you have heard about yourself from Jesus gently and frequently. Let the truth be an antidote that lets the pain go into Jesus and sets you free.*

▶▶▶ PRESENT TO WHAT'S HAPPENING INSIDE

Both consolations and desolations point toward the purpose for which Fives were created. Here we focus on consolations and desolations particular to you. This Five is studying the map of his soul and notices signposts of desolation and where mental acuity doesn't give the whole picture. Notice when Fives default and withdraw into their heads and miss gut and heart consolations and/or desolations that provide wisdom in times of decision.

The unexamined life is not worth living.
SOCRATES

> There was no talk about feelings, and certainly none of the children ever expressed anger toward each other or toward our parents. Self expression in the presence of my father evoked threat of his belt (desolation). His threat was usually enough to bring us back in line. That's how my Eight gut intelligence lost its voice and went underground along with me. I do not remember ever having a conversation with my father. My mom passed information about the children to my dad, and she made sure it was good news. I found I was safest when I withdrew alone in my room. There I listened to Broadway and classical music and pantomimed scenes or directed the orchestra (consolation). Sometimes I made up imaginary, self-scripted adventures alone or with my best friend. In my adventures, I was always the hero who saved someone's life or accomplished some remarkable and widely recognized feat (consolation).
>
> My mom was very unhappy and complained to me about my dad. I did not know what to do with her feelings or information, so I just withdrew into my head. This is where my Two began to get sidelined. There was no room for my needs (desolation). I needed to take care of my mother. This expanded into taking care of women in general, being careful not to hurt them, and hiding my needs in relationships (desolation).

Prayer Practice for Opening to God

Beloved Fives, in particular, withdraw from being present to God, others, and themselves. They think consolation can be found on their own and in their head. So when you notice yourself escaping into your head, let this breath prayer open you to God and the moment. Breathe in: "God gives wisdom." Breathe out: "I share God." Something unexpected might happen if you are present to what is.

➤ This Five found consolation in imagination. Where do you find consolation in imagining things?

➤ How does the head defense of isolation show up in this Five? How does it show up in you?

➤ Check God's motions in your head as you face into a current desolation. Is your head hiding and ignoring desolation?

▶▶▶ DESOLATIONS AND GREED OR AVARICE

Reticent and studious Fives often play it safe with non-committal mental responses like "That's interesting" or "I'll have to think about that." These responses don't require action or sharing. In fact, they can be ways of looking engaged while staying detached and stingy with what you know. Without judgment, notice where you take a pass on sharing who you are and what you know. Stay with one or two questions and let the truth settle in.

> How do you withhold yourself from others and move away from your feelings? When does gathering information, analyzing, and systematizing offer you a way to keep people at arm's length?

> How does your body constrict in desolation when you are afraid that you don't have enough information or energy? Where do you tighten and carry your fear of looking foolish?

> Are there behaviors besides withdrawal and avarice that block discernment and flowing with God's wisdom?

▶▶▶ CONSOLATIONS AND DETACHMENT

Fives can pontificate on what you know and perseverate over what you don't know. The Spirit's invitation to consolation often means engaging EQ that recognizes the importance of attaching to others and not just information. Engaging GQ opens Fives to acting on what you know. You can discern, "How much information is needed to pull the trigger?" or "Am I talking to connect or just holding forth?" Notice when the Spirit invites you into the consolation of advising others with confidence and compassion.

Fives are consoled as you follow God's Spirit out of isolation into presence and commitment. You step back and detach from the clinging, grabbing fear that tries to fill inner emptiness with information and then engage in what is really happening. True discernment flows with perspective and love—with detachment and attachment.

> Describe a situation in which you felt God inviting you to step back and detach in order to see. What happened? What consolations came to you?

> When has detachment helped you stand in FLOW that loves God with your heart, soul, strength, and mind?

SPIRITUAL RHYTHMS FOR FIVES

Those who live according to the flesh [false self] have their minds set on what the flesh [false self] desires; but those who live in accordance with the

> To know what you know and what you do not know: that is true knowledge.
> **CONFUCIUS**

Spirit have their minds set on what the Spirit desires. The mind governed by the flesh [false self] is death, but the mind governed by the Spirit [true self] is life and peace. (Romans 8:5-6, with our additions)

Being smart, educated, and knowledgeable is not the same as having a mind set on what the Spirit desires. Fives who intentionally partner with the Spirit to break false self patterns of isolation and avarice begin to develop new neural pathways of generosity and engagement. Fives who do the work to connect information to lived experience and the lives of others often discover the Spirit of wisdom working through you.

Attending to the Holy Spirit's motions of your soul on a daily basis helps Fives have wisdom that lovingly directs.

These spiritual rhythms are all ways Fives can lean into God's invitations to transformation and mind renewal. Not every practice will be God's invitation to you. Say yes to the practices that best capture your desire to be with God right now.

►►► PRACTICING PRESENCE: FIVES

Re-read the FLOW definition in the Key Terms section. Notice the presence of Trinitarian harmony.

> Father, Son, and Spirit belong and flow together.
>
> Head, heart, and gut belong and flow together.
>
> Faith, love, and hope belong and flow together.

Divine harmony calls Fives to be present to God, self, and others in ways that access heart and gut as well as head. The following meditative prayer moves through your entire created being in ways that integrate IQ, EQ, and GQ. Staying with this prayer for a season can help Fives access emotions and act with courage.

Find a comfortable and awake position. Remember that the Spirit of God dwells within you and prays for you. Ask God to give you an open and receptive head, heart, and gut.

Gut Presence: Put yourself in the presence of the Spirit. Breathe into your gut space. Notice what is happening in your body. Notice without judgment. Let your body tell you what it knows. Notice how your body reacts to tension and invasion of privacy. What does your body know and want to tell you about that? Is there something you want to do in response? Is there a place where your head goes "ready, aim, aim, aim" and fails to "fire"? Ask your gut to show you what it would be like to go "ready, aim, *fire!*" How and when does your body constrict rather than step up and stand your ground? Experience your decisiveness—your active energy. Give thanks for your mind and its ability to know and then make things happen.

Heart Presence: Put yourself in the presence of Jesus. Breathe into your heart space. Feel your tenderness. Notice your guarded heart and its need to be understood and connected. Breathe in and create even more space around your heart. Notice where you feel connected or disconnected, attached or detached. Welcome the presence of emotions; name them and breathe: "I can trust you." What is it like to trust emotions and not just thoughts? Tell Jesus what in you needs care, kindness, or a healing touch. How does Jesus respond to you?

Head Presence: Put yourself in the presence of the all-wise Creator. Move your head around on your shoulders. Feel its weight and tightness. Breathe into your intellect. Observe your life in the body: exercise, interactions, and usual postures. What does your head tell you about your body life? What questions would you like to ask your heart or gut space? What needs or desires would you like to express? What is it like to welcome new information and other mental constructs?

Pray into Your Harmony: Wisdom Lovingly Directs

"Wisdom lovingly directs" is a breath prayer that helps you engage the life-giving gut instincts of Eights: direct communication and confident action. It also opens your heart to a Two's empathy, compassion, warmth, and awareness of the needs of others.

Memorizing this prayer brings awareness of what is most true about you to real-life situations. You are more than your type. Breathe it in when you find yourself detaching from personal conversations or zoning out to conserve energy. Let go of the constriction around safety and sufficiency that keeps you stuck in your head. Open and call on your God-given, generous wisdom.

FLOW Practice for Fives

In FLOW, Fives are **F**ree, **L**oving, **O**pen, and **W**ith. You stand in the presence of the three-in-one God and integrate heart and gut with your knowing. You also relate with the three Christian virtues of faith, hope, and love. When you notice that you are constricting and stuck in your head, overthinking, and requiring others to be logical like you, return to the holy three and breathe deeply into the constriction. Freedom comes as you relax with God, with what is, and with your need to stay safe through linear rationales and distance. Open your gut and heart

> Think in the morning [Five IQ].
> Act in the noon [Eight GQ].
> Eat in the evening [Two EQ].
> Sleep in the night.
> **WILLIAM BLAKE**
> **(WITH OUR ADDITIONS)**

> Knowledge is of no value unless you put it into practice.
> **ANTON CHEKHOV**

and ask: "How can I be *open* and *with* this moment and/or this person?" At the end of the day, log what happened when you were not in FLOW. What happened when you were in FLOW? Celebrate when God's wisdom for others flowed with love through you. Confess when it didn't. Begin again tomorrow.

Practice Confession

Tell your Creator the truth about who you are. Consider what it might be like for people who live and work with you. Ponder how your false self can sabotage relationships. Confess your:

- ▶ *Vice of avarice:* how you withdraw, are stingy with yourself, withhold your presence, and hoard your energy.

- ▶ *Self-protection:* Admit where you self-protect rather than connect. Commit to the journey of presence and connection.

- ▶ *Fear of incompetence:* Ask God to help you know deep within that "safe is a place inside" and "Your life is now hidden with Christ in God" (Colossians 3:3). You are safe.

- ▶ *Hoarding:* "I don't have enough." Ask God for grace to see, "Who I am and what I have is enough."

Receive words of assurance: "Before the God of extravagant generosity, receive your abundant, connected life."

Practice the Presence of People

Let others in. Jesus is an amazing example of how to practice the presence of people. Even when he is spent and trying to rest, he knows how to engage others. Jesus practices the presence of a non-Jewish outcast woman when he is exhausted and thirsty. He practices the presence of lepers, sinners, outcasts, men, and women. He sees them and validates their worth and dignity. Spend some time leaning into generosity.

▶ When you are interrupted or asked to do more than you planned, trust God to provide you with the energy. Don't hold back; risk and give.

▶ Lean into the conversation rather than hanging back.

▶ Notice how often you sit at the back of the room or how often you lean back and cross your arms in a discussion. What messages are you sending to others?

▶ When your energy is on empty, learn to kindly extract yourself rather than withdrawing without a word to anyone. Say something like, "I wanted you to know I'm leaving now, thank you for . . . "

▶ When someone asks you a question, don't unload everything you know and don't hoard your insights. There is a middle way here.

▶ Notice how using you EQ and GQ gives you deeper understanding. Respond to others with holy wisdom, not just smarts.

Name That Feeling

Become acquainted with the feeling part of life. Connecting with others depends on your heart not just you head. Feelings are like the weather; they come and go. And they also give us

Breath Prayers

Notice your magnificent breath. Feel the oxygen fill your lungs and lift your chest. Follow your breath in and down. Take time to notice what is happening in your heart. Feel the wisdom of your created life as you breathe in: "You have formed my inward parts; I am wisely and wonderfully made . . . may my soul know that very well." Spend a few minutes with this breath prayer. Follow your breath to the liberty of not having to be the all-wise Creator.

Keep breathing into your body. Breathing in from the soles of your feet, fill your belly with breath, and continue breathing to the crown of your head. Feel your experience. Breathe into your head, your heart, and your gut. Without judgment, notice whatever comes up. If memories come, welcome them with your wise, loving strength. Stay with them. Take action to stay inside and hold yourself in a loving way. Use the breath prayers below when they fit the situation you are in.

❖ *Inhale: "Made in God's image." Exhale: "I can show up."*

❖ *Inhale: "God gives wisdom." Exhale: "I share God."*

❖ *Inhale: "Wisdom," exhale: "lovingly directs."*

information about ourselves, others, and the world around us. Jesus expressed his feelings to others. He was sad, angry, grieved, lonely, and heartbroken. Take some steps into Jesus' own heart for others.

▶ Your body will tell you about your feelings. Notice where you are stiff and achy. Pay attention to the butterflies in your stomach. What makes you blush? What feelings are tied to these body reactions?

▶ Keep a catalogue of all the feelings you felt today. Work at naming your feelings. Each day, try to name one more feeling than the day before.

▶ Notice how you go to your head when you are asked to share or when you are flooded with feelings. Breathe deeply into your heart space. Ask God to help you be generous and love with all your heart.

▶ Today, try to notice what people who live and work with you might be feeling. What information is noticing their feelings giving you? How can you respond more wisely and lovingly to them?

Practice Empathy and Compassion

Standing back and detaching to get the thirty-thousand-foot view is the unique gift of Fives. That lofty perspective can be accurate and still lack true wisdom. Godly wisdom is integrated with empathy and compassion.

▶ GQ involvement and EQ proximity take you out of the clouds and invite you to express immediate care and concern for others. Empathy beckons you to stay in the game. Don't pull away when you feel overwhelmed. Breathe and ask for eyes to see and ears to hear as God does.

▶ Ask others what they feel and not just what they think. Listen to their story all the way to the end. Express an emotion about the story that shows you understand how they feel. "That must have been . . . hard, sad, lonely."

▶ Study people who are good at expressing empathy. Put your study into practice.

Practice Detachment for the Sake of Others

Detachment can be a great thing in a crisis where a cool head is needed. Detachment lets go of fear and emotions that cloud the picture. Detachment makes room to focus on what really matters under pressure so wise action can be taken. Detachment isn't the same thing as disconnecting from others. It is possible to be detached and cool headed yet still stay connected.

▶ God the all-wise One has gifted you with wisdom. Some knowing can only be learned through detaching to do research and study. But real wisdom and knowing can be applied in ways that benefit others. Let your ability to detach and see the big picture be something you share. When you find something that really captures your attention, consider who would like to know and talk to them about it.

▶ Attachment to God's will: nothing more, nothing less, and nothing else leads to right detachment. Jesus could say, "Your will (not mine) be done" (Matthew 26:42) because he was attached to his Father above all else. Notice when you are attached to privacy, books, or ideas. Notice when you are nudged to detach from these things so you can be attached to what God values in the moment.

▶ Notice when you have a word beyond your wisdom, an insight beyond your smarts, a kindness beyond your feeling, or an energy beyond your endurance. These things come from the Spirit within you. Keep track of how God's Spirit gives you what you need in the moment even when you feel your tank is empty.

Blessing for the Beloved Five

As we close this section, take time to breathe in this blessing and create space in your soul.

May you be blessed as you open your hands and heart and as you journey to your true self.

May God the Father direct you with divine understanding.

May the heart of Jesus open you to passion and compassion for self and others.

May the Holy Spirit ground you in strong action for the vulnerable.

May the generosity of the Trinity lead you on your road while on this journey, upholding you and loving you.

Empathy for FIVES

*When peoples care for you and cry for you,
they can straighten out your soul.*

LANGSTON HUGHES

Every child should be able to know their needs matter. Early on Fives may have found that their feelings or big energy were ridiculed. It was safer to hold back than express thoughts and feelings. They survived by isolating and developing the life of the mind. Here you can explore your responses to Fives and how you can grow in empathy for them.

Empathy is a true self response that harmonizes and breaks down the we/they divide. We may find Fives retreat and go silent when we need them to show up. Or we may find Fives interesting, knowledgeable, and wise. Understanding that a Five's withdrawal and stinginess often began as a protective measure can give us compassion and receptivity in our interactions with them.

This Five describes her journey. See if you can enter into the story and engage your understanding heart.

As part of the military, I saw the world and faced danger. But I seldom tell people about what I have done. I would rather ask them questions about their experience than share my exploits. My reticence to share is rooted in my family of origin. EQ feelings and GQ passion and intensity were not acceptable in our cool—rather than hot—family system. In grade school, I dismissed my Eight and Two and lived in my mental world. I avoided my feelings by being helpful to others. It could be all about them, not me. As I grew up, I reserved my passion for ideas and debates. It took years to realize that I access my feelings through my head. I also backed away from conflict. The Harmony Triads have helped me intentionally check out my EQ and GQ. I decide when kindness and connection means sharing and engaging the heart. I try not to default to detachment and non-committal responses like, "that's interesting." I show up, expend energy, and get things done.

1. As you consider the Five story, notice:
   - What are you thinking about this Five?
   - What are you feeling about this Five?
   - What is your gut instinct about this Five?

2. When have you withheld your experience or feelings or knowledge? What was that about?

3. Have you ever constricted and tightened your boundaries in ways that shut off empathy for others? How can this experience help you have empathy for Fives?

UNDERSTANDING THE DEFENSE MECHANISM OF ISOLATION

Another beloved Five remembers how his defense mechanism of isolation began. When you get inside this story, where do you connect?

I don't think I was a particularly quiet child by nature. But my parents' message was clear, "children should be seen and not heard." In the summer we were assigned two hours of reading after lunch. I loved reading but also wanted to play. I remember sneaking outside to play. My mother found me and sent me back to read. My family had strong ideas about religion and what was right. I often had different ideas.

But if I expressed them strongly, I ended up clobbered by debate and censure. It was totally exhausting to hold my own. I learned to hold back, self-mute, and hesitate rather than jump in. I would nod my head when people talked, but not let anyone know what I thought or felt. When I was by myself, I was free to think and imagine what I wanted. But I knew I couldn't share these things with my family. It was lonely, but it was better than looking foolish and feeling misunderstood. I am so glad I'm in grad school with people who understand intellectual pursuits. When I access my gut, show up, speak up, and make a smart point, I feel alive.

1. What connections or resistances are you feeling with this Five?

2. How could you demonstrate God's love and acceptance of a Five?

3. How might you join the Holy Spirit in praying for a Five you know?

RELATING TO A FIVE

We find grace to see things from a Five's point of view when we remember that under the Five's thoughtful and reserved exterior is a tender child who learned to hide rather than express. Appreciate their objectivity, competencies, and counsel.

- Fives seldom enjoy small talk. Ask questions about ideas, work, hobbies, and what they know best.

- Fives don't want to be the center of attention or appear inadequate or foolish. Don't embarrass them or put them on the spot. If you want them to participate, give them time to prepare.

- Fives want to know what is expected of them. Don't be vague and hope they get your drift. Be clear about what you want and need.

- When Fives withdraw to conserve their energy, respect their need of privacy.

- Fives often sit at the back of the room or observe events from the outside edges. This is more comfortable than figuring out who to talk to and where to go. It doesn't mean they don't want to be included or invited.

- Invite a Five to be in their body: go to a dance class, ride bikes together, hike, or go to a museum.

The following list summarizes key characteristics of our beloved Fives. Consider your responses to these characteristics.

- *Authentic true self:* Wise
- *Compulsive false self:* Stingy
- *Virtue leading back to true self:* Detachment
- *Personality style:* Observer
- *Work style:* Thinker
- *Leadership/action style:* Systematizer
- *Relationships:* Intellectual
- *Core motivation:* Safety
- *Negative fixation:* Fear
- *Narrative:* "I won't have enough or get what I want."
- *Communication:* Ideas, theories
- *Five with a Six Wing:* More likely to be committed, dutiful, connected to a group
- *Five with a Four wing:* More sensitive, intuitive, connected to feelings
- *Basic fear:* Looking foolish, incapable
- *Basic desire:* To be in the know, capable
- *Drive:* To watch, know, analyze, and understand

Based on the description above:

1. How does it feel to be a Five? Which descriptors give clues on how to relate to Fives?

2. Is there a better way to say what is true of Fives?

3. Fives are thinkers. What is it like to receive the insights of a Five with your own head intelligence?

4. Fives fear becoming depleted by what is required of them. How can your heart EQ help sustain them in their calling?

SIXES

Faithfulness Produces Peace

Just because you're paranoid doesn't mean they aren't after you.

JOSEPH HELLER

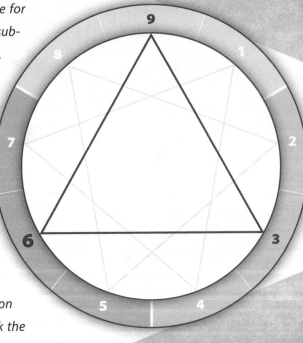

I am a loyal person who longs for a sense of belonging and looks for signs of trustworthiness in others. My friends can count on me to be loyal to them to the end. I am motivated by a desire for safety and security. I am always aware, even subconsciously aware, of what might go wrong. Perceived danger can be as real as if it were happening. I have a constant background of anxiety due to my vivid imagination. I wonder what might go wrong and don't want to be defenseless. In dangerous situations, I can withdraw or confront them head on. I can be suspicious and look for the hidden meanings and messages in people's actions. I ask questions and play the devil's advocate to keep things safe and stable. I value tradition and the common good. I don't want to rock the boat. I don't readily trust authority and don't necessarily want to be the authority. When I do trust, I am loyal to people, systems, organizations, and beliefs, sometimes to a fault.

WHO I AM AND WHO I AM NOT

Sixes bear the faithful image of a God you can trust. Your life resonates with:

The steadfast love of the LORD never
ceases,
his mercies never come to an end;
they are new every morning;
great is your faithfulness.
(Lamentations 3:22-23 NRSV)

Loyalty and support are inevitably part of a Six's story. Stories about who we are and who we are not shape what we do, who we become, and where we get stuck. Sixes often share a narrative about your loyalty, commitment, and vigilance in creating and supporting what is right. You skip over chapters of your life where fear drives your relationships or choices. This section gives you awareness of some words that shape the storyline of a Six.

▶▶▶ **BELOVED SIXES**

Spend some time with the words below that describe who Sixes are and are not. Circle the characteristics that resonate with your journey. Star words that express your gifts. Underline words that describe parts of your personality that are unusable by God in their present form. Put a checkmark beside characteristics that you *celebrate*.

Sixes Descriptive Words List

I AM		I AM NOT	
loyal	warm	disloyal	cool
devoted	kind	traitor	mean
faithful	friendly	treacherous	unfriendly
responsible	communal	irresponsible	isolated
trustworthy	cooperative	rebellious	difficult
dependable	vigilant	undependable	negligent
dutiful	awake	fickle	lights out
true blue	fearful	mixed bag	relaxed
enduring	prudent	flaky	reckless
persistent	obedient	flighty	disobedient
hospitable	careful	rude	negligent

> ➤ Which words reflect the image of God in you?

> ➤ Which words are you most attached to? Addicted to? Compulsive about?

> ➤ Which words do you resist and judge the most?

> ➤ If you opened up to the words you resist without judgment, how might your life and relationships shift?

> ➤ Journal about the words that reflect how God's faithfulness protects you.

▶▶▶ GETTING TO KNOW SIXES

Sixes are the only Enneagram number that is divided into two types. In the face of danger, each type responds differently. *Phobic Sixes* freeze, pull back, and gather with other like-minded people to support and protect yourself. *Counterphobic Sixes* prepare to engage, structure, organize, and fight your fears. Not doing anything to fight the fear scares you the most. Many Sixes share both phobic and counterphobic tendencies. This phobic Six avoids risks that brought "pain and concern to others." This counterphobic Six takes risks to prove her mettle. Notice how both Sixes are motivated by fear.

Phobic Six: I am the youngest of five kids, raised in an emotionally repressed and highly educated family. As a child, my family toured the United States. One night we stopped at a motel with a playground. My older siblings jumped off the swings at just the right moment and landed on their feet. So I took my four-year-old courage and fearlessly jumped as well. Instead of landing on my feet, I did a face-plant and hit my mouth on a rock. The remainder of the trip included dentists, awful-tasting medicine, and, when we got home, tooth extraction. Though my parents comforted me, I got the message that I was too young to be trying such things. I learned that to jump and take risks brought pain and concern to others. To this day, I hold back for fear of not being able to do something. I don't trust my body to have enough courage to risk dangerous things.

Counterphobic Six: I was raised in a household full of boys. As the only girl, I wanted to prove my bravery and intelligence. I felt driven to compete without losing or getting injured. I tried to outsmart danger by being prepared, devoted, and courageous. This gave me a sense of security and fearlessness. Looking back, I see my ardent efforts to achieve a difficult PhD followed by twenty-five years of teaching at a university were all part of overcoming the fear that I didn't have what it takes to belong to the boys' club.

> ➤ What does the "taking risks brings pain" story bring up in you?

> ➤ What does the fear of not having "what it takes" story bring up for you?

> ➤ What happens in your head, heart, and gut when you are afraid?

Breath Prayer ▶

In silence and solitude, ask God to help you see yourself clearly. Begin with breathing. Breathe in: "Made in God's image," and then breathe out: "I am courageous." Spend a few minutes with this breath prayer. Feel the safety and freedom of being made in God's image; feel the liberty of letting God be God. Breathe this prayer in and out throughout the day.

TRUE SELF AND FALSE SELF: THE LOYAL PERSON

Who we are or are not comes with expression and energy. The attitudes, behaviors, and motivations of beloved Sixes convey trustworthy presence. Your true self emerges from union with God. It knows that unshakeable safety is internal rather than external. Security comes from knowing God's Spirit camps out in the soul. The false self is the compulsive, deeply entrenched, old nature that constricts and tightens around distrust of others and fear of what might happen. This emotionally unhealthy psychological or ego self is constructed on a complex mixture of nature, nurture, tradition, taboos, and free will. This section will help you begin to recognize compulsive and impulsive false self reactions, as well as true self FLOW that opens to trust others.

True Self Sixes: Sacred Fidelity

Sixes are designed to reflect God's fidelity and commitment. Your behaviors and motivations convey non-anxious, loyal energy that loves and serves others. Sixes are reliable, vigilant, and supportive. You can be trusted to show up, shoulder responsibility, and commit to shared purposes and/or the common good. Your presence says, "I am steadfast!" A Six's insight, curiosity, organization, questions, and plans—as well as your ability to teach, anticipate problems, and prepare for potential threats—often help others reach their dreams while protecting them from what could go wrong. Healthy Sixes care about pitching in, establishing, and maintaining the values and safe spaces that keep communities and society on track. You are the steady, trustworthy bulwarks

of society. You embody God's sacred fidelity. When Sixes are present to the Spirit within, you quiet catastrophic thinking and let go of constrictive worst-case scenarios. As leaders, you acknowledge fear, befriend courage, and use your inner authority.

False Self Sixes: Get Stuck in Fear and Constrict Around Security and Survival

Compulsive, false self Sixes over-identify with hypervigilance, matters of safety, and questions about the trustworthiness of authority. False self, phobic Sixes doubt others, yourself, and the good of change. When you ignore your inner authority, you project your fears outward and onto others, creating a we/they divide. You respond to fear by pledging unquestioning allegiance to systems, traditions, predictability, and authorities you trust. When these things are challenged, your ungrounded energy can move into catastrophic thinking about, "what awful thing might happen if . . . ?" Often, you circle the wagons and withdraw to protect yourself from the bad out there. False self, counterphobic Sixes fear ever-escalating evil and expect authority to respond with glib answers and lies. You can detach from relationships and communities, becoming reactive, reckless, defiant, and fixated on hazards. Focusing on uncertain futures and dangerous people or ideologies, you can be dangerous and strike out to defend your good from the bad out there.

▶▶▶ TRUE OR FALSE SELF

As you think about your true and false self, consider the following questions. Notice without judgment what comes up for you. Journal your responses.

➤ How do true self Six characteristics show up in your relationships?

➤ Where do false self Six qualities show up in your relationships? When do you wonder, "Can he/she be trusted?" or "Are we moving too fast on this decision?" How do you rush in or run away when you don't feel safe?

> ➤ What makes you constrict and get stuck in overthinking security and survival issues? What is a cue to relax and risk trust?

> ➤ How do you know the difference between centered, true self energy and edgy, false self energy?

HARMONY: FAITHFULNESS PRODUCES PEACE

Sixes are sometimes identified as the steady troopers or loyal skeptics, but you are much more than just one number! You bear the image and harmony of the three-in-one God. When beloved Sixes integrate and harmonize, your faithful IQ loyalty flows with EQ productivity of the Three and GQ easiness of the Nine. This section creates awareness of how FLOW is the unique gift of the Harmony Triads.

In harmony and FLOW, Sixes act with effective tranquility. You trust yourself and channel caution and skeptical questions in ways that competently and effectively defend and support truth (Three EQ) and serve the common good through peaceful action (Nine GQ).

▶▶▶ MORE THAN YOUR TYPE

This story describes a Six, Nine, and Three journey to integration. This Six is letting go of his addiction to security and learning to be present to the non-anxious presence of Nine GQ and the productive Three EQ. Notice how he lets certainty go and risks letting "what if" be part of his story.

Finding Courage

After Jesus was executed, his closest friends feared their lives were on the line, so they went into hiding. In this text, a man who hadn't been courageous enough to follow Jesus during his life does something no one else has courage to do.

Later, Joseph of Arimathea asked Pilate for the body of Jesus. Now Joseph was a disciple of Jesus, but secretly because he feared the Jewish leaders. With Pilate's permission, he came and took the body away. He was accompanied by Nicodemus, the man who earlier had visited Jesus at night. (John 19:38-39)

1. How do you see a phobic and/or a counterphobic Six here?

2. When have you secretly believed in something and been afraid to tell others? What does it take for you to show up and be brave?

3. When do you hide what you think or feel from others? How has this affected you and your relationships?

As a Six, I over prepare and overthink, even though I have a PhD and have mastered many subjects. I still don't trust myself. I worry that bad things might happen. I'm afraid of making the wrong decision. I fear that those in charge are missing something important. When I'm anxious, I get flooded with self-doubt and start questioning myself and everyone else to find what's true. My Harmony Triad helps me prepare for meetings and presentations. I breathe and ask my gut and heart to contribute to my thoughts. My competent EQ and my grounded GQ help me regulate my overactive vigilance and low-grade fears. I can courageously say, "I have three intelligences. I can be clear. I can decide. I can risk!"

➤ When does fear drive you to know more authoritatively? What would it look like to trust that you have inner authority?

➤ Your effective heart helps you get the job done. Your inclusive gut risks speaking your truth to others. How would integrating EQ and GQ affect your relationships?

➤ Imagine tempering your energy for security and safety by risking love of God and neighbor. What do you see?

▶▶▶ GQ, EQ, IQ

This Six navigates a hostile work environment by moderating overly reliable energy with grounded presence and courage. She names her competency and silences angst and compulsive thoughts with breath prayers. Breath prayers open her to all three centers of intelligence and help her embrace the Six, Nine, and Three journey to integration and empathy.

Throughout my childhood, I worked hard at school. My parents had high expectations for grades and effort. They would edit my already good papers and try to make them more excellent. I heard the message, "You did well, but how about doing it this way?" Through their input I learned to doubt my own efforts, dismiss my restful Nine self and work harder like a Three. I didn't want to let anyone down. I wanted to succeed for my parents and keep authorities on my side. In the process, I lost track of me, my voice, and my inner authority.

A key turning point happened years later when my mom came to visit my new home. I had arranged the kitchen the way I liked. My mom suggested I put the dishes in another place. I said, "They are okay where they are." She got up the next morning at 4:30 a.m. and moved them to a different cabinet so I could "try it out." My limbic brain hollered, "My voice doesn't matter." I watched courage and grounded anger rise up in my body. For one of the first times ever, I expressed hurt and pain about how being doubted about something so simple made me feel I didn't have what it took to arrange my kitchen! My words contained relational intelligence (EQ), insightful questions (IQ), and patient listening (GQ). It was a blessed integrating and defining moment for me and us.

➤ When Sixes engage their gut, they ground in their body, relax their guardedness, and speak their truth. Where do you see GQ in yourself?

> ➤ When Sixes engage their compassionate and warm EQ, they connect and act effectively. Where do you see EQ in yourself?

> ➤ What is it like for you to have GQ, EQ, and IQ?

HEALING CHILDHOOD HURTS: OPENING TO COURAGE

Children are wired for resilience. Still, residual childhood baggage and messages can leak into adult Six relationships. Six children can lose the message, "I am safe." The default message you can learn is: "Don't trust yourself or anybody else." To cope, Six children became guarded, reliable troopers who work hard to keep things safe for yourself and others. This vigilance protected and mitigated against trust.

When childhood messages get triggered in adult Six interactions, then raw, ragged, unprocessed pain can erupt. Trust and decision making are sabotaged by fear. Suddenly a frightened four-year-old inside the Six begins to call the shots. Defaulting to the false self, you get stuck on the edge of overthinking, suspicion, and doubt. This can create a deep we/they division. The Harmony Triad offers a way for Sixes to be curious about how guardedness, trauma, defenses, and childhood lies affect your relationships today. Exploring your triggers means leaning into your virtue of courage.

Calming Fears

This text describes an event that terrifies Jesus' disciples. Notice the times fear is mentioned and what Jesus says and does to calm Peter's fears.

Shortly before dawn Jesus went out to them, walking on the lake. When the disciples saw him walking on the lake, they were terrified. "It's a ghost," they said, and cried out in fear.

But Jesus immediately said to them: "Take courage! It is I. Don't be afraid."

"Lord, if it's you," Peter replied, "tell me to come to you on the water."

"Come," he said.

Then Peter got down out of the boat, walked on the water and came toward Jesus. But when he saw the wind, he was afraid and, beginning to sink, cried out, "Lord, save me!"

Immediately Jesus reached out his hand and caught him. "You of little faith," he said, "why did you doubt?" (Matthew 14:25-31)

1. When has something good made you terrified?

2. When do you courageously step out in faith and then distrust God and/or your head convictions, heart abilities, and gut instincts?

3. How do you stay in the place that requires faith? When do you breathe deep and hold conflict with your Nine GQ? When do you give the benefit of the doubt with Three EQ?

▶▶▶ RECEIVING THE DISMISSED CHILDLIKE SELF

Receiving your dismissed child can heal and give inner freedom to let go of fear and open to trust again. Remember within every faithful, reliable, questioning Six is a go-with-the-flow, moderate, "all will be well" Nine that is slothful about inner work and what is happening here and now. There is also a successful, competitive, and forward-moving Three who wants to shine, direct, and be recognized for your connections, leadership, productivity, and competence. To recognize where you dismissed your childlike self with its competence and authority, pay attention to where you may have ignored your EQ and GQ.

Be curious and open your heart to this Six story. Can you see how his fearful environment created coping mechanisms of false connection to survive?

My false self Six with all its hesitations and doubt began in childhood. My father was distant and selfish. Self-gratification mattered more to him than his family. He married multiple times and never wanted to get to know me. My angry and controlling older brother used me as a punching bag. My mother had a very vindictive and explosive personality. She often expressed her feelings by using both physical and emotional violence. My loyalty to her caused me years of confusion about what love really meant. To escape fearful relational realities, I developed some devastating coping skills. Early on I was introduced to pornography. I used it to quiet my heart anxiety and meet my desire for intimacy. Porn let me escape into my head and gave me fantasy connections. I struggled with this issue into my forties, causing my wife terrible pain. My great sorrow is how my unfaithfulness caused her such suffering. I am a counterphobic loyalist. I chose a profession that helps people prepare for worst-case scenarios and death. I work out for at least an hour each day. I practice extreme sports, and I'm always prepared for bad things to happen. I never want my wife, kids, or people I care about to be unsafe like I was.

> ### *Prayer of Ignatius of Loyola* ▶
>
> *Allow this prayer of Ignatius of Loyola, which addresses the heart, head, and gut motivations of the Enneagram Triads, to become your prayer. This week, pray the mind, heart, and strength of the Trinity into your life and interactions.*
>
> > *O Christ Jesus, when all is darkness and we feel our weakness and helplessness, give us the sense of Your presence, Your love, and Your strength. Help us to have perfect trust [Six] in Your protecting love [Six] and strengthening power, so that nothing may frighten or worry us [Six], for, living close to You, we shall see Your hand, Your purpose [Three], Your will through all things [Nine].*

As you read these questions, notice where you sense God's invitation to more deeply receive your dismissed child. Write down any new insights and awareness. You are doing important and integrative work here.

➤ What was it like for this Six to be shaped by abuse and neglect? Where does this story resonate in you?

➤ Within the safety-seeking Six is a Nine who either hides out or numbs to avoid conflict, or a Nine who stubbornly digs in and refuses to move when he/she has had enough. How do you dismiss or use your gut?

➤ Worst-case-scenario Sixes have a tender Three heart that wonders, "Am I worthy of love? Am I enough?" Notice when your inner child asks these questions. Where do you dismiss or use your heart?

▶▶▶ JOURNALING YOUR DISMISSED CHILDLIKE SELF

Integrating and accessing your EQ and GQ can help you figure out what to do when you get caught in analysis paralysis and fear making a decision. Getting acquainted with your GQ gives you the ability to relax your guard. Integrating your EQ gives you confidence to choose and act. Checking out your body instincts and heart feelings gives you more than a safety checklist as you work toward harmony.

Name and journal some of your doubts and courageously explore how you learned to protect yourself by withdrawing trust and questioning loyalty. Engage your EQ and GQ and decide which questions to answer. You can return to other questions later.

➤ What is your story about finding the world unsafe? Where do you continue to dismiss Three agency and procrastinate like a Nine?

➤ What default reactions and triggers of your childhood self still operate today? Courageously explore how you began to live on high alert. Be curious about how it affects your ability to make decisions and connect with others today.

➤ Ask God to help you return to your virtue of courage. Open yourself to risks as they can bring growth, adventure, and connections.

➤ Where has your trust been repaired/healed or increased/solidified?

Sixes want to serve the common good, create community, and help people be prepared for the worst. But constantly preparing for stability and/or future catastrophic scenarios constricts spontaneity, adventure, and relationships. These things are always a risk, and risk is the other side of the coin of trust. God's invitation to love offers Sixes a spiritual practice that opens you to letting down your guard and risking trust. It may be helpful for you to read the chapter "Invitation to the Most Excellent Way" (of love) in *Invitations from God* by Adele Ahlberg Calhoun.

This week when you are triggered and feeling reticent, skeptical, or insecure about the intentions of others, decide to open and risk staying in the game. Let your inner truth and authority out. Step up and engage; things may turn out better than you imagine.

DISCERNMENT: DESOLATIONS AND CONSOLATIONS

Ignatius of Loyola taught that God's Guiding Spirit of wisdom moves in all three centers of intelligence—head, heart, and gut. When faced with a decision, Ignatius suggested noticing your consolations and desolations by asking: What does my heart feel? What does my mind think? What does my gut sense?

Consolations point Sixes toward God's faithful presence and the virtues of faith, hope, and love. Consolations are evidence that a Six is heading in the direction of IQ discernment that flows with EQ effectiveness and GQ ability to see many sides of an issue. Desolations of fear, self-doubt, and distrust stymie the FLOW of faithful discernment and alert Sixes that you have fallen into your false self and are in need of God's courage to risk decision making. (More information on Harmony Triad discernment is found in Soul Resource 5.)

Sixes experience consolations such as courageous trust, responsible relinquishment, non-anxious vigilance, peaceful questioning, productive awareness, efficient analysis, insightful ease, and loyal competence. This is freedom.

Sixes experience desolations such as fear, insecurity, hyper-vigilance, distrust, self-doubt, victim mentality, suspicion, paranoia, skepticism, indecision, and we/they thinking. These desolations leave you bound.

►►► PRESENT TO WHAT'S HAPPENING INSIDE

Both consolations and desolations point toward the purpose for which Sixes were created. This story focuses on consolations and desolations particular to Sixes. This Six is studying the

Healing Prayer

When Sixes process your wounds in the presence of the faithful God and loyal friends, you can find healing for your default fears and doubts. You move from your vice of fear—either cowardly or over-reactive—to your virtue of faithfulness.

This is a way to do healing prayer on your own. Relax into silence and solitude. Breathe deeply. Don't force it. Become present to God and yourself. Ask God to show you a past pain in your life that is still being transmitted. Express your desire for ongoing healing. Be still and wait.

❖ Imagine yourself and Jesus back in the memory. Get your bearings. Where is Jesus? Where are you?

❖ What are you feeling? (fear, unprotected, betrayed, alone, threatened, or something else)

❖ Do these feelings remind you of a time you had similar reactions? You can go with Jesus to that place and time or stay where you are.

❖ Continue to name what you feel in your experience. Ask Jesus if these feelings point to a lie you began to believe at that time. Give it a name.

❖ What is Jesus saying to you about this lie? Listen. Is there an image, word, or phrase that he speaks to you?

❖ Repeat the truth you have heard about yourself from Jesus gently and frequently. Let the truth be an antidote that lets the pain go into Jesus and sets you free.

map of his soul. He notices signposts of desolation in his sarcasm and suspicions. He recognizes how defaulting to security and survival paralyzes relationships and keeps him stuck in fight, flight, or freeze. How do consolations and desolations of this Six direct him toward healing and the presence of God?

> At my core I believe that the world cannot be trusted. The under rumble of my life is "don't trust anyone completely." Even if a situation has trustworthy attributes, I can be sarcastic and suspicious about how or when the bottom will drop out (desolation). I am so cynical (desolation). I'm learning to notice when suspicion and fear ramp up in me. I know these reactions impact my ability to decide. Even now at forty-four years of age, I wonder if I can risk another career path.

> I have to practice trust. I am risking on a spiritual friend who sees me as more than a scared Six. He reminds me that I am able and capable. His presence is opening me to heart warmth and giving me sacred confidence (consolation). I repeatedly breathe in God's promise, "Fear not, I am with you." This breath prayer helps quiet the fear-monger in my head and directs my attention to my gut instincts. Sometimes I hear my body say, "Relax, it's all right; you can trust yourself." I stay with that truth and it grounds me (consolation). Awareness of how my heart and gut are available to me is life changing. Integrating heart and body is the journey I'm on, and it gives me peace that passes understanding (consolation).

> ➤ How do sarcasm and cynicism block your discernment and bring desolation?

> ➤ Pay attention to the Spirit's motions in your head and gut instincts. When does desolation move you into catastrophic thinking and doubt? How do you act courageously and trust in consolation?

Prayer Practice for When You Feel Afraid

Sixes in particular don't want anyone to be unprepared or at risk. It is way too dangerous. So when you need courage to risk the unknown, breathe deeply into your fear and insecurity. Breathe in: "God, you are here." Breathe out: "I can risk." Let this breath prayer open you to God and the moment. Something unexpected might happen if you are present in the unknown.

▶▶▶ DESOLATION AND PROJECTION

Fearful Sixes have a default defense of projection. Projection unconsciously attributes one's own fears and issues to someone or something else. For instance, a Six who fears making the right decision might ask someone else what they think, but then that same fear imagines that the person can't know what is right either. Or a Six who is nervous about speaking up in a staff meeting might project onto everyone else, thinking that no one wants to hear what they have to say. Sixes can make what is about them about someone else. Without judgment, notice where you might be projecting your fear and distrust onto people and situations. Stay with one or two questions and come back when the answers have settled in.

> Where does projection show up for you? When does projection manifest in imagining the worst, then living in fear that the worst will ambush you?

> How does your body tell you about fear, distrust, and self-doubt? How does constricting around these things sabotage your ability to open and welcome risk and adventure?

> Are there defenses besides projection that block your discernment?

▶▶▶ CONSOLATIONS AND COURAGE

The Spirit's invitation to consolation invites Sixes to engage your GQ Nine that doesn't panic but peacefully holds options and outcomes, as well as your EQ Three that steps in to decide and act. Your non-anxious GQ and confident EQ help you choose rather than perseverate.

Sixes are consoled as you follow the Holy Spirit out of projection and fear into trust, action, and effectiveness. Non-anxious loyalty conveys faithful peace and courageous action.

> Describe a situation in which God's Spirit invited you out of distrust and into courageous action or decision making. What happened? What consolations came to you?

> When has courage helped you stand in faithful FLOW that serves God and others with your heart, soul, strength, and mind?

SPIRITUAL RHYTHMS FOR SIXES

What good is it, my brothers and sisters, if someone claims to have faith but has no deeds? Can such faith save them? Suppose a brother or a sister is without clothes and daily food. If one of you says to them, "Go in peace; keep warm and well fed," but does nothing about their physical needs, what good is it? In the same way, faith by itself, if it is not accompanied by action, is dead. (James 2:14-17)

Sixes commit. They are often people of faith with strong values and beliefs. James suggests that faith is more than having right or orthodox beliefs. Faith is validated by action, partici-pation, and decisions that love and serve others. Sixes who put your faith into practice make space for the Spirit of God to create new neural pathways and ways of responding. Old protective patterns change. Spiritual transformation is a two-part invention. The Spirit's movement within helps Sixes integrate so your faithfulness produces peace.

These spiritual rhythms are all ways Sixes can lean into God's invitations to transformation and mind renewal. Not every practice will be God's invitation to you. Say yes to the practices that best capture your desire to be with God right now.

▶▶▶ PRACTICING PRESENCE: SIXES

Re-read the FLOW definition in the Key Terms section. Notice the presence of Trinitarian harmony.

Father, Son, and Spirit belong and flow together.

Head, heart, and gut belong and flow together.

Faith, love, and hope belong and flow together.

Divine harmony calls Sixes to be present to God in your fears, doubts, and struggles with authority so you aren't immobilized by them and actually become courageous in them. Let the following meditative prayer move through your entire created being. Let it hold your IQ, EQ, and GQ together. Staying with this prayer for a season can help Sixes find God in places that are scary for you.

Find a comfortable and awake position. Remember that the Spirit of God dwells within you and prays for you. Ask God to give you an open and receptive head, heart, and gut.

Gut Presence: Put yourself in the presence of the Spirit. Breathe into your gut space. Notice what is happening in your body without judgment. Let your body tell you what it knows. Is there something your body wants to do in this prayer? Do that. Experience peace, your grounded-ness, and your ability to mediate. Give thanks that you faithfully care for the good of others. How and when does your body want to move things forward and engage? Where do you freeze up before opening to gut inspiration and passion?

Heart Presence: Put yourself in the presence of Jesus. Breathe into your heart space. Feel your tenderness. Notice your heart's need to be in trustworthy relationships. Breathe in and create even more space around your heart. Notice your desire to rely on God and on others. Invite self-compassion. What is it like to take down your guard and share your heart? Welcome your emotions. Name them and breathe: "I can trust you." What in you needs reassurance, loyalty, or a trustworthy touch? How does the God who will never leave you or forsake you respond?

Head Presence: Put yourself in the presence of the all-wise Creator. Move your head around on your shoulders. Feel its weight and tightness. Breathe into your intellect. Observe your life in your body. What does your head tell you? What is it like to trust insight rather than suspicion? Notice times when your head says, "This won't work!" Ask your head to give you faith-filled words.

Pray into Your Harmony: Faithfulness Produces Peace

"Faithfulness produces peace" is a breath prayer that helps you engage the non-anxious instinct of GQ Nine that can chill out and slow down to notice. GQ keeps you from reacting too quickly with fear or skepticism. The prayer also helps you engage the life-giving Three EQ

Coming together is a beginning [Nine GQ]. Keeping together is progress [Six IQ]. Working together is success [Three EQ].

HENRY FORD (WITH OUR ADDITIONS)

with its inspiration and effectual connection that moves toward others with warm hospitality rather than distrust and suspicion.

Memorizing this prayer brings awareness of what is most true about you to real-life situations. You are more than your type. Breathe this prayer as preparation for moments you feel threatened or unsafe. Anytime you feel triggered and are tempted to constrict and tighten around security and survival, breathe "faithfulness produces peace." Call on all your God-given faithfulness to collaboratively act.

FLOW Practice for Sixes

In FLOW, Sixes are **F**ree, **L**oving, **O**pen, and **W**ith. In FLOW you stand in the presence of the three-in-one God and integrate head loyalty with EQ and GQ. You also integrate the three Christian virtues of faith, hope, and love. When you notice that you constrict with panic or shortness of breath and want to run from the moment (phobic Six), or when you get stuck in having to rescue and fight others in the moment (counterphobic Six), breathe into the Holy Three. They have got you! Step into FLOW and be with them. Open your heart and trust that "I can love here and now." Access your gut and trust that "God will give me peace." At the end of the day, log what happened when you were not in FLOW. What happened when you were in FLOW? Celebrate when God's faithful care of others flowed through you. Confess when it didn't. Begin again tomorrow.

Practice Confession

Vulnerability and transparency about who you are before God and others is part of transformation and connection. Confess your:

▶ *Vice of fear:* ask God where it wounds you and others. Who do you trust to help you make the journey to courage and faith?

▶ *Self-doubt:* "I am not enough." Don't just freak out or rush in. Ask God to help you know that you are enough. Let the angst you feel about inadequacy lead you to trust that in Christ, "I have enough."

▶ *Judgment:* confess the narrative, "Others aren't as committed as me."

Breath Prayers

Notice your magnificent breath. Feel the oxygen fill your lungs and lift your chest. Follow your breath in and down. Take time to notice what is happening in your head. Feel the faithfulness of your created life as you breathe in: "You have formed my inward parts; I am faithfully and wonderfully made . . . may my soul know that very well." Spend a few minutes with this breath prayer. Follow your breath to liberty—you don't have to be the all-vigilant Rescuer.

Keep breathing into your body. Breathing in from the soles of your feet, fill your belly with breath, and continue breathing to the crown of your head. Feel your experience. Breathe into your head, your heart, and your gut. Without judgment, notice whatever comes up. If memories come, welcome them with your productive and faithful, non-anxious presence. Stay with them. Use your inner authority to act, risk, trust, and hold. Use these breath prayers when they suit your situation.

❖ *Inhale: "Made in God's image." Exhale: "I am not afraid."*

❖ *Inhale: "God, you are here." Exhale: "I can risk."*

❖ *Inhale: "Faithfulness," exhale: "produces peace."*

▶ *Guilt:* confess the narrative, "I can't trust myself to get it right."

   ▶ *Grudges:* the inability to forgive people who disappoint you.

Receive words of assurance: "Before a holy and righteous God, you are safe and in the clear."

Practice Love

The scariest thing a Six can do is open themselves to the insecurity and unpredictability of relationships and life. The practice of choosing to love with your GQ, EQ, and IQ moves Sixes out of isolation and toward people and action.

▶ This week, be intentionally vulnerable in at least one interaction with a colleague or friend each day. Don't hide or project disinterest on to them.

▶ Send an email, text, or note to someone that expresses your care and concern.

▶ How can you love in macro ways? Is there a justice issue that pulls at your heart? Where might you volunteer, give, and serve others for the common good?

▶ Let down your guard and ask God for the grace to trust spontaneous interactions.

▶ Where do you sense God loving others through you? What is that like for you?

Practice Scripture Memory

The anxious, obsessive mind of Sixes changes through disciplined and focused attention on words that bring faith, hope, and love rather than fear. Let verses like those below shape the narrative you tell yourself about your life in this world.

▶ 2 Timothy 1:7, "For God gave us not a spirit of fearfulness; but of power and love and discipline." (ASV)

▶ 1 Peter 5:7, "Cast all your anxiety on him because he cares for you."

▶ Psalm 37:5, "Commit your way to the LORD; / trust in him, and he will do this."

▶ Memorize St. Patrick's Breastplate or other prayers of trust.

Practice the Presence of God

In the mid-1600s, a monk named Brother Lawrence wrote a book called *The Practice of the Presence of God.* It explained how he found God in everything from prayer to peeling potatoes. Practicing the presence of God is a practice that can ground Sixes in the reality that no matter how fearful a situation, God's Spirit is present right there in real time within you.

▶ When you feel yourself constrict in fear or doubt, ask for eyes to see and ears to hear where God is. Be curious about how God might be working for good in what is happening. Can you find any evidence of love, joy, peace, grace, kindness, or patience? How might Jesus be praying for what is happening? Join him in his prayer.

▶ In Genesis 28, when Jacob's twin brother Esau wanted to kill him, Jacob ran for his life. When it became dark, Jacob finally stopped to rest in a place without a name or significance. That night, he had a dream. And when he woke up, he realized, "Surely the LORD is in this place, and I was not aware of it" (Genesis 28:16). Looking back in retrospect, where can you see that God was in a place and you were not aware of it? What do you want to say to God about this?

▶ Bidden or unbidden, God is present everywhere. Where do you have a hard time seeing God? Is it a circumstance, responsibility, or relationship? Ask the Holy Spirit to help you see where God is hiding out in plain sight. Share your God sightings with a friend.

Practice Mindfulness

The prophet Isaiah writes, "You have seen many things, but you pay no attention; / your ears are open, but you do not listen" (Isaiah 42:20). Isaiah knows that it is easy to be unaware and preoccupied. You can do a task, be with others, and not really be there at all. The biblical practice of mindfulness is a state of active, open, non-judgmental attention to what is unfolding now. It is opening to what is going on under your nose.

▶ When you find yourself worrying about the future, gently return to the present moment. What awareness is being given? What might God want you to notice in the here and now?

▶ When do you judge what is going on rather than let it unfold? Practice noticing without judgment. What happens? Is it better or worse than you imagined?

▶ When you get caught in a spiral of catastrophic thinking, take some deep breaths. Imagine rivers of water flowing from you. Let the river carry each catastrophic thought away. Don't hold on to them; let them go. Return to God and presence.

Practice Encouraging and Blessing Others

This is a courageous risk and a way to instill courage and confidence in others.

▶ Watch for what people do well, even if they just wink in the right direction, and give them encouragement.

▶ Find words to express gratitude and write an encouraging email or card.

▶ Thank people for the virtues you see in them.

▶ Write a list of people you think need encouragement. Take action to encourage them today.

Practice Celebration

Sixes will temper the seriousness of life by taking the body to experiences of fun. God directs people to regularly schedule feasts and celebrations. Dancing, music, clapping, songs, and feasting are all part of expressing joy for the goodness of God and the gift of life.

▶ When you are invited to a party, let your guard down. When people talk to you, tell them something about yourself.

▶ Engage in play. Plan ways to enjoy your life this week. Take a walk. Have lunch with a friend.

▶ Take your heart and body with you into the day. Trust that they can help you enjoy yourself. Let your heart laugh at itself and others. Tell your mouth to smile and look people in the eyes with love. Celebrating is a choice.

Practice Being Part of a Committed Group

Sixes enjoy groups where participants commit themselves to help and encourage each other in service and/or soul work. You like to meet regularly and faithfully invest in each other's growth. A group commitment affords safety that gives Sixes confidence to move beyond your fears and put your skills to work in the world.

▶ Who do you know that would relish a regular and committed time to grow their soul, share their story and engage in spiritual practices and service? Prayerfully ask a few people to join you. You can begin with one or two.

▶ Share your stories. What happens as you share your stories?

▶ Plan a project or party that helps you reach out beyond yourselves.

Blessing for the Beloved Six

As we close this section, take time to breathe in this blessing and create space in your soul.

May the Holy Three bless you with bravery in the journey to your true self.

May God the Father direct you with questions that rise from divine insight.

May the heart of Jesus open you to your own inner authority and brilliant light.

May the Holy Spirit ground you in patience and rest as you trust all will be well.

May the sacred faithfulness of the Trinity lead you on your road, steadying you and loving you.

Empathy for SIXES

Don't ask yourself what the world needs.
Ask yourself what makes you come alive, and then go do that.
Because what the world needs is people who have come alive.

HOWARD THURMAN

Every child should be able to know their caregivers are trustworthy. Early on, Sixes might have had caregivers who were preoccupied and unaware of their fears. This undermined their inner authority and made them look for external rules or authorities to keep them safe. Or caregivers may have guarded Six children so closely that they became either risk averse or risk takers. Here you can explore your responses to Sixes and how you might grow in empathy and seeing them as God does.

Empathy is a true self response that harmonizes and breaks down the we/they divide. For instance, you may think the hyper-vigilant guardedness of Sixes makes them hard to know. Their questioning might slow things down and make you uncomfortable. Or you may find Sixes are truly supportive friends. Understanding how a Six became fearful and skeptical can open compassion and receptivity in your interactions with them.

In this Six's journey, she did everything she could to be dutiful, and still she felt invisible. Allow compassion for this Six to rise in you.

I am the only daughter in a family of five children; I have two older and two younger brothers. My mother started teaching high school when my youngest brother began first grade. In this patriarchal home, my duties were to clean the house and begin dinner preparation every night. Even though I excelled in athletics, my identity became attached to a stable, ordered, neat household where I provided for everyone else's well-being. I sometimes felt invisible, but if I worked hard, I might get thanks for being loyal to the family. For some reason, I began to dismiss my Three competitive competencies and I focused on being busy at home. My mother's scorn and some of my brothers' disapproval was scorching. I still try to avoid criticism and ward off my fears by being loyal and hard-working.

1. As you consider this Six story, notice:
   - What are you thinking about this Six?
   - What are you feeling about this Six?
   - What is your gut instinct about this Six?

2. Where can you find a collaborative, peace-keeping child in this hard-working Six?

3. Have you ever constricted around doing your duty and being committed to others in ways that kept you from yourself? What was it like for you?

4. A Six's questioning IQ and commitment to order and stability make them focus on a thousand future contingencies. This mitigates against being fully present in the moment. How can you be a safe person who reassures and encourages Sixes to let down their guard and engage?

UNDERSTANDING THE DEFENSE MECHANISM OF PROJECTION

Another Six story reveals how projection became a defense. Notice how you are thinking, feeling, and reacting to this Six.

I was brought up in a military family; my dad was an Army Captain who "defended the country against tyrants."

My motto is, "Keep your friends close and your enemies closer." This may be the reason I went into police work. I don't let people out of my sight. It's not just the criminals I'm watching. I don't trust my partner to fill out forms accurately, and I watch my own back on every call. At home, I sweat over the bottom line; the kids getting what they need; the dog having tags and shots. I check and recheck my wife's to-do list. The problem is I don't trust myself, and that is why I distrust others and work hard to keep the world safe.

1. This Six says his motto is, "Keep your friends close and your enemies closer." What connections and resistances are you feeling with this Six?

2. In your interactions with Sixes, how can you compassionately lower their need to be on guard?

3. How might you join your heart to the Holy Spirit's prayer for a Six you know?

RELATING TO A SIX

We find grace to see things from a Six's point of view when we remember that under the dutiful, self-doubting, and distrusting exterior of a Six is a gentle child who felt unsafe.

- Sixes build trust over time, and it takes practice for them to do this. Be vulnerable, purposeful, and consistent in your connection. Take initiative and share your story.

- If you like to push the envelope and drop everything to be spontaneous, remember that Sixes are working hard to maintain stability, traditions, and the common good. Bring reliability along with your spontaneity.

- Accept that Sixes ask questions to lower their anxieties. Listen and validate their perspective. They see what could go wrong. They can steer you right.

- When you see a Six respond with their inner authority rather than look to others, affirm them and the good they bring.

- Decision-making can be difficult for Sixes. Be patient with them and let them know you have confidence in their ability to choose well.

The following list summarizes key characteristics of our beloved Sixes. Consider your responses to these characteristics.

- *Authentic true self:* Loyal
- *Compulsive false self:* Fearful
- *Virtue leading back to true self:* Courage
- *Personality style:* Joiner
- *Work style:* Relator, good at creating systems that serve people

- *Leadership/action style:* Teamster, community builders
- *Thinking style:* Group minded
- *Relational style:* Loyalist
- *Core motivation:* Security, survival
- *Negative fixation:* Fear
- *Communication:* Agreeable, dutiful
- *Six with a Five wing:* More introverted, intellectual, cautious
- *Six with a Seven wing:* More playful, spontaneous, innovative
- *Basic fear:* Insecurity
- *Basic desire:* Security
- *Drive:* Seek the common good, certitude, reassurance, security, and support; test the loyalty of others; stand up for truth

Based on the description above:

1. How does it feel to be a Six? Which descriptors give clues on how to relate to a Six?

2. Is there a better way to say what is true of a Six?

3. Sixes care about and invest deeply in belonging to and building communities that serve God and/or the common good. They are disappointed when others don't commit like they do. How does understanding this drive help you empower and appreciate what Sixes can bring?

SEVENS

Joy Is Deeply Stable

Joy is prayer. Joy is strength. Joy is love.
Joy is a net of love by which you can catch souls.

MOTHER TERESA OF CALCUTTA

I view life as an adventure. I want to be on the go, experiencing new and exciting things. I constantly think of the next trip, the next idea, or the next opportunity. People say I am the life of a party. I am enthusiastic and spontaneous and give myself wholeheartedly to what I enjoy. Conversely, if I find things boring and difficult, I will look for a way out. My imagination is a nonstop playground. I love to connect ideas and information and envision something new. It's fun to get involved in projects at the beginning when things are fresh and the playing field wide open. When painful or hard things happen, I try to change the channel by distracting myself and thinking of other things. I avoid pain. I am optimistic, and I am counting on living a fun and enjoyable life.

WHO I AM AND WHO I AM NOT

Sevens bear the image of the God of all joy. Your life resonates with Nehemiah 8:10: "Go and enjoy choice food and sweet drinks, and send some to those who have nothing prepared. This day is holy to our Lord. Do not grieve, for the joy of the LORD is your strength."

Gladness and pleasure are inevitably part of a Seven's story. Stories about who we are and who we are not shape what we do and don't do, who we become, and where we stall out. Sevens often have a story about fun, excitement, spontaneity, and adventure. You skip over the painful and difficult chapters of your life. This section offers awareness of some words that shape the narrative of a Seven.

►►► **BELOVED SEVENS**

Spend some time with the words below that describe who Sevens are and are not. Circle the characteristics that resonate with your journey. Star words that express your gifts. Underline words that describe parts of your personality that are unusable by God in their present form. Put a checkmark beside characteristics that trigger you.

Sevens Descriptive Words List

I AM		I AM NOT	
joyful	naive	joyless	jaded
fun	youthful	serious	old
happy	whimsical	sad	routine
free	energetic	rigid	lethargic
spontaneous	animated	predictable	expressionless
enthusiastic	active	dull	passive
bubbly	alert	flat	asleep
playful	exciting	workaholic	bland
funny	interesting	solemn	tedious
witty	multi-talented	humorless	modest
quick-witted	friendly	slow	hostile

➤ Which words reflect the image of God in you?

➤ Which words are you most attached to? Addicted to? Compulsive about?

➤ Which word do you avoid or rationalize the most?

➤ If you opened up to the words you ignore, without judgment, how might this shift help you relate to yourself and others?

➤ Journal about the words that reflect God providing for all that you need and want.

▶▶▶ GETTING TO KNOW SEVENS

A Seven shares the journey that shaped her. Early on, this Seven felt most alive and satisfied when she was having fun. Notice how even as a child she made plans to play with others.

> As a child, I was an obedient, happy-go-lucky, caring girl. I don't remember causing anyone trouble; I always wanted to entertain or be entertained. I did not like being alone and wanted to be with others most of the time. I would feel impatient and sad when there wasn't anybody to do things with. I did not play well alone. I always got the comment "talks too much" on my report cards. I would plan adventures to draw kids into relationship. Mud, scrapes, hideouts, and making applesauce from the apple trees in the medium between the traffic lanes! I did whatever took my fancy and captured my imagination.

➤ What does this Seven childhood story bring up in you?

➤ What is your memory of your first Seven experience?

➤ What is like for you to think you made others laugh or have a good time?

> **Breath Prayer**
>
> *In silence and solitude, ask God to help you see yourself clearly. Begin with breathing. Breathe in: "Made in God's image," and then breathe out: "God fills me." Spend a few minutes with the sufficiency of this breath prayer. Feel the goodness and freedom of being made in God's image; feel how reflecting God can fill your inner emptiness. Breathe this prayer in and out throughout the day.*

TRUE SELF AND FALSE SELF: THE JOYFUL PERSON

Who we are or are not comes with expression and energy. The attitudes, behaviors, and motivations of beloved Sevens convey gladness and freedom. Your true self emerges from union with God and contentedly trusts you have enough life and joy. The Seven's false self is the compulsive, deeply entrenched old nature that constricts and tightens to avoid pain or boredom. It is the psychological or ego self that is a complex mixture of nature, nurture, and choices. This section will help you begin to recognize compulsive and impulsive false self reactions, as well as true self FLOW that loves God, others, and self.

True Self Sevens: Sacred Joy

Sevens are designed to reflect God's infinite capacity for joy, enthusiasm, and delight. You are optimistic, spontaneous, high-spirited, playful, versatile, and adventuring. Your presence says, "joy ride." Healthy Sevens are able to channel and focus your vitality and vision so you can persevere in accomplishing your dreams and goals. When you are present to God, you can let go of the need for more (experiences, stuff, or diversions). In presence, centered Sevens soften your hearts, accept your limits, and aren't afraid to suffer. In solidarity with Jesus, "a man of sorrows" (Isaiah 53:3 ASV), you can joyfully receive what is mundane or broken. True self Sevens don't say yes to every opportunity, desire, or experience—even when you want to! You can be sober minded and still embody sacred joy, which is the door to your virtue of sobriety. Sober people know you are and have enough.

False Self Sevens: Constricted in Distractions, Gluttony, and Escape Plans

False self Sevens are compulsive and impulsive about your joy. Your rationalization is "more joy—less pain." This addiction to joy often leads to FOMO (Fear Of Missing Out). FOMO fuels an over-extended, scattered, undisciplined, addictive lifestyle that gobbles up adventure and excess. When Sevens constrict around fears of being limited, bored, deprived, or taken down by the dark side, you generate more choices and rationalizations for why happiness, excitement, busyness, stimulation, and keeping your options open are best. Over-identification with joys and highs defends Sevens from pain. Highs can sublimate deprivation and divert responsibility. Highs can land Sevens smack in the middle of your vice of gluttony and its fear that you never have enough. Sevens can become addictive personalities who tighten and constrict around your comforts and escapes. This affects your ability to handle real problems, responsibilities, routines, and long-term commitments. False self Sevens also resist the hard work that leads to self-awareness and growth because it is a pain.

▶▶▶ **TRUE OR FALSE SELF**

As you think about your true and false self, consider the following questions. Notice what comes up for you; notice without judgment. Which questions particularly invite you to do some inner work and journal your responses?

Reacting to Pain

In this text Jesus is teaching about the trajectory of his own story and its culmination in pain and suffering. Peter exemplifies our resistance to the place of hardship in our story. Ponder your reactions to painful life situations.

> He then began to teach them that the Son of Man must suffer many things and be rejected by the elders, the chief priests and the teachers of the law, and that he must be killed and after three days rise again. He spoke plainly about this, and Peter took him aside and began to rebuke him.
>
> But when Jesus turned and looked at his disciples, he rebuked Peter. "Get behind me, Satan!" he said. "You do not have in mind the concerns of God, but merely human concerns." (Mark 8:31-33)

1. How do you find yourself responding to Jesus' teaching?

2. How do you respond to suffering and being rejected? How do your own plans and schemes close you down to hearing what God is saying to you?

3. Peter hoped following Jesus would give him something more than suffering. Maybe he'd be part of Jesus' inner circle when he came into his kingdom. Where does your mind get caught up in daydreams you want to have happen?

➤ Where do true self Seven characteristics show up in your relationships with others?

➤ Where do false self Seven qualities show up in your relationships with others? How does fear of pain or boredom show up: "This is no fun"? How does avoiding limits and downs sabotage your relationships: "Oh, let's not talk about that stuff"? How do plans and ideas distract you from what is important or help you avoid negative feelings?

➤ Where does your gluttony for experience constrict your ability to be present to your pain? What is a cue to relax your constricting urge to escape?

➤ How do you tell the difference between centered, true self energy and distracted, false self energy?

HARMONY: JOY IS DEEPLY STABLE

Sevens are often characterized as the joyful number, but you are much more than just one number! You bear the image and harmony of a three-in-one God. When beloved Sevens are present to your GQ and EQ intelligence, you harmonize and your joy flows with One stability and Four depth. This section creates awareness of how FLOW is the unique gift of the Harmony Triads.

In harmony and FLOW, a Seven's gift of joy flows with grounded-ness and compassion. Your ebullience and optimism are balanced by perseverance and stability (One GQ) and the depth and ability to hold life's pains (Four EQ).

▶▶▶ MORE THAN A TYPE

In this story a Seven suffered so much trauma that she sublimated her pain. Heart creativity (Four) helped this Seven become present to her feelings. Joy that is deeply stable rather than ephemeral integrates a Four's depth and a One's non-judgmental grounded-ness. Notice how EQ and GQ open this Seven to discernment and empathy for herself and others.

> Everyone I've ever loved has devastated me, either by hurtful actions or by dying. My high school boyfriend was shot in the face and died. When the grandmother I spent every day with died, an aunt angrily asked me, "What are you crying for?" I tried to stop crying and couldn't. A couple months later I found my mom's boyfriend beating the crap out of her. I don't remember feeling anything again until I started going to church with my cousins. They attended an apostolic Pentecostal church, and I joined the choir and band. I played the heck out of my trumpet. That was my Four heart space that went deep and creative and kept me from imploding. When I was playing music, I could feel something.
>
> Over time, my pattern of not wanting to feel pain mutated into feeling nothing. The Enneagram has helped me realize that in order to feel joy and happiness, I have to commit to feeling sadness and pain. I said "commit" because it's a conscious effort for me. I can stick my toe into the waters of sorrow, but as soon as I feel the wetness, I'm on to something more enticing. I'm learning to notice when I want to forget my childhood rather than go through

a process of remembering and noticing and dealing with it. My Four space helps me embrace both sorrow and joy. The unhealthy One in me wants to avoid mistakes and be good and perfect. As I give myself room to notice without judgment, I become grounded. And I receive the grace God has for me and my mistakes.

> ➤ When has your pain or need been dismissed by you or by others? Where do you want to forget your childhood or sublimate, avoid, and hide so you won't implode?

> ➤ How might you engage EQ creativity and/or beauty to get in touch with your own neglected pain?

> ➤ Where would your GQ help you keep hanging in there so that you find the joy in what is, rather than what isn't?

▶▶▶ IQ, EQ, GQ

Another Seven describes her Seven, One, and Four journey to integration. Notice how a life of coping is transformed through accessing the Harmony Triads.

> I have not always focused on transformation. Most of my life I have lived in my full throttle Seven without accessing my EQ or GQ. I didn't want to feel the pain, so I dismissed my feelings and gut responses. I navigated sexual abuse, marital dysfunction, divorce, and life transitions through escape, diversion, and planning some new adventure. Now I am discovering that my true self Seven is beautiful and not just an escape artist. When I flow with my heart Four (EQ), I bring balance and beauty to my world. I can also bear the pain I find there. When I flow with my gut One (GQ), I stand up for myself and what I need. I also persevere when it is hard. Integrating heart and gut is changing me and my relationships.

Life As It Is

The Bible passage offers opportunities for the Seven to integrate your EQ and GQ. No one escapes life's ups and downs. Embracing life's pleasures and pain takes a deep heart and a stable gut. Slowly read the text below; notice what you resist and what you embrace.

> There is a time for everything,
>> and a season for every activity under the heavens:
>> a time to be born and a time to die,
>> a time to plant and a time to uproot,
>> a time to kill and a time to heal,
>> a time to tear down and a time to build,
>> a time to weep and a time to laugh,
>> a time to mourn and a time to dance,
>> a time to scatter stones and a time to gather them,
>> a time to embrace and a time to refrain from embracing,

> ➤ When Sevens engage their gut and become grounded, they are present to what is really going on. Where do you see GQ in yourself?

> ➤ When Sevens engage their heart, they moderate their head-tripping and go with people into dark places to bring hope. Where do you see EQ in yourself?

> ➤ What is it like for you to have GQ, EQ, and IQ?

HEALING CHILDHOOD HURTS: OPENING TO SOBRIETY

Children are wired for resilience. Still, residual childhood distress leaks into our adult Seven relationships. Seven children can completely lose the message, "You will be taken care of." The default message you can learn is, "It's not okay to depend on anyone for anything." Seven children coped by escaping, clowning around, and presenting a happy face. These defenses brought pleasure that protected and mitigated against feeling pain or slogging through difficulty.

Prayer of Ignatius of Loyola

Allow this prayer of Ignatius of Loyola, which addresses the heart, head, and gut motivations of the Enneagram Triads, to become your prayer. Invite the strength, heart, and mind of the Trinity into your life and interactions as you pray it this week.

> *It is my will to win over the whole world, to overcome evil with good [GQ] to turn hatred aside with love, to conquer all the forces of death—whatever obstacles there are that block the sharing of life between God and humankind. Whoever wishes to join me in this mission [IQ] must be willing to labor with me, and so by following me in struggling and suffering [EQ] may share with me in glory.*

a time to search and a time to give up,
a time to keep and a time to throw away,
a time to tear and a time to mend,
a time to be silent and a time to speak,
a time to love and a time to hate,
a time for war and a time for peace. (Ecclesiastes 3:1-8)

1. How do your "escape attempts" prevent you from experiencing the fullness of life and authentic relationships with others?

2. Ecclesiastes describes life as it really is, not as you want it to be. Where are you being invited to embrace a part of your life that is unpleasant? How might you draw on your Four EQ to enable you to descend into that bit of darkness?

3. How would your One GQ bring perseverance to endure and weather all these various mountains and valleys?

Sometimes a traumatic memory or ethical lapse lays like a weight on your shoulders triggering the false self message of escape. Unprocessed pain can sabotage the FLOW of a Seven's joy. When that happens, an avoidant four-year-old self inside you looks for escapes and comforts. Defaulting to the false self, you get stuck in gluttony, addiction, and escapism. The Harmony Triad offers Sevens a way to reclaim your virtue of sobriety by being courageous and curious about how you indulge pleasure to block trauma.

▶▶▶ RECEIVING THE DISMISSED CHILDLIKE SELF

Receiving your dismissed child can heal and give you freedom to be sober and stay in the moment. Remember, within every light-hearted, positive, have-a-good-time Seven there is a deep, soulful Four who is anxious about your worth and fears being abandoned. There may also be a judgmental, uptight, controlling One who doesn't want to make any mistakes. To recognize where you dismissed your childlike self's depth and stability, pay attention to where you may have ignored your GQ and EQ.

Listen as this Seven shares her story. Notice how she hid the deep feelings of the Four inner child who wasn't protected and where she used both being chipper and a good girl in order to cover her secret.

> In early childhood, I recall a fun yet dramatic little girl that danced and daydreamed. My parents were strong disciplinarians who believed children should be seen and not heard. We were never encouraged to express our feelings. If my enthusiasm bubbled over or my feelings were too sad or angry, I was given a time-out. I was not to be a problem. I was to be okay. In fact, I was a good girl who longed for a pleasant environment and I kept my room clean and ordered. I didn't cause trouble and made straight As, which brought immediate attention. I see One gut organization, Four heart feelings, and Seven happiness in my early years. But sexual abuse at age seven left me feeling unprotected, ashamed, and confused by the intrusion into my body. I felt unsafe and began to keep secrets because revealing dark truths did not stop the unthinkable. It appeared that no one was going to defend or protect me. So I tried to figure out how to cope with my pain and not lose the validation my parents gave to "happy, carefree" me.

> As a teenager, I experienced my Seven to the exclusion of the rest of my triad. Pain was a dirty word, and sadness was to be avoided. I was the chipper cheerleader and wanted to have all the fun I could—without going too far away from the good little girl my parents were proud of. I buried my Four because pain and melancholy weren't acceptable ways to live. If I slipped into the hovering sadness, I feared I'd never come out. My romantic relationships were often with men who embodied order and needed my sense of fun to balance their serious side.

As you read these questions, notice where you sense God's invitation to more deeply receive your dismissed child. Write down any new insights and awareness. You are doing important and integrative work here.

➤ This Seven received validation for being happy and carefree. Imagine what it's like to need to be carefree and happy when you don't feel that way. Where does this story resonate in you?

➤ How does this Seven experience her One GQ? How do you dismiss your gut?

➤ Notice when your Four inner child's sadness was not allowed. Where do you dismiss your heart EQ?

▶▶▶ JOURNALING YOUR DISMISSED CHILDLIKE SELF

Integrating and accessing your GQ and EQ can help you relax your flight and pleasure instinct so you can discern how to show up and stay put in any given moment. Getting reacquainted with EQ depth creates connection and ability to hold the pain. Integrating GQ stability and perseverance brings a sense of how to assert the right sort of control. Checking out what your heart feels and your gut senses offers a path to harmony and a life that can hold both joy and sorrow.

Name and journal some of your hurts and purposefully explore when you began to defend yourself with an inner event planner that just partied through. Engage your EQ, taking time to acknowledge what your heart is feeling, and your GQ, following what is right for you. Feel free to choose among the questions and return to other questions at another time.

➤ What is your story about not being taken care of? Where do you continue to dismiss your deep feelings and grounded-ness because of fear or past trauma? What default reactions and triggers of your childhood self still operate today?

➤ What addictions and compulsions keep you from feeling pain? What are they about? Where in your life right now are you headed out the door, hoping to avoid some uncomfortable relationship or commitment?

➤ Ask God to give you a desire to return to your virtue of sobriety so you can find childlike enough-ness in the moment. Notice when a moment is enough. What is happening?

➤ Where has your ability to be truly lighthearted and truly deep and real been repaired/healed or increased/solidified?

Spontaneous and lively Sevens have a default for pleasure and instant gratification. Embracing God's invitation to weep is counterintuitive for you. After all, weeping feels terrible and takes you down. Sevens need spiritual practices that help integrate your EQ and GQ so you can lean into the seasons of sorrows and pain when circumstances aren't happy. During those seasons, it is completely appropriate to weep. In fact, even God weeps. To discover your compassionate and deep heart, it may be helpful for you to ready the chapter "Invitation to Weep" in *Invitations from God* by Adele Ahlberg Calhoun.

When you fear being limited, bored, or forced to encounter unpleasant events and pessimistic people, you have just been given an opportunity to grow. You can open up to

God and what is really going on. You can carry your hope with you and have conversation with the person who triggers you. You can enlarge your heart EQ through sadness, tears, and discomfort. You can find solidarity with Jesus' sufferings, compassion, and perseverance. Watch how embracing your pain can actually deepen your joy and fuel your desire to bring life's goodness to others.

DISCERNMENT: DESOLATIONS AND CONSOLATIONS

Ignatius of Loyola taught that God's Guiding Spirit of wisdom moves in all three centers of intelligence—head, heart, and gut. When making a decision, Ignatius suggested noticing your consolations and desolations by asking: What does my heart feel? What does my mind think? What does my gut sense? The answer to these questions gives you evidence of how the Spirit is at work in you.

Consolations point Sevens toward God's presence and a joy that is not based on sublimating bad things. Consolations are evidence that a Seven is heading in the direction of joy (IQ) that is deeply (EQ) stable (GQ). Desolations of fear, which distort the FLOW of God's joy, invite Sevens to notice how the Spirit is directing you to an inner freedom that endures with hope. (More information on Harmony Triad discernment is found in Soul Resource 5.)

Healing Prayer

When Sevens face your wounds in God's healing and joyful presence, you discover that your hopes and fears are both welcomed and honored. Jesus gives Sevens a place to put your pain, gluttony, and feelings of scarcity. He holds out the possibility of having a sober joy, a contentment that doesn't depend on events, and an optimism that brings hope into darkness. But you will need to come to Jesus for healing. With Jesus, your vice of gluttony is transformed into your virtue of sobriety.

This is a way to do healing prayer on your own. Relax into silence and solitude. Breathe deeply. Don't force it. Become present to God and yourself. Ask God to show you a past pain in your life that is still being transmitted. Be still and wait. When something comes to mind, follow this simple trail of healing prayer.

❖ *Imagine yourself and Jesus back in the memory. Get your bearings. Where is Jesus? Where are you?*

❖ *What are you feeling? (sad, afraid, limited, controlled, the need to escape, or something else)*

❖ *Do these feelings remind you of a time you had similar reactions? You can go with Jesus to that place and time or stay where you are.*

❖ *Continue to name what you are thinking and feeling in your experience. Ask Jesus if there is a lie you began to believe at that time. Give it a name.*

❖ *What is Jesus saying to you about this lie? Listen. Is there an image, word, or phrase that he speaks to you?*

❖ *Repeat the truth you have heard about yourself from Jesus gently and frequently. Let the truth be an antidote that lets the pain go into Jesus and sets you free.*

Sevens experience consolations such as integrated joy, holy optimism, good fun, reflective spontaneity, responsible adventure, passionate enthusiasm, receptive emptiness, and solidarity with those who experience pain. You can be free!

Sevens experience desolations such as gluttony, addiction to self, hyperactivity, impulsivity, procrastination, overextension, scatteredness, superficiality, and fear of pain. In desolation Sevens lack empathy, commitment, and discipline. You are bound.

▶▶▶ PRESENT TO WHAT'S HAPPENING INSIDE

Both consolations and desolations point toward the purpose for which Sevens were created. This Seven is studying the map of her soul and how she erected walls. She notices signposts of desolation and pain that make her wonder if she is even capable of love. Notice the consolations and desolations that can lead this Seven toward wholeness.

I'm not sure if I am capable of love (desolation). I take care of my husband and kids and want what's best for them. I want them to be genuinely happy. But love them . . . I haven't loved anyone in years! With all the pain in my childhood, I just put up a wall that no one, not even my children, have been able to penetrate. I hate to admit it. It makes me sound crazy (desolation). I've literally put up a wall around my heart space. No wonder I have such a hard time believing God loves me. Still, I find that the Harmony Triads help me stay with all the pain, sorrow, and disappointments in ways that lead to health and integration. My Seven is kicking and screaming as I look at my ugly and broken life. I am staying with my Four depth of experience and One perseverance. My breath prayer is, "God, I love you; God, I trust you." This prayer is doing a work in me (consolation).

> *Prayer Practice for Finding Joy*
>
> *Sevens often feel the desolation of life draining away when they are bored, down, in pain, and slogging through. When you feel desolation, intentionally breathe into your frustration and exasperation. Breathe in: "This is the day the Lord has made." Breathe out: "I will rejoice and be glad in it." Let this breath prayer open you to finding your joy in what is.*

➤ How does not feeling safe enough to express your pain lead you into desolation?

➤ Pay attention to how God's Spirit moves in your EQ and GQ to bring you into stable joy. Do you get fearful and run away from the desolations? Or do you open yourself to the consolations that bring freedom?

▶▶▶ DESOLATION AND SUBLIMATION

Free-spirited and enthusiastic Sevens have a default defense of sublimation. Sublimation resists bringing difficult things into conscious awareness. To keep hard things at bay, Sevens occupy yourself with lots of plans (some good and some escapist). These strategies may involve excessive stimulation or activities that push conflict and hardship out of awareness. But sublimation doesn't work forever. Difficult things keep popping up from the depths of the unconscious like a beach ball that won't stay underwater. Without judgment, look at your life patterns and notice how sublimation shows up in you.

> ➤ When do you push difficult things out of your awareness by thinking up things to do? How do you distract yourself from what is important? How has spontaneity and a blithe word dismissed someone's pain?

> ➤ How does your body constrict in desolation? Where do you carry your fear of pain and being trapped?

> ➤ Where does collecting false joys and planning for more close you off from consolations and the FLOW of God's joy?

> ➤ Are there defenses besides sublimation that block your discernment?

▶▶▶ CONSOLATIONS AND SOBRIETY

The Spirit's invitation to consolation often engages your steadfast GQ that helps you become present to the entire EQ range of emotions, not just joyful ones. Joy that arises from the depths and perseveres through all the vagaries of life is, in the words of St. Francis of Assisi, "joy unspeakable."

Sevens are consoled as you follow God's Spirit out of gluttony and move into the beauty and mess of life with sobriety, attention, and perseverance. Sober Sevens recognize what you have is already enough; you do not need more. Sobriety gives you the ability to hold the whole range of human experience with hope that is undiminished and undeterred by any internal or external circumstance.

> ➤ Describe a situation in which you felt the Holy Spirit inviting you to let go of the fear of missing out and the image of yourself as the measure of fun and no-limits living. What happened? What consolations came to you?

> ➤ When has sobriety helped you stand in FLOW that enables you to bring God's joy to others with all your heart, soul, strength, and mind?

SPIRITUAL RHYTHMS FOR SEVENS

So I tell you this, and insist on it in the Lord, that you must no longer live as the Gentiles do, in the futility of their thinking. They are darkened in their understanding and separated from the life of God . . . due to the hardening of their hearts. Having lost all sensitivity, they have given themselves over to sensuality so as to indulge in every kind of impurity, and they are full of greed.

That, however, is not the way of life you learned when you heard about Christ. . . . You were taught, with regard to your former way of life, to put off your old self, which is being corrupted by its deceitful desires; to be made new in the attitude of your minds; and to put on the new self, created to be like God in true righteousness and holiness. (Ephesians 4:17-24)

Quick-witted and optimistic Sevens can love to over-indulge. Paul suggests that being greedy and needing to experience everything can harden hearts and sensitivity. He also holds out hope for developing new attitudes and living into our true selves. A Seven's true self leans into the joy that holiness and righteousness actually give.

Attending to the Holy Spirit's motions of the soul on a daily basis enables Sevens to move from your fear of confinement into a centered place, where you are held in God's joyful heart and live from a joy that is deeply stable.

These spiritual rhythms are all ways Sevens can lean into God's invitations to mind renewal and sobriety. Not every practice will be the one for you. Say yes to the practices that best capture your desire to be with God right now.

▶▶▶ PRACTICING PRESENCE: SEVENS

Re-read the FLOW definition in the Key Terms section. Notice the presence of Trinitarian harmony.

> Father, Son, and Spirit belong and flow together.
>
> Head, heart, and gut belong and flow together.
>
> Faith, love, and hope belong and flow together.

Divine harmony calls Sevens to be present so you can intentionally learn to be joyful in *all* things. Sevens who are present to God and others with head, heart, and gut can integrate and lean into joyful wholeness. Let the following meditative prayer move through your entire created being so it holds you together. Staying with this prayer for a season can give Sevens the moderation that comes from GQ and EQ.

Find a comfortable and awake position. Remember that the Spirit of God dwells within you and prays for you. Ask God to give you an open and receptive head, heart, and gut.

Gut Presence: Put yourself in the presence of the Spirit. Notice what is happening in your body. Notice without judgment. Let your body tell you what it knows. Is there something your body wants to do in this prayer? Do that. Experience your stable joy. Give thanks for its enduring nature. How and when does your body react rather than focus and persevere? When do you divert your attention to other ideas instead of observing what your body tells you about needs, pains, or wounds?

Heart Presence: Put yourself in the presence of Jesus. Breathe into your heart space. Feel your tenderness. Notice your heart's need to be held and cherished. Breathe in and create even more space around your heart. Notice and welcome your vulnerability and dismissed pain. Breathe: "This is also me." Invite self-compassion. What in you needs care, a word of encouragement, or a healing touch? Imagine naming these things in the presence of Jesus who delights in you. How does Jesus respond to you?

> *Head Presence:* Put yourself in the presence of your all-wise Creator. Move your head around on your shoulders. Feel its weight and tightness. Breathe into your intellect. Observe your life in the body. What does your head tell you about you? How could your mind help you recognize when your plans and strategies keep you in your ego rather than inner freedom? What questions would you like to ask your heart space? What is it like to trust your heart—to give your heart rather than guard your heart?

Pray into Your Harmony:
Joy Is Deeply Stable

"Joy is deeply stable" is a breath prayer. This prayer helps you engage the life-giving stability of the One that is principled, disciplined, organized, and responsible, as well as the life-giving heart of the Four that is reflective, authentic, deep, and empathetic.

Memorizing this prayer brings awareness of what is most true about you to real-life situations. You are more than your type. Breathe this prayer when you want to avoid conflict, sublimate pain, escape a boring meeting, or ignore a project that needs to be finished. Anytime you are triggered and tempted to constrict around fears of being trapped and bored, open up and breathe, "joy is deeply stable." Open to God and call on the joy that is deeply stable.

FLOW Practice for Sevens

In FLOW, Sevens are **F**ree, **L**oving, **O**pen, and **W**ith. You stand in the presence of the three-in-one God and integrate head, heart, and gut in your loving. You also relate with the three Christian virtues of faith, hope, and love. When you notice that you are constricting and stuck in escapist thinking, when you crave more of something (or everything), when you sidestep pain in yourself and others—this is the moment to breathe, be with the Spirit, and ask for the gift of inner freedom. Open your heart and gut and ask, "What am I trying to escape? What am I avoiding

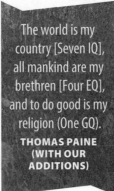

The world is my country [Seven IQ], all mankind are my brethren [Four EQ], and to do good is my religion (One GQ).

THOMAS PAINE (WITH OUR ADDITIONS)

by not staying put?" FLOW happens as you hold and welcome these things into your conscience along with the deep, unshakeable, divine joy that holds everything together. At the end of the day, log what happened when you were not in FLOW. Celebrate when God's love for others flowed through you. Confess when it didn't. Begin again tomorrow.

Practice Confession

Vulnerability and transparency about who you are before God and others is part of transformation and emotional health. Confess your:

- ▶ *Vices:* of gluttony and self-indulgence.
- ▶ *Rationalization:* "More is better. I don't have enough."
- ▶ *Fear:* of pain, sadness, and deprivation.
- ▶ *Addictions:* to comfort, food, alcohol, exercise, pornography, adventure, diversions, or highs.
- ▶ *Escape strategies:* humor, changing the subject, planning, or fantasizing.

Receive words of assurance: "In the presence of the God who died for you and smiles on you, you stand free and clear."

Practice Fasting

Sevens can hate being deprived. Reframe your understanding of fasting. Fasting is a way to give your entire self to God in the moment. It helps you curb the voracious appetite for more. Instead of filling your internal void with adventures and stuff, you create a space to seek God and God alone. Fasting is a practice that helps you lean into sobriety, moderation, and full attachment to God—without dependence on substances or escapes that are harmful to life.

Fasting includes many things such as refraining from food, watching TV, using digital devices, shopping, criticism, alcohol, going everywhere, seeing everyone, or staying up late. Choose one to practice this week.

Choose a compulsion that hinders freedom to receive life as it is. Ask God to give you grace to let go of this for a specific amount of time. What is it like for you?

Practice Fixed-Hour Prayer

Many religions have fixed hours for prayers. Old and New Testament Jews went to the temple to pray at specific hours of the day. Early Christians did the same. Muslims are called to prayer at particular hours. Monastic communities interrupt their duties with prayers at specific hours of the day. For people who are easily distracted, fixed hour prayer opens a door to being present to God throughout the day. Download the app *Pray as You Go* to your smartphone. Use the daily prayers found in the Divine Office or *The Divine Hours* by Phyllis Tickle. These prayers don't depend on spontaneity or ingenuity. Relax into the prayers and let them carry you back to FLOW.

Practice Sobriety and Simplicity

Sevens often pack their life to the brim. There are no margins, buffers, or limits. More is better. "More" is the Seven's medication for "deprivation neurosis." Simplicity and sobriety address limitless over-choice and consumerism.

Breath Prayers

Notice your magnificent breath. Feel the oxygen fill your lungs and lift your chest. Follow your breath in and down. Take time to notice what is happening in your head. Feel the joy of your created life as you breathe in: "You have formed my inward parts; I am joyfully and wonderfully made . . . may my soul know that very well." Spend a few minutes with this breath prayer. Follow your breath to the joy that you have enough and are enough.

Keep breathing into your body. Breathing in from the soles of your feet, fill your belly with breath, and continue breathing to the crown of your head. Feel your experience. Breathe into your head, your heart, and your gut. Without judgment, notice whatever comes up. If memories come, welcome them with your deeply stable joy. Stay with them. Use the breath prayers below when they fit the situation you are in.

- ❖ *Inhale: "Made in God's image."*
  Exhale: "God fills me."

- ❖ *Inhale: "A time to weep."*
  Exhale: "A time to laugh."

- ❖ *Inhale: "The Lord is my shepherd."*
  Exhale: "I have everything I need."

- ❖ *Inhale: "Joy is," exhale: "deeply stable."*

▶ Shop only one day a week. Observe "buy nothing" days.

▶ Clean out your closets. Organize clutter. Keep surfaces clear. Pack up stuff and give it away. What does not filling up every space do for you?

▶ Spend some evenings alone.

▶ Listen to your body. Eat only when you are hungry. Sleep when you are tired.

Practice "No Spontaneous Yeses"

Sevens are quick to go for more. You can say yes to so many experiences, options, responsibilities, relationships, and adventures that you lose yourself. You overload and can't remember what matters and what you need.

Take the next two weeks to have, "No spontaneous yeses." When someone asks you to do something, say, "Give me a minute." Take that minute to think, "Why do I want to do this?" or "Is my yes keeping me from something I need to do?" Decide whether you really want to say yes or no. No can be a boundary that helps you restore your soul. When has saying no given you life? Keep a mental list of each time.

Practice Stability

Stability is the practice of being committed to a community and/or long-term relationships. Stability in work and life creates joint responsibilities, projects, experiences, and assignments that call for everyone to invest and persevere.

▶ Talk to God about the friends, church, or organizations you want to stick with over the long haul.

▶ Imagine how stability could enhance your life and relationships.

▶ Don't over-promise. Be upfront about what you will deliver.

▶ Stability commits to a reasonable number of things and observes human limits. It works against the fear of missing out and grounds you in community.

Practice Empathy and Compassion

Your gifts of optimism and joy are better received when people recognize your ability to go into deep places (EQ) and persevere with them (GQ).

▶ Take time to listen to other people's stories.

▶ Express your heart concern and care for those suffering hardship.

Blessing for the Beloved Seven

As we close this section, take time to breathe in this blessing and create space in your soul.

May the Holy Three bless this non-indulgent, joyful journey home to your true self.

May God the Father direct you with insight as you consider your commitments.

May the heart of Jesus, the man of sorrows, infuse you with joy and be your solidarity in suffering.

May the Holy Spirit ground you to live with limits and deprivations.

May the joyful sobriety of the Trinity lead you on your road, upholding you and loving you.

Empathy for SEVENS

[There are] moments when it is clear—if I have the eyes to see—that the life I am living is not the same as the life that wants to live in me. In those moments I sometimes catch a glimpse of my true life, a life hidden like the river beneath the ice. . . . What am I meant to do? Who am I meant to be?

PARKER PALMER

Every child needs to be dependent. Early on, Sevens may have found that depending on caretakers hurt; it wasn't a good idea. To survive, they took on the role of the happy-go-lucky child, took care of themselves, and cheered everyone up. Here you can explore your responses to Sevens and how you might grow in empathy, seeing them as God does.

Empathy is a true self response that harmonizes and breaks down the we/they divide. You may find Sevens to be flighty, unreliable, and superficial. Or you may absolutely revel in their upbeat enjoyment of almost everything. Understanding how a Seven's gluttony for experiences and over-the-top optimism developed can create compassionate and empathetic interactions with them.

This Seven describes her journey. See if you can enter into the story and engage your understanding heart.

In college, I lived in a dorm where my room faced the elevators. I always left my door open so people could come in and visit. I loved having people around, using my Seven ability to plan and encourage. I also used my

Four ability to read others' emotions and create deep relationships, filling my need to be important. When I focused on having solutions for others though, I avoided working on myself. My mantra to open my heart and gut is enlightenment, presence, and discernment. Enlightenment is found when I am present to my experience and to God. Presence and enlightenment bring discernment and harmony.

1. As you consider the Seven story, notice:
   - What are you thinking about this Seven?
   - What is your gut instinct about this Seven?
   - What are you feeling about this Seven?

2. When have you filled your life up with people, advice giving, and planning adventures to feel happy and important?

3. Have you ever constricted around avoiding pain or an uncomfortable situation? What was that like for you?

4. Why do you think Sevens find it easier to come up with a plan or make a joke than be present to and open about their fears or pain? How can this give you empathy for Sevens?

UNDERSTANDING THE DEFENSE MECHANISM OF SUBLIMATION

Another Seven illustrates how his defense mechanism affects his day and the difference it makes to integrate his Seven IQ with One GQ and Four EQ.

My job is networking and making deals happen. Getting people to buy into my projects is an amazing head rush. I text, talk, drive, think, and plan what's next all at once! As an addictive personality, I like my

wine, my travel, my adventures, and my comforts too much. I don't like negativity or limits or being told what I can't do. That's me in my juice. Working with the Harmony Triads is hard for me because it means admitting my autopilot self can be spacey, listen poorly, and suggest ideas all day long with no follow through. Harmony Triads have shown me that I need my One GQ to center, commit to the team agenda, and get the job done. Honestly, it can feel like death to lean into my One, saying no to things I want, but I see how it stabilizes my life and relationships. I also am learning to use my Four EQ. Landing deals is not just about having a good time. It works best when I form some deep connections. But deep connections can disappoint and hurt. Hey, I'm learning, and it's all good.

1. This Seven enjoys his "head rush" and sublimates negativity or limits by keeping busy with plans. What connection or resistances do you have to him?

2. What do you think is behind this Seven's frenetic pace?

3. How could you enter into the joy of a Seven in a grounded way?

4. How might you join the Holy Spirit in praying for a Seven you know?

RELATING TO A SEVEN

We find grace to see things from a Seven's point of view when we remember that under the playful exterior of a Seven is a fearful child who escaped into activities and optimism to protect themselves.

- Sevens want you to play and join in their fun rather than dampen it. Take yourself less seriously and delight in their delight.

- When a Seven expresses pain or disappointment, be gentle and encourage them that this is good thing.

- Sevens can have a hard time sitting in meetings and sticking with tasks. When they crack a joke or suggest a diversionary tactic derailing the discussion, invite them to stay with you through the boring and tough stuff. Build in some breaks and fun.

- Sevens like variety and new experiences. They manage things by walking around. Don't expect them to sit at their desks all day.

- If you want a Seven to listen to something hard or something that requires a decision, give them room to respond later so they don't minimize it in the moment.

- Sevens like to be happy, but they don't want responsibility for your happiness. That creates an expectation that saps their joy.

The following list summarizes key characteristics of our beloved Sevens. Consider your responses to these characteristics.

- *Authentic true self:* Joyful
- *Compulsive false self:* Gluttonous
- *Virtue leading back to true self:* Sobriety
- *Personality style:* Cheerful, optimistic

- *Work style:* Animator
- *Leadership/action style:* Cheerleader
- *Thinking style:* Positive
- *Relational style:* Gregarious, talkative
- *Relationships:* Social
- *Core motivation:* Happiness, variety
- *Negative fixation:* Escapism, gluttony
- *Narrative:* "This is boring or painful; I'm out of here!"
- *Communication:* Enthusiasm, stories, humor
- *Seven with a Six wing:* More moderate, persistent, attentive to duty
- *Seven with an Eight wing:* More aggressive, competitive, controlling
- *Basic fear:* Pain, deprivation
- *Basic desire:* Satisfaction, fulfillment
- *Drive:* Avoid missing out on adventure; desire freedom and exciting experiences; reject pain or boredom; need to be occupied

Based on the description above:

1. How does it feel to be a Seven? What descriptors give clues on how to relate to a Seven?

2. Is there a better way to say what is true of Sevens?

3. Sevens are fun, creative, and energetic. What is it like to meet the optimism of a Seven with your own openness and delight?

4. Sevens want to be appreciated for their ability to bring joy and find paths of fulfillment. How can you express your appreciation for a Seven?

SOUL RESOURCES

PART IV

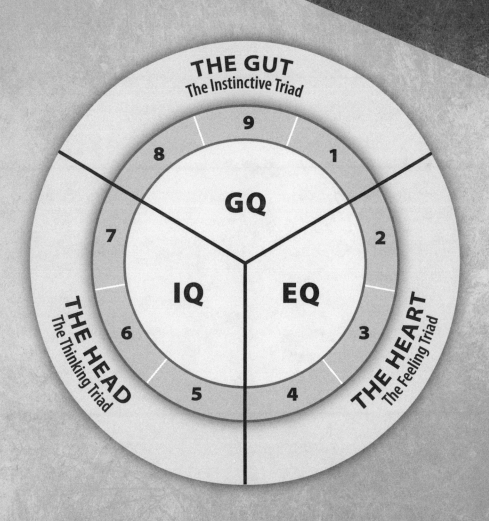

THE GUT
The Instinctive Triad

THE HEART
The Feeling Triad

THE HEAD
The Thinking Triad

GQ

IQ

EQ

9

8

1

7

2

6

3

5

4

Soul Resource 1

STOP FOR HARMONY

What I want to do I do not do, but what I hate I do.

ROMANS 7:15

STOP IS AN ACRONYM that opens you to transformation in the midst of your life. It can give you awareness of default reactions and return you to presence to God and others so you can FLOW with love of God and neighbor.

Many of your triggers and reactions are so automatic you don't even realize they are happening. Words you didn't intend to say fly out of your mouth. You wish you could take your actions back. You need help to STOP.

Under stress and in the heat of the moment, there is always a tiny sliver of time when you can send your ego energy in a different direction and return to your true self. STOP opens you to the help of the holy three-in-one God who designed your brain with neural plasticity to transform and renew your mind. Transformation cannot happen unless you stop, notice a trigger, and open. Opening makes space for the Spirit. God's Spirit can give grace in a split second! Grace can override the reactionary fight, flight, or freeze responses of the brain's amygdala and develop new neural pathways to the prefrontal cortex where responses such as love, joy, and peace originate. The Spirit partners with you to help you notice how you constrict around wounded and

broken places in yourself or others. The Spirit can help you let go of constriction and open you to a new response. Transformation of ingrained habitual reactions happens incrementally over time as you practice new ways of responding.

STOP is a sign you can recognize in the moment and then follow these steps:

See: ask God to give you eyes to see.

▶ Take a deep breath.

▶ What does your Enneagram number automatically see here?

▶ Seek to visualize things from another perspective.

Triggers: notice without judgment.

▶ What just happened in you?

▶ What got you out on the edge of your number?

▶ Where did you leave your true self behind? If you don't have time to really think this through now, notice and come back to this trigger later.

Open: access your head, heart, and gut. Breathe into your harmony; it will loosen your constriction around your false self. Think about:

► What does my head IQ think about this?

► What does my heart EQ feel about this?

► What is my gut instinct GQ about this?

Presence: intentionally return to God's presence.

► What is God's invitation in this moment?

► Intentionally give your full presence to reality as it is. What do you see and hear?

► What would it look like to be free in this present moment? Choose where your presence and energy will go.

► What would God's presence within you do right now?

REFLECTION

1. Where in your current life are you likely to have opportunity to practice STOP?

2. What makes it most difficult for you to let go and move into presence where you stand in the FLOW of God's love?

3. What is it like to realize that God is with you, sustaining you and loving you through the hardships, triggers, and heartaches?

You can work with these questions in moments when you are and are not triggered. It's impossible to answer all the questions in a sliver of time. Still, by God's grace, you can STOP and notice what triggered you. The more you STOP, the more your awareness grows. The more awareness you have, the more you can be present to God in the moment. It is being present to the Spirit that helps you change your default autopilot. Remember, you can always return to a difficult encounter and debrief your trigger later in the presence of God, who is ready to help you become your beautiful, integrated, beloved, true self.

EIGHTS STOP

> The arc of the moral universe is long, but it bends toward justice.
> **MARTIN LUTHER KING JR.**

When Eights sense your constrictive demand-and-attack energy coming online, you need a practice to help you relax your default power-up muscle. To experience your own emotional climate, you need to make choices to power down, detach, and observe through your Five IQ and open up to care through your Two EQ. STOP is a practice that can redirect your intensity.

See

Where am I tensing up, hardening, mad, bullying, and pushing against?

Triggers

This needs to be done now! I'm finished! That isn't fair. I'm stronger. Get out of the way.

Open

Head: How can I learn from and collaborate with others? Do I have to do this alone?

Heart: Is my intensity sabotaging my goals and relationships?

Gut: How much power do I need to use in this moment?

Presence

Notice how you are either all in and present, or you pull away and are not present at all. Living in the presence of God and staying present to yourself and others with love is its own sort of strength. Paul writes about how strength in the inner being keeps you attached to others in love:

> I pray that out of his glorious riches he may strengthen you with power through his Spirit in your inner being, so that Christ may dwell in your hearts through

faith. And I pray that you, being rooted and established in love, may have power . . . to grasp how wide and long and high and deep is the love of Christ . . . that you may be filled to the measure of all the fullness of God. (Ephesians 3:16-19)

Let Paul's prayer shape your understanding of your strength. When you are triggered and start to pull away, ask for power "in your inner being" to stay engaged, vulnerable, and caring. What happens when you relax and let something unfold?

NINES STOP

> You cannot find peace by avoiding life.
> **MICHAEL CUNNINGHAM**

When Nines sense you are procrastinating, powering down, and closing up shop, you need a practice that wakes you up and helps you stay engaged. STOP is a practice that points Nines toward Three EQ action and Six IQ courage and concern for the common good. STOP is a practice that helps you show up, not numb out.

See

Where am I falling asleep to conflict? Decisions? Tasks? Difficult conversations? Desires?

Triggers

I'm ready for a break. This is too much. Don't push me. I'm fine!

Open

Head: How can I be courageous in this moment? What does loyalty to others ask of me?

Heart: Is my heart awake to what I want and what I can achieve?

Gut: How can I make true peace happen? What work is necessary for peace in this situation?

Presence

Nines who practice staying present to things you want to avoid can change your relationships and world. You bring your mediating self to problems and difficult relationships and steadfastly work for the common good. You embody, "You (God) will keep in perfect peace / those whose minds are steadfast, / because they trust in you" (Isaiah 26:3).

ONES STOP

> Goodness is the only investment that never fails.
> **HENRY DAVID THOREAU**

When Ones sense you have constricted around having to be right and make things better, you need a practice to silence your internal critic and relax your judgment. To dismantle anger and resentment requires practice. STOP helps Ones open to the levity of Seven IQ, which lightens up and laughs at personal foibles. A One's Four EQ invites you out of perfectionism and gives you permission to create, color outside some lines, and lean into inner freedom.

See

Where did I just tense up, constrict my body and lose my easy goodness? Where do I refuse to admit I am wrong?

Triggers

I am resentful. I am angry about this. I am feeling critical and defensive.

Open

Head: Step back. What is the worst that can happen if things don't go my way? Can I hear my tone of voice and sense my judgmental vibe? Do these reactions help or sabotage what I want?

Heart: What do I feel besides anger? Is it hurt? Disappointment? Lack of appreciation? How can I be tender to myself?

Gut: Where am I experiencing life as a full-body blow? Am I clenching my jaw or grinding my teeth? Where am I carrying my anger?

Presence

Become present to reality, the God of all perfection. Love covers a multitude of sins. Let go of how you want others to be better and be present to the God who makes things new: "He who was seated on the throne said, 'I am making everything new!' Then he said, 'Write this down, for these words are trustworthy and true'" (Revelation 21:5). Feel the relief of not having to make everything better and new.

TWOS STOP

> If you live for people's acceptance,
> you'll die from their rejection.
> **LECRAE**

When Twos feel you have constricted around having to help someone, you need a practice that relaxes and/or dismantles your overzealous hovering, pleasing, and pride about loving better than anyone else. You need a practice that helps you STOP and detach from the needs and responses of others so you can attach to your own needs. You need a way to integrate Five IQ that contemplates what you can and can't do with your Eight GQ that can say no and hold your ground.

See

Where am I anxious? Distressed at lack of connection? Tight and hurt?

Triggers

I am not getting the response I want. Someone doesn't seem to need me. I am not feeling appreciated.

Open

Head: Step back. Can I interpret people's reactions in another way?

Heart: What do I need right now? Is my love about getting something I need?

Gut: Breathe into tightness. Do I need to use my voice and agency in asking for something I need?

Presence

Become present to the reality that God is utterly devoted to you: "Let the beloved of the LORD rest secure in him, / for he shields [you] all day long, / and the one the LORD loves rests between his shoulders" (Deuteronomy 33:12). Let go of how you want others to love you and be present to the God who carries you. What happens as you rest between God's shoulders?

THREES STOP

> I've always been in the right place and time.
> Of course, I steered myself there.
> **BOB HOPE**

When Threes notice you have constricted around image and success, you need a practice to relax your overdoing, overworking, and overcompensating productivity. You need a way to lay down your addiction to vainglory and access your loyal and curious Six IQ as well as your pause-and-see Nine GQ. STOP is a practice to help Threes open where you constrict and get stuck in competition, performing, and looking good.

See

Where am I stressed, anxious, and feeling shame about outcomes and how I come across?

Triggers

I feel like a failure. I need to impress. I want to win. I can work harder. I am frustrated by their ineptness.

Open

Head: Step back. Have I lost sight of what and who matters most?

Heart: How does my need to impress and win affect connecting to others?

Gut: Breathe into any body tightness or constriction. Where can I let go of image and lean into the inner freedom and peace of my authentic self?

Presence

Focus on the reality that God's love for you is not attached to your doing. You have nothing to prove: "Do nothing out of selfish ambition or vain conceit. Rather, in humility value others above yourselves" (Philippians 2:3). Let go of your need to win or succeed and be present to God and others in what is. What happens then?

FOURS STOP

> Sometimes I pretend to be normal. But it gets boring. So I go back to being me.
> **ANONYMOUS**

When Fours feel you have constricted around being unique and are anxious about being abandoned, you need a practice to relax your envy, exaggerated emotions, and the feeling that you have a fatal flaw. STOP is a practice that helps Fours access your less serious Seven IQ and more stable and objective One GQ.

See

Where am I stressed and worried that I am not worthy of love and belonging?

Triggers

I fear abandonment. I am not connecting. No one understands me.

Open

Head: Remember that joy can live next to sorrow. Lighten up.

Heart: Am I over-dramatizing what I feel and/or what is happening? Am I anxious that someone will leave me? Am I bored?

Gut: Breathe into any body constriction. Where can I breathe into anxiety? What would happen if I accepted the ordinary in and around me? How can I lean into the freedom of my beautiful true self?

Presence

Become present to the reality that "God has said, / 'Never will I leave you; / never will I forsake you'" (Hebrews 13:5). You are a one-of-a-kind wonder. Open your heart to the goodness, beauty, and uniqueness in the life you have.

FIVES STOP

> Educating the mind without educating the heart is no education at all.
> **ARISTOTLE**

When Fives notice you have constricted and fear looking foolish or being sucked dry by people and responsibilities, you need a practice that stops your default withdrawal response. STOP is a practice that helps Fives access your Two EQ so you stay engaged. STOP also helps Fives lean into the agency and decisiveness of your Eight GQ. Be curious about why you want to escape interacting.

See

What is happening that makes me want to withdraw into my head?

Triggers

They will suck me dry. I feel like my privacy is being invaded. I need to be alone! This is too much emotion and or conflict for me.

Open

Head: Consider the wisdom of checking out my GQ and EQ.

Heart: Can expressing feelings create connections that nourish me and others? How can I participate and share? This is a stretch for my heart, but it won't kill me.

Gut: What boundary do I need to hold? How can I step up with voice, leadership, and agency?

Presence

Contemplate the distinction between intelligence and true wisdom: "The wisdom that comes from heaven is first of all pure; then peace-loving, considerate, submissive, full of mercy and good fruit, impartial and sincere" (James 3:17). Divine wisdom happens through presence to God's Spirit, who gives you good fruit such as mercy, impartiality, and sincerity for the sake of others.

SIXES STOP

> It is not death that man should fear,
> but he should fear never beginning to live.
> **MARCUS AURELIUS**

When Sixes sense your constrictive "threat meter" is on high alert, you need a practice to curb your get-to-safety default. You need a practice to help you relax your fears and open to other perspectives. STOP is a practice that nurtures a Six's inner authority. It helps you embrace your "I can do it" Three EQ and your "see it from every side" Nine GQ.

See

Is something making me feel guarded, paralyzed, or afraid of making a decision?

Triggers

I don't trust these people. This isn't a safe place. I question this authority and their motives. These people aren't doing their duty.

Open

Head: What does the loyal skeptic in me think? How could I be less guarded?

Heart: How can I be courageous and trust that taking a risk could bring me connections I want? How do I open up and love in this moment?

Gut: Relax. Breathe. What inner voice of catastrophic thinking can I speak peace to? What could go right if I went with the flow? How can I step up and use my mediating voice?

Presence

Become present to the reality that ultimate safety is to be held in God's heart. It is to be "hidden with Christ in God" (Colossians 3:3). Security is grounded within you. Notice what happens when you ground your fear default in the God who holds you. What changes happen? What risk-taking parts of you open up inside?

SEVENS STOP

> Folks are usually about as happy as they
> make their minds up to be.
> **ABRAHAM LINCOLN**

When Sevens notice you are constricting around future options, fun, and escape strategies, you need a practice to help you stay present to what is happening right now—especially if what is happening now is unpleasant and painful. STOP opens spacey Sevens to your Four EQ with its ability to hold pain and dive deep into life. STOP also grounds Sevens in your One GQ sense of responsibility. STOP opens Sevens to the whole of life so you really don't miss it.

See

What is happening that makes me feel trapped? Avoidant? Indulgent? Bored?

Triggers

How much longer? I want out! This is depressing.

Open

Head: How can I think about being here? What will my presence bring?

Heart: What could happen to me if I would feel their pain with them? How can I experience relationships deeply and authentically?

Gut: Where do I need objectivity and stability? What good am I missing because I lack discipline?

Presence

Being present to the presence of God, others, and self is a practice that can actually lead Sevens into deep joy. Joy goes deep. Joy is big enough to hold sorrow and still be full rather than empty: "You believe in him (Christ) and are filled with an inexpressible and glorious joy" (1 Peter 1:8). Notice how presence frees you to experience more of God and more of life.

SOLITUDE AND SILENCE

*Nurture the IQ, EQ, and GQ
of the True Self*

*When he opened the seventh seal, there was
silence in heaven for about half an hour.*

REVELATION 8:1

SILENCE AND SOLITUDE create space to intentionally remember who you are, receive who God is, and contemplate what really matters in life.

The spiritual practices of silence and solitude serve a different purpose than "time and space for me." Silence and solitude create a space where voices that prop up the false self persona go mute. Alone and in quiet, the mirror of responses ceases. With no one to impress and nothing to prove, there is room for truth—room to be present to God and God's voice alone.

Enneagram types respond to silence and solitude differently. Here are reactions we have heard. Notice which comments resonate as true for you.

EIGHTS

▶ "Silence and solitude are a battle. But I practice ten minutes of silence every day whether I want to or not."

▶ "I don't get what I am waiting for in silence and solitude. I don't like to wait."

▶ "Silence and solitude have helped me monitor my anger and false self energy."

NINES

▶ "Silence and solitude feel comfortable, but they can fuel my disappearing act."

▶ "I don't like to be the focus of things. Silence and solitude is a reprieve."

▶ "It is important for me to differentiate between silence and solitude and sloth."

ONES

▶ "Silence and solitude are another place to fail. They don't seem to make anything better."

▶ "What if I do silence and solitude wrong? What if nothing happens?"

▶ "Silence seems punitive to me."

▶ "In silence, my inner critic goes wild."

TWOS

▶ "This is too difficult and uncomfortable!"

▶ "I don't help anyone by being quiet and alone."

▶ "I had to be silent as a child and I don't like it."

    ▶ "Talking helps me more than silence."

THREES

    ▶ "This isn't productive or a good use of my time. It makes me feel guilty."

    ▶ "If I do silence and solitude, people will think I'm lazy and wonder what's up."

    ▶ "Retirement introduced me to the goodness of silence and solitude. Too bad it took me so long to like it."

FOURS

    ▶ "Something is missing in my relationship with God; maybe silence and solitude will give me the experience I seek."

    ▶ "I hope practicing silence and solitude will make me wiser, deeper, and more extraordinary."

    ▶ "Silence and solitude keep me from the dark side."

    ▶ "Silence and solitude take me to the dark side."

FIVES

    ▶ "When I grew up, banishment from others was my punishment."

    ▶ "I can't get enough of silence and solitude. It's the safest place in the world."

    ▶ "Sometimes solitude makes me lonely. I have to intentionally turn my heart to listen to God rather than my thoughts."

SIXES

    ▶ "In silence my mind is flooded with decisions, plans, agendas, security issues, and questions. It doesn't feel restful to me."

▶ "When I'm nervous, I go silent—does that count as silence?"

▶ "Silence and solitude in a place of my choosing is one of the safest places on earth."

▶ "I find God in silence."

SEVENS

    ▶ "Silence and solitude are *boring*."

    ▶ "I can't concentrate when I am silent and alone."

    ▶ "Silence and solitude make me think about doing other things. It's hard for me to be present there."

EXPLORING YOUR RESPONSES TO SILENCE AND SOLITUDE

We live, in fact, in a world starved for solitude, silence, and privacy, and therefore starved for meditation and true friendship.

C. S. LEWIS

1. As a child, what was your experience of silence and solitude? Consider a situation where you were subjected to silence and solitude; where was God in that experience? Where was God not in the experience? Ask God to heal you and help you let go of anything that keeps you from embracing silence and solitude. Ask God, "What can we do about this together?"

2. Talk to God about what it is like for you to practice solitude and silence today, how you try to avoid silence and solitude, and where you feel your attempts to find time alone get sabotaged. Listen. How does God respond to what you have said? Is there more that you want to say to God about this?

3. Tell God what happens inside of you when you are free from the weight of noise, distractions, people, projects, and technology. You might want to pray: "O God of silence and words, how can I make space for you beyond the noise?"

4. Get in touch with your desire for silence and solitude. Have a conversation with God and a friend about where you can go to experience your desire to be with God and God's desire to be with you.

5. Have a conversation with God about which center is hardest for you to bring into the quiet: Head? Heart? Gut? Is the place that is hardest an undernourished center of intelligence? Is it your dismissed childlike self? Listen. How is God inviting you into new ways of being alone and quiet in presence?

SILENCE AND SOLITUDE MEDITATION

We need to find God, and he cannot be found in noise and restlessness. God is the friend of silence. See how nature—trees, flowers, grass—grows in silence; see the stars, the moon, and the sun, how they move in silence. . . . We need silence to be able to touch souls.

MOTHER TERESA

Jesus of Nazareth's ministry began with forty days of fasting in silence and solitude in the desert. At the end of that time, he faced three temptations to power up and take things into his own hands. Notice the temptations to the false self: to secure his survival (IQ), impress the crowds (EQ), and take the easy path to power and control (GQ).

Then Jesus was led by the Spirit into the wilderness to be tempted by the devil.

After fasting forty days and forty nights, he was hungry. The tempter came to him and said, "If you are the Son of God, tell these stones to become bread."

Jesus answered, "It is written: 'Man shall not live on bread alone, but on every word that comes from the mouth of God.'"

Then the devil took him to the holy city and had him stand on the highest point of the temple. "If you are the Son of God," he said, "throw yourself down. For it is written:

"'He will command his angels
        concerning you,
and they will lift you up in their hands,
so that you will not strike your foot
        against a stone.'"

Jesus answered him, "It is also written: 'Do not put the Lord your God to the test.'"

Again, the devil took him to a very high mountain and showed him all the kingdoms of the world and their splendor. "All this I will give you," he said, "if you will bow down and worship me."

Jesus said to him, "Away from me, Satan! For it is written: 'Worship the Lord your God, and serve him only.'"

Then the devil left him, and angels came and attended him. (Matthew 4:1-11)

1. What sort of discussion do you want to have with Jesus about his temptations and the temptations that confront you in silence and solitude?

2. What does it mean that he refuses to do things in his false self?

3. How might silence and solitude make you less susceptible to the temptation for security and survival? To impress and get approval? To power up and take control?

Soul Resource 3

RETURNING PRAYER FOR HARMONY

GOD, *the Master, The Holy of Israel,*
has this solemn counsel:
"Your salvation requires you to turn back to me
and stop your silly efforts to save yourselves.
Your strength will come from settling down
in complete dependence on me—
The very thing you've been unwilling to do."

ISAIAH 30:15 *THE MESSAGE*

RETURNING PRAYER is a way of coming back home to God and ourselves. We leave the "far country" and our false self efforts and return to who God made us to be. Returning prayer begins with returning to body awareness. We remember that we are inhabited by the Spirit of God. As we become present in our bodies, we can breathe into our hearts so they open up and return to a place of listening to God.

Returning prayer is found in Psalm 131:1-2 (NRSV):

> O LORD, my heart is not lifted up,
>   my eyes are not raised too high;
> I do not occupy myself with things
>   too great and too marvelous for me.
> But I have calmed and quieted my soul,
>   like a weaned child with its mother;
> my soul is like the weaned child that
>   is with me.

This quiet meditative prayer leads the psalmist into a trusting, open place. Like an active weaned child, he returns home to God, the mother, in whose arms he is protected and freely beloved. Being with God's motherly presence, there is no need for words. Being held by God calms, soothes, and harmonizes. That is enough until he runs off again to play.

Returning to God with quiet and prayerful meditation can develop, strengthen, and expand neural circuits. You don't have to be saying or doing something for the Spirit to work within. When you practice returning prayer at the day's end, look back and see where in stress you let God hold you and calm your EQ, IQ, and GQ so you could act in your true self.

FIVE TO TWENTY MINUTE PRACTICE

1. Return to God by leaving what you are doing for five to twenty minutes. You may

want to set a timer so you can relax into God and let the quiet overtake you. Think of a word or name of God that invites you to return to presence; for example: Father, Jesus, Holy Spirit, Mother, Truth, Keeper, Protector, Friend, Healer, Mighty God, Comforter, Savior, or Shepherd. Let that word or name act as a handle or placeholder. Sometimes the word or image you need is one you have least access to. Listen to your dismissed child. Does that child want you to use a particular word for God?

2. Get comfortable. Move your head in circles to release your neck and close your eyes. Sit with the name or image for God. Rest within. Sit and wait.

3. When thoughts or distractions interrupt you, gently return to God with your word. Return again and again. Continue to be with God. As you do this, you create new neural pathways that help you enter into being with God more easily. When your time of being with God is over, rest in silence with your eyes closed for a few minutes.

4. Close with this returning prayer: "In returning and rest you shall be saved; / in quietness and in trust shall be your strength" (Isaiah 30:15 NRSV).

REFLECTION

1. What was returning prayer like for you?

2. How do your head, heart, and gut respond to the notion that God is present and changing you as you return and lean into being with God?

3. What is it like to let go of wordy prayers?

4. Where did you sense harmony during this prayer?

MINDFUL BODY HARMONY

*Do you not know that your bodies are temples of
the Holy Spirit, who is in you, whom you have received from God?*

1 CORINTHIANS 6:19

MINDFUL BODY PRAYERS transform you as you receive harmony in your created body. Bodies don't lie. They tell all. Your soul's current address is your earthly body. Connecting your body to your mind in prayer opens this moment to integrating IQ, EQ, and GQ.

In the Christian tradition, God is in solidarity with people. In fact, God comes with skin on, in the person of Jesus. Jesus let go of divine prerogatives. He experienced vulnerability, stress, exhaustion, thirst, and tears in his body. He was bruised, violated, tortured, and pinned naked to a cross. Jesus' hands touched people's bodies with compassion. At the communion table, Jesus says, "This is my body given for you" (Luke 22:19). Even now, Jesus chooses to be incarnated in your body! When you go into places of strength and weakness, vigor and depletion, or life and death, the presence of Jesus Christ is in you.

In his book *Anatomy of the Soul,* Christian psychiatrist Curt Thompson explains how practicing a simple body scan can increase GQ, IQ, and EQ connectedness: "Neuroscience research confirms that mindful, meditative exercises that stretch and challenge the attentional mechanism of your brain enhance the integration of the prefrontal cortex."

MINDFUL HARMONY PRACTICE

Breathing is one of the fundamental practices of the body. You can't live without breathing. It is no different with your soul. You can't live on one breath of God either. God is the oxygen of your soul. Connecting body breath to God is a spiritual practice.

A 2016 study revealed a neural circuit in the brainstem that seems to play the key role in the breathing-brain control connection. The circuit is part of what's been called the brain's "breathing pacemaker" because it can be adjusted by altering breathing rhythm (slow, controlled breathing decreases activity in the circuit; fast, erratic breathing increases activity), which in turn influences emotional states. "Take a deep breath" is solid advice; research suggests that slowing your breathing can help regulate blood pressure via your heart rate. The study evaluated the "Relaxation Response," which refers to a method of engaging the parasympathetic nervous system to counteract the nervous system's "fight or flight" response to stress.

Go ahead and practice your breathing.

1. Find a comfortable position, one that keeps you open and relaxed. Breathe deeply; receive your breath as a gift of God. Breathe in the goodness of your breath.

2. Become aware that you breathe the breath of God by the will of God. Feel the strength of your breath, the dependence of your breath, God's gift, God's miracle of your breath. Take time to stay with your breath.

3. Breathe in the words from Psalm 139:14-15:

I praise you because I am fearfully and
     wonderfully made;
   your works are wonderful,
   I know that full well.

My frame was not hidden from you
     when I was made in the secret place,
   when I was woven together in the
     depths of the earth.

BODY SCAN AND GQ WISDOM

1. Become aware of the crown of your head; feel it, sense it, don't think about it, be aware of it, feel it. Continue bringing this attentive awareness to every part of your body. Sense your forehead, your eyes, nose, mouth, jaw, and neck. Don't hurry. Continue down to the soles of your feet, body part by body part. When you reach the soles of your feet, move slowly back up again in the same way.

2. Sense the goodness of your body's strength. Be gentle with your body's weakness. Anytime you get distracted, return gently to where you fell away from body presence.

3. Consider what part of your body you are grateful for. Lay your hand on that part of your body. (Or lay your hands on it in your mind.) Thank God for the gift of that part. Feel your gratitude for this part of your body. Say thank you for its faithful service to you. Stay with that gratitude, allowing the memories of the good things this part of your body has done for you. Breathe in that gratitude. Stay for a minute.

4. Now notice where your body feels under stress, overworked, burdened, sad, and desolate. Imagine that Jesus comes and asks your body to tell him the truth about what's been going on. Look at Jesus and ask him for grace to hear the truth from your body. How does your body answer? What does your body say about your life right now or about past pain? Imagine Jesus' healing power coming to that part of your body through his words or loving touch.

5. Notice if there is a part of your body/temple that has been ignored. Stuck in old patterns? Addicted to destructive behaviors? Overworked and under rested? Express your desire to honor your body and give it what it needs. What does Jesus say to you about how to care for this part of your body? Ask Jesus for grace to live with respect and joy in your body.

HEART CONNECTION AND EQ

We often think the head rather than the heart knows. We know God loves us, but we don't feel it. We know friends care, but our hearts can't seem to take in their love. Since 1991 the HeartMath Institute (www.heartmath.org) has been researching and developing reliable, scientifically based tools to help people bridge the connection between their head and heart. We have adapted their pattern for connecting head and heart.

1. Focus your attention on your heart and breathe a little deeper than normal; in for five or six seconds and out five or six seconds.

2. *Heart breathing:* Imagine breathing through your chest. Picture yourself slowly breathing in and out through your heart area. Expand and open your heart with each breath.

3. *Heart feeling:* Remember a time or a person who made you feel happiness, goodness, joy, appreciation, or love. Maintain your heart focus and continue breathing. Reconnect with this experience; breathe it in. How do you feel? Do you notice more space around your heart or a greater sense of ease, well-being, and openness? Stay with your feeling for a few minutes.

4. Breathe in gratitude for this person or event. Breathe out praise to God. Take a walk with God and gratitude. Let openness to that person deepen.

Mindful body prayer is a way the Spirit works to help you put off old destructive reactions and put on new healthy responses. Your body and brain were actually designed by God to help you transform. Default neural pathways and destructive habits can change. Dr. Thomas put it like this: "Neuroplasticity is the brain's ability to create new neurons, make new neural connections, and prune those it no longer needs. The neuroplasticity Triad of aerobic activity, focused attention exercises, and novel learning experiences all play vital roles in increasing the brain's level of malleability."

How wonderful that the God who breathed life into us from the beginning continues to breathe life into us today. Breathe in God's life; it can renew your mind and heal your heart.

EXAMEN AND HARMONY

Search me, God, and know my heart [EQ];
test me and know my anxious thoughts [IQ].
See if there is any offensive way in me [GQ],
and lead me in the way everlasting.

PSALM 139:23-24 (WITH OUR ADDITIONS)

IGNATIUS OF LOYOLA developed the spiritual practice of the examen as a way to help members of the Society of Jesus receive God's love and discern God's call and direction. The examen opens and awakens you to the Spirit's movement and motions of your soul. It opens you to God, your three intelligences (head, heart, and gut), and the truth they reveal.

Still, some of us have resistance to any kind of practice that has the word *exam* in it. We have had "examinations" before and came out wanting. Do any of the reactions below resonate with you or your number?

Eights: "I already know how to be hard on myself and kick my can down the road. I don't need more introspection when there is so much to do."

Nines: "The examen sounds intense. I'm fine."

Ones: "I live with an internal loudspeaker of judgment. The word *examen* just sets me up to fail."

Twos: "I like focusing on others. Can I do the examen with others?"

Threes: "I don't have much time. How long will the examen take?"

Fours: "Will the examen take me deeper into my own darkness? Too much dark, and I can't find the light."

Fives: "Where can I read about the examen?"

Sixes: "Where do I find the examen in the Bible? How will it help me discern?"

Sevens: "The word *examen* makes me think, 'It's time to take your medicine.'"

The examen is actually a gift that helps you see you and God at the same time. It is the gift of God's loving eye on you and his presence with you. The examen intentionally calls you to awareness of how God's Spirit moves in and through your experiences and your body, mind, and heart to reveal motivations and desires and give direction. This can take time. Your heart may feel something before your head thinks it. Your gut may sense God moving but not know how to articulate it. Paying attention to the Spirit's motion in your head, heart, and gut can bring discernment about your desires and the things that give your life.

The psalmist writes, "Take delight in the LORD, / and he will give you the desires of your heart" (Psalm 37:4). God has put deep desires in your heart. It is up to you to see and name those desires. Your God-given desires inform your purpose, call, and daily choices. They shape where you go, who you meet, and what you do. God-given desires fit who you are and bring you energy and life. Spiritual discernment requires attention to what gives you life. Frederick Buechner writes, "The place God calls you to is where your deep gladness and the world's deep hunger meet."

The examen reviews your experiences and interactions in the presence and light of God. It is a way to replay your day or week and notice how you were with God and others. The examen helps you:

▶ See where your true self IQ, EQ, and GQ showed up, and where you missed it.

▶ Pay attention to consolations that lead you toward God. You notice consolations by asking, "Where today did I experience places of deep gladness, love, joy, peace, patience, kindness, goodness, faithfulness, gentleness, self-control, or life?"

▶ Recognize desolations. Desolations can drain life away. They are places of human frailty, resistance, sorrow, and addiction to self. Desolation often accompanies the bully of shame and lies of the evil one such as, "You are not enough," or "You are bad." You can notice desolations by asking, "Where today did I experience fear, anger, pride, gluttony, addiction, or deceit?" Desolations don't always lead you away from God. They can lead you back to God as well.

You often first experience consolations and desolations in your gut brain or heart brain. The neurons in your body and heart start sending information to your brain. You may recognize this information as colds sweats, hot flashes, hair-raising fear, a lump in your throat, clenched fists, tears, a stiff neck, heart break, heart joy, a queasy gut, headaches, elation, or illnesses with no preceding cause. These body and heart signals can be God's way of starting a conversation that looks beneath the surface of your tasks and transactions to what is really affecting and guiding your life. What fears and blocks do the desolations reveal? What joys, desires, and aptitudes do the consolations reveal?

Naming your consolations and desolations in the presence of God's unconditional love is safe. God isn't waiting with a lightning bolt in his hand to zap you. God's love is strong enough to hold the whole truth of you. In fact, God never stops seeing you as a very good creation. Lean in. Let the cues of consolation and desolation in your body and heart bring you divine wisdom.

EXAMEN SACRED READING

The psalm writer examines his desolations and finds a way through to consolations, God, and freedom.

> While I kept silence, my body wasted
> away
>   through my groaning [desolation] all
>   day long.
> For day and night your hand was heavy
>   upon me;
>   my strength was dried up as by the
>   heat of summer.
> Then I acknowledged my sin to you,
>   and I did not hide my iniquity;
> I said, "I will confess my transgressions
>   to the LORD,"
>   and you forgave the guilt of my sin.
> Therefore let all who are faithful
>   offer prayer to you;

at a time of distress, the rush of mighty
    waters
  shall not reach them.
You are a hiding place for me;
  you preserve me from trouble;
  you surround me with glad cries of
    deliverance.
I will instruct you and teach you the way
    you should go;
  I will counsel you with my eye
    [consolation] upon you. . . .
  Steadfast love surrounds those who
    trust in the LORD.
Be glad in the LORD and rejoice
    [consolation], O righteous,
  and shout for joy, all you upright in
    heart. (Psalm 32:3-11 NRSV, with
    our additions)

1. When has repressing or denying the truth about yourself brought desolation? What did that desolation feel like?

2. When has confessing the truth about you brought freedom and a sense of reconnection to God and others?

3. How does the image of God in this psalm ground the songwriter in truth about God and self?

4. What is it like to have God for a hiding place?

5. What else stands out to you in this psalm?

EXAMEN PRACTICE

> O God, gather me
>   to be with you
>   as you are with me.
> **TED LODER,** *GUERRILLAS OF GRACE*

1. Tell God you long to know the whole truth of your beloved-ness. Ask for grace to name

and see what is going on inside you. Thank God that he is already with you.

2. Gently name a desolation, a place you feel the absence of your true self or the absence of God or the absence of God's pleasure. Take time to notice where your heart or body constrict. Listen. What do your EQ and IQ tell you?

3. Confess without judgment: "Today I fell into my false self and constricted when I [fill in the blank]. Forgive me and make me new." If you sense the absence of God, put yourself in solidarity with Jesus on the cross. Pray: "Jesus, you know forsakenness. I am one with you in my forsakenness."

4. Gently name a consolation, a place you feel the presence of God and your true self. What are you grateful for? What are you grateful for about yourself? What do you love the most? Receive and enjoy your consolations. Where do you sense God's pleasure? What do you want to say to God about this? Where did EQ and GQ give you guidance and wisdom today? Thank God for your body and gut intelligence.

5. Keep track of your desolations and consolations over the next month. What keeps showing up? How do your desolations and consolations help you name God-given desires and how you were made for God's glory?

AN EXAMEN FOR BEDTIME OR THE END OF THE WEEK

> In repentance and rest is your salvation,
> in quietness and trust is your strength.
> **ISAIAH 30:15**

Don't allow the bully of shame to lead your nightly examen. Answering these questions in the presence of God can give you eyes to see patterns of deep gladness and deep distress. Let what your life is saying to you open a discussion God wants to have. Say, "Oh God, let me abide with you as you already abide with me."

1. Ask to be with God as God is with you.

2. Gently name desolations: What was your low? Where did your false self show up? How did you ignore what your heart (EQ) or body (GQ) brain tried to tell you? What was life draining (lack of connection, envy, anger, fear, or addictions)? When did your joy lose traction? What interactions had the opposite of the Good Spirit's fruit?

3. Confess without judgment: "Today, I fell into my false self and constricted when I [fill in the blank]. Forgive me and make me new."

4. Gently name your consolations: What was your high today (this week)? When were you in your true self? When did you listen to what your heart (EQ) or body (GQ) brain told you? What was life giving, and what gave you deep gladness? Where did you experience the fruit of the Spirit?

5. Looking deeply into your consolations and gladness is important, but it can be confusing. Did you want to be an entrepreneur or end up in management? Look deeper. What is your desire to start things about? Is there an invitation to join someone who is starting something? Listen to God around your desire. Suppose that children give you life and you never had any. Look deeper still. Ask God how your gladness can be unleashed in a way you haven't yet imagined. There is no plan B for anyone. The Holy One is not stumped by where you are now. Start listening, noticing, and paying attention to what gives you life. Respect your heart brain and body brain and all that they try to tell you.

6. Pray: "Today I found life, light, and joy in [fill in the blank]. Ground me in gratitude."

Soul Resource 6

WELCOMING PRAYER

A Path to Harmony

> *"Abba, Father," he [Jesus] said,*
> *"everything is possible for you. Take this cup*
> *from me. Yet not what I will, but what you will."*
>
> **MARK 14:36**

WELCOMING PRAYER is a portable prayer that turns the ordinary activities of daily life into your spiritual practice. It is a way to welcome God into unbearably hard places, delightful places, and boring places. The prayer always involves a little "death" to your need to control reality. This death and detachment from control allows you to receive reality as it is and find God in what is.

Welcoming prayer pulls you out of your default reactions and reveals where you need the Spirit to reclaim your true self right now. It is a living path that connects each triad to God. God created us for connection. Our need for affection and approval from others (Heart Triad energy), security and survival in life and relationships (Head Triad energy), and control or agency in decisions and life (Gut Triad energy) is hardwired into your DNA. Without the connection that comes from affection, you fail to thrive. Without the security that builds trusting relationships, you resort to fight or flight. Without agency to make free choices, you live someone else's reality. Affection, security, and control matter!

However, anyone's need for affection, security, and control can become inordinate and insatiable. When we feel we don't have enough approval, safety, and agency, our behaviors and motivations become reactionary, impulsive, and compulsive. We try to coax, coerce, and cajole reality and the people in it into being what we want and need. This is the moment we need a prayer to help us dismantle our false self energy. We need a prayer that puts us in the presence of God for transformation—*under* the circumstances.

Paul writes in Romans 12:2, "Do not conform to the pattern of this world, but be transformed by the renewing of your mind. Then you will be able to test and approve what God's will is—his good, pleasing and perfect will." Disordered compulsions are the pattern of this world. Welcoming prayer renews the mind by letting go of disordered compulsions and staying in the moment with Jesus. Welcoming prayer takes us into the worst or best of experiences and offers Jesus our need for security, affection, and agency. Letting go opens us to other possibilities.

FOUR MOVEMENTS OF WELCOMING PRAYER

▶ I let go of my desire for security and survival. Welcome, Jesus, welcome.

▶ I let go of my need for approval and affection. Welcome, Jesus, welcome.

▶ I let go of my desire for control and power. Welcome, Jesus, welcome.

▶ I let go of my desire to change this reality. Welcome, Jesus, welcome.

PRAYING GUT RESPONSES

Bodies speak.

1. Notice when your muscles tighten, when your head throbs, when your stomach drops, when your face flushes, or when you walk into a room and your heart stops. Bring your full attention; go to that place. Focus on what you are experiencing. Open to it and welcome God into it.

2. Without judgment, look more deeply at your body's response. Notice if your reaction is about anger, resentment, control, or the need to change reality.

3. In the presence of God, open to whatever it is you sense your body telling you. Don't force anything. When you can name what your body is saying, gently let go and say, "I release my need to have power and control. Welcome, Jesus, welcome." These words are a small death to your agenda and your way. Don't underestimate the power of this dying process. It is what the Holy Spirit uses to transform you.

PRAYING HEART RESPONSES

Hearts speak.

1. Notice how you feel when your connection to others breaks. Feel how your heart aches, breaks, and palpitates. If the lack of approval or affection is bringing you anxiety or shame, it's time to focus, welcome, and let go.

2. Breathe deeply, slowly, and rhythmically. Let your abdomen rise and fall. This will open a space in your distress for God.

3. Visualize the person(s) that distresses you. How are you wanting them to respond to you? Express the emotions you are feeling in the presence of Christ. Commit the person to God's care.

4. Release your anxiety, shame, and distress at being disconnected with these words: "I let go of my need for affection and approval. Welcome, Jesus, welcome. I consent to your work in me!"

5. If you have time to stay with the prayer, you might imagine Jesus welcoming you and speaking his approval and love over you.

PRAYING HEAD RESPONSES

Thoughts speak.

1. Welcoming prayer can't happen in theory or with something that isn't real for you now. Consider where you can't turn off your thoughts or are stuck in analysis paralysis. Where are you perseverating and engaging in catastrophic thinking? Where are you stuck in stinking thinking and dark, bitter thoughts that won't let go? Welcome Jesus into your thoughts.

2. Notice where your mental activity centers on fear and issues of safety and security. Welcome what comes up.

3. Slow down your breathing and let it relax your body. A relaxed body makes it easier to put your mind at ease. It also sends a signal to fearful thoughts that things may turn out different than you imagine.

4. Gently say, "I let go of my need to be safe and secure. Welcome, Jesus, welcome. Come order my thoughts with your truth. Welcome."

PRAYING TO RECEIVE REALITY AS IT IS

We can only find God in what is—not in what is not. The last movement of the welcoming prayer surrenders to God and reality. The prayer is, "I let go of my need to change reality, and I receive reality as it is right now. Welcome, Jesus, welcome."

When we are resistant to what is happening in the moment, we try to force it to become something else. Welcoming prayer works with our resistances as well as with the anger, shame, anxiety, and fear that surfaces throughout the day. If you are resisting letting go, pray, "Welcome into my resistance. Welcome, Jesus, come set me free."

Welcoming prayer dismantles autopilot triggers. Welcoming prayer interrupts instinctive false self responses and opens a space for being with Jesus and what is in the moment.

IMAGINATIVE PRAYER

Nurture Head Intelligence (IQ)

*So if the Son sets you free,
you will be free indeed.*

JOHN 8:36

IMAGINATIVE PRAYER is a way to find yourself in God's sacred story. It is a way to enter the presence of God through your imagination. Some of us were taught that imagination cannot be trusted—in fact, it should be distrusted because it can lead you astray. We may also have learned that emotions are to be distrusted as they are irrelevant to truth. Facts and right belief are what matter and give one maturity. Cognitive understanding is important, but if it is all we have, we are woefully at sea with what it means to be human.

Scripture gives ample evidence that knowing God is not just an exercise in left-brain thinking. Strange and unusual experiences of God fill the pages of the Bible. These experiences don't always come with a "this means that" attached to them. People are left to make meaning out of experiences, images, and encounters. This is risky. Still, God seems quite comfortable with this risk. Consider how the following people made meaning from experiences that weren't just a compilation of facts.

- Abraham had an angel stay his hand.
- Jacob wrestled with an angel of God.
- Moses saw a burning bush, stood on holy ground, and saw the back of God.
- Balaam heard God speak through the voice of a donkey.
- Samson felt God's strength.
- Elijah saw God drop fire from heaven and heard God whisper.
- Isaiah saw God high and lifted up, and his train filled the temple.
- Ezekiel saw the Glory depart from the temple.
- Daniel had dreams.
- Mary talked with an angel.
- Joseph had dreams.
- The Magi had dreams.
- Peter, James, and John saw Moses and Elijah when Jesus was transfigured.
- Paul was caught up to the seventh heaven.
- John saw heaven opened.

Imaginative prayer is a way to enter God's story by using your three intelligences in imaginative ways. During sacred reading, notice what is happening in your:

Head: How do you imagine the scene? Observe the sights, sounds, tastes, smells, and interactions happening around you.

Gut: Do you have an instinctive response to people or the situation?

Heart: Do you have an emotional response to people or the situation?

What do you see about yourself in this situation? How do you want to respond to God in prayer? The sacred story becomes a point of departure for prayer. You may even sense that God is setting the agenda for your prayer through the reading.

IMAGINATIVE PRAYER PRACTICE

Luke describes Mary's openness to a strange and unusual experience and how it holds God's call within it. Ask God to help you pray your experience of this story. Imagine you are in the room with Mary. Be watchful and savor the encounter. Be alert to attachments Mary has to release.

> In the sixth month of Elizabeth's pregnancy, God sent the angel Gabriel to Nazareth, a town in Galilee, to a virgin pledged to be married to a man named Joseph, a descendant of David. The virgin's name was Mary. The angel went to her and said, "Greetings, you who are highly favored! The Lord is with you."
>
> Mary was greatly troubled at his words and wondered what kind of greeting this might be. But the angel said to her, "Do not be afraid, Mary; you have found favor with God. You will conceive and give birth to a son, and you are to call him Jesus. He will be great and will be called the Son of the Most High. The Lord God will give

him the throne of his father David, and he will reign over Jacob's descendants forever; his kingdom will never end."

> "How will this be," Mary asked the angel, "since I am a virgin?"
>
> The angel answered, "The Holy Spirit will come on you, and the power of the Most High will overshadow you. So the holy one to be born will be called the Son of God. Even Elizabeth your relative is going to have a child in her old age, and she who was said to be unable to conceive is in her sixth month. For no word from God will ever fail."
>
> "I am the Lord's servant," Mary answered. "May your word to me be fulfilled." Then the angel left her. (Luke 1:26-38)

1. How does your head IQ imagine this scene? What stood out to you? What do you want to say to God about what stood out to you?

2. What attachments did Mary need to release to give a full yes to God? What do you want to say to God about your attachments?

3. What was happening in your body GQ? Did you have any instinctual responses? What do you want to say to God about your gut response to this story?

4. What did you feel as you watched the scene unfold? What was your heart EQ telling you? Where did you feel consolations such as warmth, presence, faith, hope, or love? Where did you sense desolations such as fear, absence, or disordered attachments? What do you want to say to God about your consolations and desolations?

5. Is God giving you an invitation in this story?

PRACTICING THE PRESENCE OF GOD

You have seen many things, but you pay no attention; your ears are open, but you do not listen.

ISAIAH 42:20

PRACTICING THE PRESENCE of God, self, or someone else means honoring them with the full attention of your head, heart, and gut. Presence gives you eyes to see and ears to hear more than you already know.

Hurry makes presence difficult. When our bodies, minds, and hearts speed toward what's next, we aren't present to *now*. It takes presence to give what is true and best about us. The Harmony Enneagram reveals how pushing our energy also pushes us to edginess. Literally, going with default reactions moves us to the edge of the circle and lands us in our vice and false self energy. It is presence to God and others that returns us to the center where virtues and giftedness restore harmony.

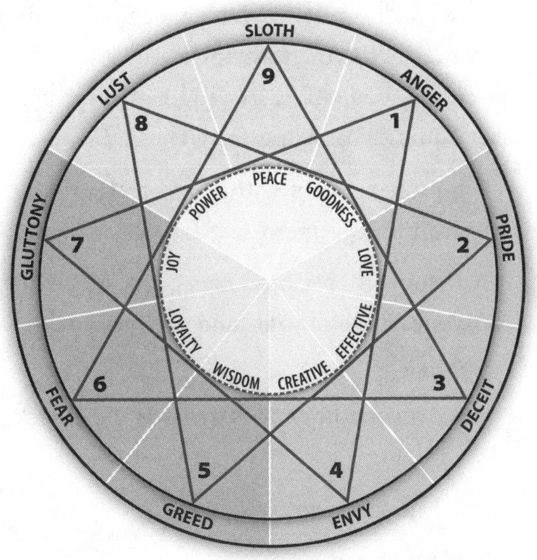

Figure 11. Harmony Enneagram: Being pushed to our edges

EDGINESS OF EACH NUMBER

The alliteration below may help you remember what leaving presence and landing on your edge looks like for your number.

Eights: Powering up and prosecuting hinder presence

Nines: Powering down and procrastinating hinder presence

Ones: Punitiveness and perfectionism hinders presence

Twos: People-pleasing and possessiveness hinder presence

Threes: Performance and pragmatism hinder presence

Fours: Personalizing and posing hinder presence

Fives: Pontificating and privacy hinder presence

Sixes: Paranoia and paralysis hinder presence

Sevens: Playing and preoccupation hinder presence

Moving back to presence happens with intention, awareness, and prayer. Thomas Keating puts it like this: "Consent to God's presence and action within."

INDIVIDUAL OR GUIDED PRACTICE WITH A SPIRITUAL DIRECTOR, COACH, OR THERAPIST

Posture

Posture affects presence. Experiment with postures that help you stay open and awake in prayer and meditation. Try some of these postures. Notice what works for you.

▸ Sit on a chair with your feet on the ground, legs uncrossed, and back straight.

▸ If you have back problems, try lying with your back on the ground with your calves on a chair.

▸ Sit on the floor, legs crossed, and back straight.

▸ Stand with arms raised.

▸ Lie prostrate.

▸ Walk.

Breath

Because breath is automatic, we don't think about it until we are out of breath. Breathing with intention brings awareness of your body and helps put you in the present. Once you find your comfortable posture, breathe in: "God, you are here," and breathe out: "I am here." Or breathe in: "Good Spirit, help me notice," and breathe out: "without judgment." Settle into the presence of God and yourself before you answer the questions that follow.

Presence

The following questions are designed to help you identify where you lose presence. Read all the questions for your number(s) before you respond. (If you are doing this with a spiritual friend or spiritual director, they can read you the questions.)

GUT CENTER (GQ): EIGHTS, NINES, AND ONES

Listen to where these traits and your own particular defense mechanism show up in your story:

▸ **Core motivation:** power and control

▸ **Negative fixation:** anger and guilt

▸ **Narrative:** "I've had enough" or "I haven't done enough"

Eights Defense Mechanism: Denial. This is the refusal to accept reality. Denial pretends that pain, weakness, and feelings don't exist. In the presence of God, notice without judgment:

▸ When do you react without thinking?

▸ In the heat of the moment, how do you ignore tenderness and vulnerability? When have power and control dismissed cool-headed and warm-hearted responses?

▸ How does anger show up and dismiss everything and everyone with, "I've had enough"? When does guilt show up saying, "I haven't done enough"?

▸ How do anger and control affect your body? What is your earliest memory of these feelings? What insight does this give you?

▸ Where do you want the Spirit to help you stay centered and present in your life today?

Nines Defense Mechanism: Narcotization. This means using food, drink, entertainment, or repetitive patterns of thinking and doing to "put oneself to sleep." In the presence of God, notice without judgment:

▶ When have you done what someone else wanted without paying attention to your desire? When do you set aside real priorities for something/someone else?

▶ When has stubbornness kept you stuck?

▶ What are you angry about? Where does passive-aggressive anger say, "I've had enough"? When has guilt shown up saying, "I haven't done enough"?

▶ How does your body respond to discomfort, stress, or conflict? What is your earliest memory of this feeling? What might that tell you?

▶ Where do you want to ask for the Spirit's help to stay centered and present in your life today?

Ones Defense Mechanism: Reaction formation. This is feeling one thing and expressing the opposite to control emotion. In the presence of God, notice without judgment:

▶ When have you judged what is right and wrong, who is good and bad?

▶ How do you scold and compare yourself to high standards?

▶ Where does anger show up saying, "I've had enough"? When has guilt shown up saying, "I haven't done this right enough"?

▶ What is your inner critic saying to you today? What happens in your body as you answer these questions? What is your earliest memory of feeling anger and guilt? What might that tell you?

▶ Where do you want to ask for the Spirit's help to stay centered and present in your life today?

HEART CENTER (EQ): TWOS, THREES, AND FOURS

▶ ***Core motivation:*** approval and affection

▶ ***Negative fixation:*** shame and anxiety about humiliation and disconnection

▶ ***Narrative:*** "I am not enough" or "I must prove my worth"

Twos Defense Mechanism: Repression. This is suppressing "unacceptable" feelings and needs and converting them into other oriented energy. In the presence of God, notice without judgment:

▶ How does your "I am indispensable" narrative show up? When do you use flattery and give to get attention? How do you respond when people don't respond to your care?

▶ Where does shame show up and say, "I am not enough"? Where are you over-serving to prove "I am enough"?

▶ What do you need now? Who do you need to support you? What would it be like for you to tell them you need their support?

▶ What happens in your body as you answer these questions? What is your earliest memory of this feeling of suppressing your feelings and needs? What might that tell you?

▶ Where do you want to ask for the Spirit's help to stay centered and present in your life today?

Threes Defense Mechanism: Identification. This is taking on a role so completely that you lose contact with who you really are. In the presence of God, notice without judgment:

- How do you live in a "fake it to make it" mode? Where are you managing your image? How have you lost yourself in a role, task, or a job? When do you feel like a human *doing* rather than a human *being*?

- Where are you being deceitful?

- What are you feeling right now? Where are you aware of shame and humiliation? Where do shame and guilt show up and say, "I am not enough"? How are you working to prove, "I am enough"?

- What happens in your body as you answer the questions? What is your earliest memory of trying to prove who you are? What might that tell you?

- Where do you want to ask for the Spirit's help to stay centered and present in your life today?

Fours Defense Mechanism: Introjection. This is unconsciously incorporating the characteristics of a person or object into one's behavior, presentation, and psyche in order to appear more unique. In the presence of God, notice without judgment:

- Where am I aloof and presenting a unique image?

- Who and what do I envy? What ordinary things am I ignoring or dismissing? What is missing from my life right now? Who is misunderstanding me?

- What is shame saying to me? Where is distress saying, "I'm not special"? Where does shame show up and say, "I am not enough"? How do you try to prove, "I am enough"?

- What happens in your body as you answer these questions? What is your earliest memory of not being enough? What might that tell you?

- Where do you want to ask for the Spirit's help to stay centered and present in your life today?

HEAD CENTER (IQ): FIVES, SIXES, AND SEVENS

- *Core motivation:* security and survival

- *Negative fixation:* fear and dread

- *Narrative:* "I won't have enough" or "I'll get what I want"

Fives Defense Mechanism: Isolation. This can be physical withdrawal from others, but it also includes staying in your head and withdrawing from your emotions. In the presence of God, notice without judgment:

- How are you stingy with others? Where are you withholding yourself from others? Who are you ignoring that evokes emotion in you? Why?

- How do you isolate physically to avoid contact with someone? When do you retreat into your head to escape feeling? How do you get stuck in reading and study and lose sight of people? Where do you minimize desire? How are you ignoring a felt sense?

- When do you think, "I don't have enough"? What are you trying to get "no matter what it costs" (it could be privacy, time, or data)?

- What is happening in your body as you consider these questions? What is your earliest memory of this feeling? What might that tell you?

▶ Where do you want to ask for the Spirit's help to stay centered and present in your life today?

Sixes Defense Mechanism: Projection. This is attributing your inner concerns and fears to others and external situations. In the presence of God, notice without judgment:

▶ Who do you project your fears and feelings on to?

▶ What situation has grown larger in your mind? Where are you carrying on an internal dialogue of doubt and questioning? What decision are you afraid to make? What are you scared, alarmed, or anxious about?

▶ Do these questions keep you from taking action? Why do you think, "I don't have enough"? What are you trying to get "no matter what it costs"?

▶ What happens in your body when you consider these questions? What is your earliest memory of feeling fearful? What might that tell you?

▶ Where do you want to ask for the Spirit's help to stay centered and present in your life today?

Sevens Defense Mechanism: Rationalization. This is staying in your head and explaining away or justifying feelings and behaviors to avoid pain or responsibility. In the presence of God, notice without judgment:

▶ Whose feelings and needs are you forgetting about? What pain are avoiding?

▶ Where are you using activities and future plans to avoid pain or negative feelings? How are your ideas and plans distracting you from what is important to you? How does reframing what's happening help you discover what is true and necessary?

▶ How are new options and possibilities hurting you and the people you care about? Why do you think, "I don't have enough"? What are you trying to get "no matter what it costs" (it could be fun, excitement, pleasure, or escape)?

▶ What is happening in your body as you consider these questions? What is your earliest memory of this feeling? What might that tell you?

▶ Where do you want to ask for the Spirit's help to stay centered and present in your life today?

Once you have a sense of where you lose presence, you have the opportunity to practice being present. Choose a place you lose presence to feelings (EQ), thoughts (IQ), instincts (GQ), people, God, or yourself. This week, keep practicing sending edgy default energy back toward centered presence. Keep track of what happens as you practice. Where do you see new harmonies emerging?

WORK STYLES AND HARMONY

Do nothing out of selfish ambition or vain conceit.
Rather, in humility value others above yourselves, not looking
to your own interests but each of you to the interests of the others.

PHILIPPIANS 2:3-4

MISUNDERSTANDING OF EXPECTATIONS, roles, responsibilities, strategies, goals, allocation of scarce resources, personality, or political differences easily ignite conflict and/or criticism. Conflict and criticism beget more conflict and criticism, making it abundantly evident that harmonious work environments don't happen by accident. In fact, in organizations people often try to assess who will win the conflict and survive the criticism. Then to protect their own interests, they move to support the side they think will win.

Harmonious work cultures take intention and attention. They get built day by day with empathy and understanding about what inspires and drains employees. Moving toward empathy and collaboration happens as people learn to:

▸ Separate the sting of conflict or criticism from the kernel of truth hidden in the sting.

▸ Understand that criticism can be about the critic's pain and not just about you.

▸ Distinguish between deserved criticism and feeling bad about criticism.

▸ Listen to the issue behind the issue.

▸ Ask questions rather than defend. For example, "How could I have done that better?"

▸ Bless rather than curse.

The Harmony Enneagram can help regulate responses to conflict and criticism. Recognizing and appreciating the varied working styles, perspectives, strengths, and weaknesses of co-workers provides insight into how to moderate expectations and judgments, as well as build foundations that create cultures of reconciliation and harmony. Cultures that can hold and make space for different voices and values discover that varied perspectives bring richness and develop synergistic creative work spaces. When people feel received, they tend to respond from a true self place rather than a false self trigger.

Recognizing response patterns in yourself and others is a crucial step in reaching for harmony. Think of the people you work with as you read these descriptions. Notice the IQ (head), EQ (heart), and GQ (gut) that people bring. How can you use your own IQ, EQ, and GQ to understand what makes them tick?

GUT TRIAD (GQ): GROUNDED AND STABLE

In general, gut people want to make the world where they live and work just and fair. To that end, they will begin and press their initiatives forward. To move things along, they may push, bully, control, and express anger in overt or covert ways. Gut people are not afraid to sacrifice relationships to attain goals. When conflict heats up, Eights and Ones take ground. Nines may duck and cover but be angry that people can't get along.

Eights: The Powerful Person; Activist, Director

Inspiring: new challenges, compelling vision, justice issues, having autonomy, being in control, lead from strength. This motivation can be perceived as a threat to turf or people.

Draining: talk without action, lack of strong leadership, not to be in a place of influence, having to wait to make decisions

Work style: entrepreneur, assertive, boss, voice of the underdog

Value add: execution, action, accountability, push through

Desire: respect, results, fairness, agency, and control

Under stress and criticism: power up, pull away, bully, get vindictive and harsh

Response to goals: buy in and work hard if they helped set the goal, pull away if they don't like what leadership does, sacrifice relationships for goals

Nines: The Peaceful Person; Mediator, Negotiator

Inspiring: peaceful interactions and initiatives, collaboration, kindness and diplomacy, peacemaking and peacekeeping

Draining: conflict, pressure, arguments

Work style: receptive, accepting, accommodating, easygoing

Value add: see all perspectives, bring everyone's voice to the table

Desire: peace of mind, inner stability

Under stress and criticism: don't show up, procrastinate, become passive-aggressive, seek peace at any price

Response to goals: if they don't feel they are making progress with a goal they may check out, numb out, withdraw

Ones: The Good Person; Reformer, Idealist

Inspiring: truth-tellers, making things better, reforming, commitment to what is godly, good, ethical, and fair

Draining: unethical leadership, favoritism, slipshod work, criticism

Work style: quality control, educator, dedicated to improving people and processes

Value add: improving systems, managing people, moral compass for the organization, discernment

Desire: respect, affirmation and appreciation for hard work

Under stress and criticism: get angry, work twice as hard, become critical, judgmental, harsh, resentful, refuse interaction with "bad" others, overly sensitive

Response to goals: work hard toward goals they believe in, judge others and how they work or don't work toward goals

HEART TRIAD (EQ): CONNECTED AND RESPONSIVE

In general, heart people want to keep connections strong even in conflict. They move toward others, even their enemies, and try to collaborate to find a win/win solution. When conflict gets too intense, Twos and Fours tend to give ground, sacrificing goals and themselves for the sake of relationships. Threes will often hold out for goals, bargain, and press for the right people to be on the bus.

Twos: *The Loving Person; Helper, Giver*

Inspiring: care for others, offering help to people and systems, being needed

Draining: feeling unneeded, unappreciated, and unsupported; putting tasks ahead of people

Work style: project focused, people oriented, need centered

Value add: seeing what is needed and filling the need

Desire: to please people, be recognized and appreciated by coworkers and those they serve

Under stress and criticism: become overly sensitive, feel used, complain, criticize, gossip, become vindictive toward those who don't appreciate them

Response to goals: not receptive to goals that put tasks before people; choose affiliation over organizational goals at nearly every turn, which can feel like they aren't with the program

Threes: *The Effective Person; Leader, Achiever*

Inspiring: big goals, measurable outcomes, systemic and personal success, achievement, applause, leadership, and productivity

Draining: lack of direction, no definition of success, unsupportive and/or unenthusiastic colleagues

Work style: take charge, efficient, task oriented, competitive, energetic, connector

Value add: goal setting, efficiency, follow through, team building

Desire: to please the system, be successful, impress, gain recognition, and achieve their goals

Under stress and criticism: feel hurt, spin failures to look like success, put unrealistic expectations on others, tasks come first, workaholism

Response to goals: want total buy-in and to see others as committed to the goal as they are, want productivity and effectiveness around goals, will do what it takes to make things happen, sacrifice connection for goals

Fours: *The Original Person; Creative, Designer*

Inspiring: creative and meaningful work, deep connections, special assignments, opportunity to create unique experiences

Draining: routine, repetition, rules, lack of freedom, too many meetings, conformity, lack of space for original contributions, lack of appreciation

Work style: expressionist, unique ideas and contributions

Value add: creativity, identifying what's missing, empathy, discernment, see things in a creative new way

Desire: freedom, responses for significant contributions, lasting connections

Under stress and criticism: feel distress and self-doubt, withdraw, don't give support, try to maintain connections, over-dramatize situation

Response to goals: don't resonate with goals that require conformity of action, looking for their own unique way to respond, sacrifice goals for connection

HEAD TRIAD (IQ): FARSIGHTED AND CURIOUS

In general, head people want to avoid conflict with all its pain and emotional wear and tear.

They will become prickly, dig in, and entrench around cherished ideas and ideals. They will marshal authorities and research to prove their position and hope this wins the day. If it doesn't, Fives may withdraw, Sixes may refuse compromise and instead blame or attack the process and people, and Sevens will find a way to escape conflict by minimizing and changing the subject.

Fives: The Wise Person; the Wise Observer

Inspiring: intellectual growth, research, teaching, training, apologetics, working toward significant or groundbreaking contributions in their field

Draining: being forced to share and connect with others, brainstorming, when people are unprepared and wasting time, meetings

Work style: thinks things through, systematizes information

Value add: analysis, big picture

Desire: privacy, space, connection based on ideas

Under stress and criticism: overthink, pontificate, prognosticate, marshal data to prove their position, listen poorly, detach from others

Response to goals: back goals they understand, may think about the goals more than act on the goals, will sacrifice connections for goals

Sixes: The Loyal Person; the Loyal Opposition

Inspiring: commitment to cause and common good, asking the right questions, responsibility, duty, security

Draining: threat to self or common good, lack of clear directives, untrustworthy authority

Work style: team player, agreeable, don't want to compete, buy in

Value add: contingency, ask the hard questions, see the worst-case scenario, planning, discernment

Desire: trustful, truthful, committed and loyal relationships, want people to do their duty and follow through

Under stress and criticism: feel unsafe, fearful, guarded, untrusting; conflict and stress bogs them down in analysis paralysis, catastrophic thinking; they slow down processes and decisions with "what ifs"

Response to goals: may initially question and push back on goals; if they trust the leader's motives, they will commit and do their duty courageously; if they don't trust the leader, they will entrench in their position; don't expect their support

Sevens: The Joyful Person; Cheerleader

Inspiring: variety, creativity, options, opportunities; work isn't everything—make things fun

Draining: limits, close supervision, repetition, paperwork

Work style: social, strategic, visionary, out-of-the-box thinker

Value add: ideas, innovation, fun, enthusiasm, optimism; we can do this

Desire: to avoid negativity and pain, to hang with those who are having a good time

Under stress and criticism: minimize, distract themselves with plans, strategies, addictions; fantasize and come up with escape strategies, refuse to take serious things seriously

Response to goals: have trouble staying focused on collective goals that require sacrifice and endurance, get sidetracked by short-term goals that are more satisfying

BRINGING HARMONY TO WORK RELATIONSHIPS AND GOALS

All nine numbers bring a unique perspective to work and relationships. Organizational systems often default to the CEO's leadership style when setting goals, hiring, firing, and measuring success. The following suggestions can help move work cultures into transformative places.

1. Intentionally hire people from different triads and form teams that have representation of IQ, EQ, and GQ triads.

2. Train your employees, volunteers, and team members in the Harmony Enneagram, letting the language of harmony shape your culture. A culture that has a safe language for virtues and vices, and strengths and weaknesses, as well as an appreciation for various styles of working, is a culture that can communicate in conflict on difficult issues and learn how to discern.

3. Ask leaders, managers, employees, and volunteers to notice true and false self energy and what triggers their reactions. Where do they find it hard or easy to receive input from a particular triad or number? What do they want to do about that?

4. Conflict often issues from misunderstanding about expectations, goals, personality styles, roles, responsibilities, or lack of alignment. In conflict, familiarize yourself with what happens to various numbers. Use the descriptions listed above. Can you recognize triggers and respect a variety of responses to goals?

ORGANIZATIONAL ISSUE PRACTICE EXERCISE

▶ Choose an issue or decision for discussion. Divide employees into head, heart, and gut triads according to their number.

▶ Ask head people to talk about how they think heart people will go at addressing the issue. Have each group present their ideas and ask heart people to respond.

▶ Ask the heart people to address how the gut people will go at the issue. Have each group present their ideas and ask gut people to respond.

▶ Ask the gut people to address how the head people will go at the issue. Have each group present their ideas and ask head people to respond.

▶ What insights do you gather? What is it like to see from another's perspective?

▶ Now choose an issue or decision for discussion and divide the group into Harmony Triads. Have each group present their findings. How are things different when you are in a Harmony Triad? What was easier and what is harder?

PRAYER FOR LEADERSHIP

Let me have too deep a sense of humor
    ever to be proud.
Let me know my absurdity before I act
    absurdly.
Let me realize that, when I am humble, I
    am most human,
    most truthful,
    and most worthy of your serious
    consideration.

Soul Resource 10

HARMONY TRIADS

A Quick Guide for Helping Professionals and Their Clients

Table 10.1. Harmony Triad Summary for Eights, Twos, and Fives

	EIGHTS	TWOS	FIVES
Center of Intelligence	Gut • Reflect God's strong protection, self-worth • Fair amount of energy needed for action • Use power to make life how it "should be"	Heart • Reflect God's loving nurture • Embody divine love • Warm-hearted, empathic, self-sacrificing, relate easily, nurture generously, love unconditionally	Head • Reflect God's wisdom • Use intellect at the service of others • Objective, curious, innovative, and focused
Authentic Self	Powerful	Loving	Wise
Thinking Style	Dialectical	Relational	Analytical
Relational Style	Decider	Giver	Intellectualizer
Action Style	Director	Helper	Systematizer
Life Force Energy	Outward/Active • Alert, decisive action to make things happen in the world	Reconciling/Balancing • Careful and nurturing thriving	Inward/Receptive • Grounded presence bearing witness with empathy and understanding
Life Force Energy, Constricted	Unrestrained and unrestricted action and aggression	Narrow and amplified rigidity	Withdrawal and inertia
Most Instinctive Need	Power and Control	Approval and Affection	Security and Survival
Afflictive Emotion	Anger	Distress and anxiety over perceived loss of connection	Fear
Movement Relative to Others	Against Assertive	Toward Compliant	Away Withdrawing
Emotional Regulation (how one responds in conflict)	Sustaining and Expressing • Voicing concerns, feelings, and positions • Intensifying and amplifying their positions to be understood and get what they want	Reframing and Shifting • Shifting away from conflict • Seeking connection and how the relationship or situation can be fixed	Containing and Concealing • Become rational, analytic • Suppressing feelings, distancing from emotion to stay "objective" • Finding intellectual solutions and reasonable action steps
Difficulty in Emotional Regulation	Not hearing other points of view, amplifying conflict situations	Avoiding necessary confrontation and exploration of issues at hand	Not addressing depth and meaning of feelings, discounting feelings

Table 10.2. Harmony Triad Summary for Nines, Threes, and Sixes

	NINES	THREES	SIXES
Center of Intelligence	Gut • Reflect God's peace • Accepting, trusting, stable, good-natured, kindhearted, relaxed, easygoing, supportive, and non-judgmental • Create acceptance and ease	Heart • Reflect God's effectiveness • Motivating, energizing, connected, adaptable, achievement-oriented, magnetic, ambitious, competent, and motivational	Head • Reflect God's fidelity and commitment • Loyal energy, reliable, hardworking, responsible, insightful questions, curiosity, security, certainty, and predictability
Authentic Self	Peacemaker	Achiever	Loyal
Thinking Style	Holistic	Effective	Group Minded
Relational Style	Accommodator	Producer	Loyalist
Action Style	Reconciler	Motivator	Teamster
Life Force Energy	Inward/receptive non-judgmental engagement. Peaceful action	Outward /active servant leadership. Reproduction from presence and connectedness	Reconciling/balancing non-anxious vigilance. Loyal competence
Life Force Energy, Constricted	Unrestrained and unrestricted action and aggression	Narrow and amplified rigidity	Withdrawal and inertia
Most Instinctive Need	Power and Control	Approval and Affection	Security and Survival
Afflictive Emotion	Anger	Distress/Shame	Fear
Movement Relative to Others	Away Withdrawing	Against Assertive	Toward Dutiful/Questioning
Emotional Regulation (how one responds in conflict)	Refraining and Shifting • Shifting away from conflict and going to the positives • Looking for better alternative and restructuring the situation	Containing and Concealing • Become rational and analytic • Suppressing feelings, distancing from emotion to stay "objective" • Finding intellectual solutions and reasonable action steps	Sustaining and Expressing • Voicing concerns, feelings, and positions • Intensifying and amplifying their positions to be understood and get what they want
Difficulty in Emotional Regulation	Avoiding necessary confrontation and exploration of issues at hand	Not addressing depth and meaning of feelings, discounting emotions	Questioning other points of view, amplifying conflict situations

Table 10.3. Harmony Triad Summary for Ones, Fours, and Sevens

	ONES	FOURS	SEVENS
Center of Intelligence	Gut • Reflect divine goodness • Recognize dignity of others • Conscientious, balanced, and responsible • Committed to a life of service and integrity	Heart • Reflect holy origin • Original, introspective creativity, authentic, sensitive, mysterious, self-revealing, emotionally honest, deep, intuitive, and personal	Head • Reflect God's infinite capacity for joy • Enthusiastic, delight, optimistic, spontaneous, and adventuring • Focused vitality and vision
Authentic Self	Good	Creative	Joyful
Thinking Style	Idealist	Individualist	Positive
Relational Style	Improver	Sensitizer	Responder
Action Style	Stabilizer	Personalist	Cheerleader
Life Force Energy	Reconciling/Balancing • Efficient and effective thriving	Inward/Receptive • Grounded presence • Bearing witness with empathy and understanding	Outward/Active • Decisive action to make things happen in the world • Alert calm
Life Force Energy, Constricted	Narrow and amplified rigidity	Withdrawal and artistic sublimation	Unrestrained and unrestricted, action and aggression
Most Instinctive Need	Power and Control	Approval and Affection	Security and Survival
Afflictive Emotion	Anger	Distress over perceived loss of connection	Fear
Movement Relative to Others	Against Dutiful/Compliant	Away Withdrawing	Toward Assertive
Emotional Regulation (how one responds in conflict)	Containing and Concealing • Suppressing feelings and distancing emotions to stay "objective" • Finding intellectual solutions and reasonable action steps	Sustaining and Expressing • Voicing concerns, feelings, and positions • Intensifying and amplifying their positions to be understood and get what they want	Reframing and Shifting • Shifting away from conflict and going to the positives • Looking for better alternative and restructuring the situation
Difficulty in Emotional Regulation	Not addressing depth and meaning of feelings, discounting feelings	Internalizing other points of view, amplifying conflict situations	Avoiding necessary confrontation and exploration of issues at hand

Soul Resource 11

DISCOVERING YOUR ENNEAGRAM TYPE

THIS ASSESSMENT TOOL is a self-administered inventory based on reading nine descriptive paragraphs and choosing one or two that most resemble you.

Find a quiet and comfortable place that is free from distractions. Take some deep breaths to help you slow down and be present. If you are anxious, we want you to know that *you* are masterfully created by God; anything you experience through this personality instrument can work for your good.

You might like to ask God to open you to things you have not seen in yourself before. A simple prayer like this is enough: "Jesus, I want to see. Holy Spirit, illuminate my heart, mind, and instincts. Amen."

The nine paragraphs—found on the title page for each number—reflect each type's overall filter or view of life. There is no "better" number than you are. Don't choose who you wish you could be. Slowly read through *all* the paragraphs. Don't worry or overthink if you feel torn between two numbers. You are more than a type and may resonate with more than one number. Which description(s) seem to describe you best?

Once you discover your Enneagram style, note where your type lands in the Triads diagram. Harmony Triads recognize three different and equally important kinds of intelligence—an intelligence of the heart or feeling (Twos, Threes, and Fours), of the head or thinking (Fives, Sixes, and Sevens), and of the body or instinct/gut (Eights, Nines, and Ones). These three centers of intelligence are available to all of us, though we tend to prefer one over the others.

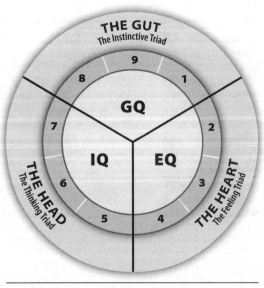

Figure 12. Harmony Triads: Three centers of intelligence

You can also take an online assessment (for a fee) designed by Dr. Jerome Wagner. It will take you about thirty to forty minutes. It can be found at enneagramspectrum.com or wepss.com. While we believe this is a highly accurate test, its results depend solely on your input. In our experience administering the test to hundreds of people, usually 20 percent have results that do not ultimately match their number. We want to add that we don't think this is the fault of the test. When people answer from their work persona or when they are exhausted or stressed, their answers are skewed and camouflage the truer picture of their resourced true self and less-resourced false self. Walking through the results with someone familiar with your life and/or a spiritual director or friend is the path to optimum understanding and insights for transformation.

SMALL GROUP DISCUSSION ON EMPATHY

THIS SOUL RESOURCE is an opportunity to explore your resistances and openness to the ways other numbers go about their lives. Each Enneagram number reflects one of the attributes of God. We need the presence of each number in their true selves to help reflect God's image in the world. True self calls to true self. False self calls to false self. This chapter can help you recognize where each number triggers your false self. Let the Holy Spirit lead your time together in ways that heal, bring compassion, and lead you in using the STOP practice that keeps you in your true self.

GUIDELINES FOR LEADING THE DISCUSSION

We hope the Empathy section at the end of each chapter can help you open your head, heart, and gut with love for each beloved Enneagram number.

You may also want to read one of the Scripture passages in each chapter that applies to that number and answer the questions that follow. If you want to expand your discussion, include the antidote to the false self of each number. Ask how the antidote resonates with the people of that number.

Remind participants to use "I" statements that reflect their own thoughts, feelings, and gut instincts. Don't blame numbers for their false self. Seek to understand how this number triggers your false self and where the call to the true self is difficult for each number.

EIGHTS

▶ Eights have big energy. When do you have big energy? What is it like for you to express that energy?

▶ How do Eights trigger your false self?

Antidote to the Eight's false self: Eights have force that blows right through limits. The apostle Paul was a strong, challenging force in the early church, and, at times, this force stirred things up in unhelpful ways. The antidote to Paul's untamed power came through a "thorn in my flesh" (2 Corinthians 12:7), a desolation that made him feel weak and limited him. Paul prayed the weakness would be removed. It wasn't removed, and his limits taught him that the Lord's "'power is made perfect in [his] weakness.' Therefore, I will boast all the more gladly about my weaknesses, so that Christ's power may rest on me" (2 Corinthians 12:9).

▶ What do you think it means to have a "thorn in my flesh"? What is yours?

▶ How can you be present to an Eight in their weakness? Do you have any experience of this? Can you feel for others who struggle with looking weak?

NINES

▶ Nines have mediating, collaborating tendencies. When do you have mellow instincts? What is it like for you to express yourself in this way?

▶ How do Nines trigger your false self?

Antidote to the Nine's false self: Jesus is clear about the antidote to the disordered need for peace at all costs. He says, "The kingdom of heaven has been advancing with force. And forceful people are taking hold of it" (Matthew 11:12 NIRV). Life isn't all chill. Some things need action. They need to be taken "hold of." A Nine that lays hold of their Three energy is a force for harmony in the world.

▶ What does it mean to you to forcefully take ground and energetically take "hold of" something?

▶ How can you encourage Nines to wake up to what God and this world are asking of them?

ONES

▶ Ones are energized when they can help people, organizations, and life work better. When are you energized by these things? What is it like to express yourself in this way?

▶ How do Ones trigger your false self?

Antidote to the One's false self: When we fly, flight attendants tell us in an emergency to secure our own oxygen mask first. Then we help children and others with their masks. To help bring goodness to the world, Ones need to secure their own true self goodness first. Inner freedom from judgment comes as Ones change their wardrobe: "Therefore, as God's chosen people, holy and dearly loved, clothe yourselves with compassion, kindness, humility, gentleness and patience. Bear with each other and forgive one another if any of you has a grievance against someone. Forgive as the Lord forgave you" (Colossians 3:12-13).

▶ When Paul says, "Clothe yourselves with compassion, kindness, humility, gentleness and patience," what is he asking you to do?

▶ How can you encourage Ones to live from a place where they know they are already "holy and dearly loved"?

TWOS

▶ Twos have loving energy. When are you energized by love for others? What is it like to express love to others?

▶ How do Twos trigger your false self?

Antidote to the Two's false self: Paul is clear about the antidote to the disordered need to please one person and then the next and the next. He writes, "Am I now trying to win the approval of human beings, or of God? Or am I trying to please people? If I were still trying to please people, I would not be a servant of Christ" (Galatians 1:10). God hasn't assigned Twos, or any other number, the care and pleasing of the world. Jesus invites beloved Twos to simply do what they can to serve as they can—not as they can't.

▶ What does "trying to please people" look like in your life?

▶ How can you encourage Twos to do only what God assigned them to do?

THREES

▶ Threes are energized to move and produce. How do these traits manifest in you? What is it like for you to want to do and make things happen?

▶ How do Threes trigger your false self?

Antidote to the Three's false self: Threes can struggle with grandiosity and how to be the superhero who saves the day. Human beings come with limits of energy, commitments, rest, family responsibilities, and more. Paul's antidote to the disordered need to perform, compare, compete, and max out your limits is found in 2 Corinthians:

> We do not dare to classify or compare ourselves with some who commend themselves. . . . We, however, will not boast beyond proper limits, but will confine our boasting to the sphere of service God himself has assigned to us . . . Neither do we go beyond our limits by boasting of work done by others. . . . For we do not want to boast about work already done in someone else's territory. . . . For it is not the one who commends himself who is approved, but the one whom the Lord commends. (2 Corinthians 10:12-18)

▶ How does this text speak to your need to produce and live large?

▶ How can you appreciate a Three's energetic productivity and not feed their addiction to praise?

FOURS

▶ Fours are energized by beauty and their creative juices. Where do you have creative energy? What is it like for you to make beauty and create?

▶ How do Fours trigger your false self?

Antidote to the Four's false self: An antidote for a Four's introjection and envy is found in the book of Proverbs: "A heart at peace gives life to the body, / but envy rots the bones. . . . Gracious words are a honeycomb, / sweet to the soul and healing to the bones" (Proverbs 14:30; 16:24). "Gracious words" offer an antidote to the devouring envy of a Four. Opening their heart to what is true and beautiful in themselves and to an imperfect reality moderates their envy.

▶ What stands out to you about this proverb?

▶ How can you encourage a Four that they are enough just as they are?

FIVES

▶ Fives find thinking and learning energizing. When do you feel energized by learning something new? What is it like for you to express what you have learned?

▶ How do Fives trigger your false self?

Antidote to the Five's false self: Fives can isolate to fill their inner emptiness with the rush of learning something new. The trouble is, "new" doesn't last or fill the emptiness. The antidote to a Five's greediness for another hit of information is found in knowing and being known by God. In Psalm 139:1-6, the psalmist contemplates the wonders of being fully known by God.

You have searched me, LORD,
   and you know me.
You know when I sit and when I rise;
   you perceive my thoughts from afar.
You discern my going out and my lying
      down;
   you are familiar with all my ways.
Before a word is on my tongue
   you, LORD, know it completely. . . .
Such knowledge is too wonderful for me,
   too lofty for me to attain.

At the end of the psalm, the psalmist invites God to search him even though God already knows him: "Search me, God, and know my heart; / test me and know my anxious thoughts. / See if there is any offensive way in me, and lead me in the way everlasting" (Psalm 139:23-24). The Creator's infinite knowing provides Fives with a safe place to accept their wisdom as God's gift for themselves and others.

 ▶ What stands out to you about the ways God knows you? When was the last time you invited God to search you?

 ▶ How might this Scripture help Fives understand what knowing is for?

SIXES

 ▶ Sixes are energized by communities that help others flourish. When do you feel energized by serving communities? What is it like for you to engage for the common good?

 ▶ How do Sixes trigger your false self?

Antidote to the Six's false self: Paul writes to his timid and loyal friend Timothy about his fears. Notice how Paul suggests the antidote to disordered fear is to "fan into flame the gift of God, which is in you."

I am reminded of your sincere faith, which first lived in your grandmother Lois and in your mother Eunice and, I am persuaded, now lives in you also. For this reason I remind you to fan into flame the gift of God, which is in you through the laying on of my hands. For the Spirit God gave us does not make us timid, but gives us power, love and self-discipline. . . . Preach the word; be prepared in season and out of season; correct, rebuke and encourage—with great patience and careful instruction. (2 Timothy 1:5-7; 4:2)

 ▶ What stands out to you in this text?

 ▶ Where can you encourage a Six to fan their gift into a flame?

SEVENS

 ▶ Sevens are energized by joy and vision. How do joy and vision give you energy? What is it like for you to express joy and cast vision for the future?

 ▶ How do Sevens trigger your false self?

Antidote to the Seven's false self: The antidote that gives Sevens a bigger picture of joy is found in James 1:2-4: "Consider it pure joy, my brothers and sisters, whenever you face trials of many kinds, because you know that the testing of your faith produces perseverance. Let perseverance finish its work so that you may be mature and complete, not lacking anything."

 ▶ What brings you a sense of "not lacking anything"?

 ▶ How can you encourage a Seven to look for "joy" in their trials?

GRATITUDES

THIS BOOK IS NOT AN INDIVIDUAL EFFORT. It is built on the foundations of our Enneagram teachers: Evagrius Ponticus, Ramon Llull, Ignatius of Loyola, Alice Fryling, Ginger Lapid-Bogda, Dee and Pat Aspell, Father Richard Rohr, David and Caron Loveless, Rich Plass, Claudio Naranjo, Andreas Ebert, Don Riso, Russ Hudson, Michael Naylor, Beatrice Chestnut, Helen Palmer, Thomas Condon, Kathleen Hurley, Suzanne Stabile, Sandra Maitri, Suzanne Zuercher, and Roxanne Howe-Murphy. To the late Dr. David Daniels, thank you for introducing us to harmony! A special thanks to Dr. Jerome Wagner whose countless hours of training at Loyola University have deeply influenced us and the work we have done in this book. We are grateful for the many voices from the oral tradition embodied in this book. Your ideas, teachings, and writings are a gift to the four of us, and hopefully through us to many others.

From the Calhouns: We are so grateful to friends who have spoken truth to us as we worked on the book. Thank you Annaliese Calhoun for reading and editing and giving us a Six perspective on our efforts. Thank you Tim and Michele Breen and Ross and Emily Jones for friendship along the way. Thank you Mark and Lynda Davies, Carla and Roger Peer, Karen Bere, Julie Baier, Ana Sisson, and Jim and Ruth Nyquist for your prayers. Thank you to Ruth Haley Barton and the Transforming Center who have consistently invited us to teach the Enneagram. Thank you to the staff at Highrock Church who supported us and reminded us, "You can do this!" Thank you Alice Kim, Susie Skillen, Janet Anderson, Abby Rice, Barbara Shingleton, Drew Hunter, and Carmen Maianu for consistently asking, "How is it going?" It has been a gift to coauthor this book with our dear friends Scott and Clare. We are grateful for the experience of co-creating with these remarkable people.

From the Loughriges: Thank you to Doug and Adele for the generous invitation to write with you and especially for never giving up on us in the midst of our dark night. Thank you Crossroads Church for allowing these pastors to discover harmony with you these past twenty-seven years. To the elders (and golden friends) at Crossroads, Shawn and Kathleen Loughrige, Don Coppo, Charles and Jill Theodorovich, Jacques Short, and Matt and Silvia Blossom, for "being all up in it" on this Enneagram journey and making the time and space for us to bring it to the wider world. Thank you Bonnie Wemple for the intercessions that kept us alive. Thank you to our children Sara, Ian, Josiah, and Libbie, and grandchildren Dante, Lorenzo, Adriana, Kiersten, and Ford who have survived our false self compulsions. We pray you continue to become your magnificent selves. Thank you to the Transforming Center and our spiritual rhythms teacher and guide Dr. Ruth Haley Barton. Your investment in us as individuals and pastors cannot be calculated. To all of the above: you are God's instruments of faith, hope, and love.

From all of us: Thank you to all who shared your IQ, EQ, and GQ autobiographies. Your honesty, courage, and generosity will help transform people who God loves that you will never meet. You made this book possible, and we are in awe of your inherent greatness! To all of you who read the first manuscript and then gave us such constructive feedback, we are so grateful for your helpful input and loving encouragement. Our editors, Cindy Bunch and Elissa Schauer, got their arms around our book and guided our process toward the book we have today. We are grateful they risked on this handbook and a new way of imagining the Enneagram with Harmony Triads.

For all who take this journey, may the Holy Spirit bring deep transformation toward your inherent glory, and may God receive all the glory!

For information about workshops and retreats
with Adele, Doug, Clare, and Scott, go to
spiritualrhythmsfortheenneagram.com

NOTES

INTRODUCTION

4   *Scott, Clare, Doug, and Adele employ Harmony Triad:* To find out more about training events with the authors, see enneagramharmonytriadstransform.com.

5   *Intriguing current research suggests:* To learn more about gut and heart intelligence, read Richard E. Cytowic, "The Pit In Your Stomach Is Actually Your Second Brain," *Psychology Today,* January 17, 2017, www.psychologytoday.com/us/blog/the-fallible-mind/201701 /the-pit-in-your-stomach-is-actually-your-second-brain; and Rosemary K.M. Sword and Philip Zimbardo, "Stress and Your Heart," *Psychology Today*, April 27, 2016, www .psychologytoday.com/us/blog/the-time-cure/201604/stress-and-your-heart. Also check out Justine Sonnenburg and Erica Sonnenburg, "Gut Feelings—the 'Second Brain' in Our Gastrointestinal Systems," *Scientific American*, May 1, 2015, www.scientificamerican.com /article/gut-feelings-the-second-brain-in-our-gastrointestinal-systems-excerpt/; and Ed Decker, "Your Heart and Stomach May Be Smarter Than You Think," *Rewire Me*, December 3, 2013, www.rewireme.com/brain-insight/your-heart-and-stomach-may-be -smarter-than-you-think.

7   *Just "studying" the Enneagram:* David Daniels, MD, "How Do We Actually Change?," drdaviddaniels.com, May 17, 2017, www.drdaviddaniels.com/how-do-we-actually -change/; and "Working with the Harmony Triads," *EANT Talk Journal Online*, May 2012, www.enneagramassociation.org/TALK/may2012/TALK-ourteachers.05-12.html.

8   *Projects of personal transformation:* Dallas Willard, *Renovation of the Heart: Putting on the Character of Christ* (Colorado Springs. CO: NavPress, 2012), 58.

9   *Evagrius was a theologian:* You can read more about Evagrius in Virginia Wiltse and Helen Palmer, "Hidden in Plain Sight: Observations on the Origins of the Enneagram," *International Enneagram Journal* 4 (2011): 41-42.

9   *see fig. 6:* Diagram from Wikimedia Commons, accessed January 31, 2018, https:// commons.wikimedia.org/wiki/File:Ramon_Llull_-_Ars_Magna_Fig_1.png.

11   *If we do not transform our pain:* Richard Rohr, *Things Hidden: Scripture as Spirituality* (Cincinnati, OH: St. Anthony Messenger Press, 2007), 25.

11   *This section provides spiritual rhythms:* Over eighty different disciplines are available in Adele Ahlberg Calhoun, *Spiritual Disciplines Handbook*, rev. ed. (Downers Grove, IL: InterVarsity Press, 2015).

12   *blind spots and hot spots:* Jerry Wagner, "Working with our Sweet Spots, Blind Spots, and Hot Spots" session at the International Enneagram Association Global Conference XVI, Fort Lauderdale, FL, July 29-31, 2011.

15   *interior freedom from sin:* Kevin O'Brien, SJ, *The Ignatian Adventure* (Chicago: Loyola Press, 2011), 191.

15   *"spoiled children" or a "false lover":* O'Brien, *The Ignatian Adventure*, 191.

PART I: THE GUT TRIAD

18   *In fact, there are more neurons:* Richard E. Cytowic, "The Pit in Your Stomach Is Actually Your Second Brain," *Psychology Today,* January 17, 2017, www.psychologytoday.com/us /blog/the-fallible-mind/201701/the-pit-in-your-stomach-is-actually-your-second-brain.

EIGHTS

20   *Spend some time with the words below:* The descriptive words list for each Enneagram number, which you will find at the beginning of each Enneagram number chapter, is derived from Jerome Wagner, PhD, Enneagram Spectrum Training and Certification Program, www.enneagramspectrum.com; used by permission.

22   *If you can't call the shots:* description adapted from Clare Loughrige, *The Enneagram Personality Styles: A Tool for Self-Knowledge and Spiritual Transformation* (CreateSpace, 2007), 18.

25   *It is my will:* Ignatius of Loyola in Joseph A. Tetlow, *Choosing Christ in the World* (Chestnut Hill, MA: Institute of Jesuit Sources, 1989), 173, with our additions.

25   *Take, Lord, and receive:* Ignatius of Loyola, "Suscipe," Loyola Press, www.loyolapress.com /our-catholic-faith/prayer/traditional-catholic-prayers/saints-prayers/suscipe-prayer -saint-ignatius-of-loyola?, accessed July 2018, with our additions.

26   *"Invitation to Wait":* Adele Ahlberg Calhoun, *Invitations from God* (Downers Grove, IL: InterVarsity Press, 2011), 135-51.

28   *These desolations leave you bound:* Clare Loughrige, *Motions of the Soul: The Enneagram and Ignatian Spirituality* (CreateSpace, 2012), 23-24.

NINES

39   *A Nine in a "whatever" state:* description adapted from Clare Loughrige, *The Enneagram Personality Styles: A Tool for Self-Knowledge and Spiritual Transformation* (CreateSpace, 2007), 22.

42   *May it please:* Ignatius of Loyola in William J. Young, trans., *Letters of St. Ignatius of Loyola* (Chicago: Loyola University Press, 1959), 257, with our additions.

44   *"Invitation to Participate in Your Own Healing":* Adele Ahlberg Calhoun, *Invitations from God* (Downers Grove, IL: InterVarsity Press, 2011), 23-36.

45   *These desolations leave you bound:* Clare Loughrige, *Motions of the Soul: The Enneagram and Ignatian Spirituality* (CreateSpace, 2012), 26-27.

46   *move is called* narcotization: as defined by Kurt Lewin, "Enneagram Theory: Psychological Defense Mechanisms and the Enneagram," The Enneagram in Business, theenneagramin business.com/theory/enneagram-theory-psychological-defense-mechanisms-and-the -enneagram, accessed August 2018.

ONES

57   *But your suppressed anger leaks:* description adapted from Clare Loughrige, *The Enneagram Personality Styles: A Tool for Self-Knowledge and Spiritual Transformation* (CreateSpace, 2007), 26.

62 *Grant me, O Lord:* Thomas à Kempis in Leo Shirley-Price, trans., *The Imitation of Christ* (London: Penguin Books, 1952), 164, with our additions.

64 *"Invitation to Admit I Might Be Wrong":* Adele Ahlberg Calhoun, *Invitations from God* (Downers Grove, IL: InterVarsity Press, 2011), 110-20.

64 *These are signs that Ones:* Clare Loughrige, *Motions of the Soul: The Enneagram and Ignatian Spirituality* (CreateSpace, 2012), 28-29.

PART II: THE HEART TRIAD

74 *There are more neurons:* Rosemary K. M. Sword, Philip Zimbardo, "Stress and Your Heart," *Psychology Today,* April 2017, www.psychologytoday.com/blog/the-time-cure/201604 /stress-and-your-heart.

TWOS

78 *Dependent on others' approval:* description adapted from Clare Loughrige, *The Enneagram Personality Styles: A Tool for Self-Knowledge and Spiritual Transformation* (CreateSpace, 2007), 30.

81 *Take, Lord, and receive:* Ignatius of Loyola, "Suscipe," Loyola Press, www.loyolapress.com /our-catholic-faith/prayer/traditional-catholic-prayers/saints-prayers/suscipe-prayer -saint-ignatius-of-loyola?, accessed July 2018, with our additions.

83 *"Invitation to Forgive":* Adele Ahlberg Calhoun, *Invitations from God* (Downers Grove, IL: InterVarsity Press, 2011), 121-34.

84 *The desolations that make:* Clare Loughrige, *Motions of the Soul: The Enneagram and Ignatian Spirituality* (CreateSpace, 2012), 31-32.

THREES

96 *You can become:* description adapted from Clare Loughrige, *The Enneagram Personality Styles: A Tool for Self-Knowledge and Spiritual Transformation* (CreateSpace, 2007), 34.

100 *Father, I dedicate:* Ignatius of Loyola, "Dedication of the Day," Catholic Online, www.catholic .org/prayers/prayer.php?p=607, accessed July 2018, with our additions.

102 *"Invitation to Follow":* Adele Ahlberg Calhoun, *Invitations from God* (Downers Grove, IL: InterVarsity Press, 2011), 37-54.

103 *This is bondage:* Clare Loughrige, *Motions of the Soul: The Enneagram and Ignatian Spirituality* (CreateSpace, 2012), 34-35.

FOURS

114 *Envy is the Four's vice:* description adapted from Clare Loughrige, *The Enneagram Personality Styles: A Tool for Self-Knowledge and Spiritual Transformation* (CreateSpace, 2007), 38.

118 *God, at his most vitally active:* Pierre Teilhard de Chardin. *Hymn of the Universe* (New York: Harper and Rowe, 1969), 271, with our additions.

120 *"Invitation to Remember":* Adele Ahlberg Calhoun, *Invitations from God* (Downers Grove, IL: InterVarsity Press, 2011), 168-81.

121   *These characteristics express:* Clare Loughrige, *Motions of the Soul: The Enneagram and Ignatian Spirituality* (CreateSpace, 2012), 37-38.

FIVES

134   *To solve problems:* description adapted from Clare Loughrige, *The Enneagram Personality Styles: A Tool for Self-Knowledge and Spiritual Transformation* (CreateSpace, 2007), 42.

138   *Eternal Word:* Ignatius of Loyola, "Prayer for Generosity," in Michael Harter, SJ, ed., *Hearts on Fire: Praying with Jesuits* (Chicago: Loyola Press, 2004), 58, with our additions.

139   *"Invitation to Practice the Presence of People":* Adele Ahlberg Calhoun, *Invitations from God* (Downers Grove, IL: InterVarsity Press, 2011), 55-69.

140   *These desolations leave you:* Clare Loughrige, *Motions of the Soul: The Enneagram and Ignatian Spirituality* (CreateSpace, 2012), 40-41.

SIXES

153   *Focusing on uncertain futures:* description adapted from Clare Loughrige, *The Enneagram Personality Styles: A Tool for Self-Knowledge and Spiritual Transformation* (CreateSpace, 2007), 46.

157   *O Christ Jesus:* Ignatius of Loyola, Jesuit Prayer, February 8, 2015, https://jesuitprayer.org /2015/02/08/?c=43, with our additions.

158   *"Invitation to the Most Excellent Way":* Adele Ahlberg Calhoun, *Invitations from God* (Downers Grove, IL: InterVarsity Press, 2011), 182-197.

159   *These desolations leave you:* Clare Loughrige, *Motions of the Soul: The Enneagram and Ignatian Spirituality* (CreateSpace, 2012), 43-44.

164   *Memorize St. Patrick's Breastplate:* Saint Patrick's "Breastplate" Prayer, Prayer Foundation, www.prayerfoundation.org/st_patricks_breastplate_prayer.htm, accessed July 2018.

SEVENS

172   *False self Sevens also resist:* description adapted from Clare Loughrige, *The Enneagram Personality Styles: A Tool for Self-Knowledge and Spiritual Transformation* (CreateSpace, 2007), 50.

175   *It is my will to win:* Ignatius of Loyola in David L. Fleming, *Draw Me into Your Friendship* (Boston: Institute of Jesuit Sources, 1996), 85, with our additions.

177   *"Invitation to Weep":* Adele Ahlberg Calhoun, *Invitations from God* (Downers Grove, IL: InterVarsity Press, 2011), 85-100.

179   *You are bound:* Clare Loughrige, *Motions of the Soul: The Enneagram and Ignatian Spirituality* (CreateSpace, 2012), 46-47.

180   *joy unspeakable:* Francis of Assisi, *The Little Flowers of St. Francis of Assisi* (London: Ballantyne, Hanson & Co., 1908), 247.

SOUL RESOURCE 3

199 *Returning prayer is a way:* Clare Loughrige, *Motions of the Soul: The Enneagram and Ig-natian Spirituality* (CreateSpace, 2012), 60.

SOUL RESOURCE 4

201 *Neuroscience research confirms:* Curt Thompson, M.D., *Anatomy of the Soul* (Carol Stream, IL: Tyndale House Publishers, 2010), 172.

201 *A 2016 study revealed:* David DiSalvo, "How Breathing Calms Your Brain, And Other Science-Based Benefits of Controlled Breathing," *Forbes*, November 29, 2017, www.forbes .com/sites/daviddisalvo/2017/11/29/how-breathing-calms-your-brain-and-other-science -based-benefits-of-controlled-breathing/#140cc91c2221.

203 *Breathe in gratitude:* In this section, we adapted some general research from the HeartMath Institute, heartmath.org, to create our material.

203 *Neuroplasticity is the brain's:* Thompson, *Anatomy of the Soul*, 172.

SOUL RESOURCE 5

205 *The place God calls:* Frederick Buechner, *Wishful Thinking: A Seeker's ABC* (San Francisco: HarperCollins, 1973), 87.

SOUL RESOURCE 8

213 *Practicing the presence:* Clare Loughrige, *Motions of the Soul: The Enneagram and Ignatian Spirituality* (CreateSpace, 2012), 68-71.

214 *Consent to God's presence:* Thomas Keating, "The Method of Centering Prayer," Contemplative Outreach, Ltd., www.contemplativeoutreach.org/sites/default/files/private/method _cp_eng-2016-06_0.pdf, accessed July 2018.

SOUL RESOURCE 9

218 *Separate the sting of conflict:* Bullet points taken from a talk by Dave Swaim to a Highrock Church Network (Arlington, MA) staff gathering, January 30, 2018.

222 *Let me have:* Daniel A. Lord, "Prayer for Humility," in Michael Harter, SJ, ed., *Hearts on Fire: Praying with Jesuits* (Chicago: Loyola Press, 2004), 39.

SOUL RESOURCE 10

223 *A Quick Guide:* Clare Loughrige, compiled by Lorilyn Wiering, inspired by David Daniels, "Working with the Enneagram Triads," The Enneagram Triads, ©iEnneagram Motions of the Soul Training and Certification Course, June 2017, www.drdaviddaniels.com/articles/triads.

Training and Certification

®iEnneagram Harmony
Triads Practitioner

MOTIONS
OF THE SOUL

©iEnneagram Motions of the Soul is an
**International Enneagram Association Accredited
Certification** that will equip you to train others in
your setting. This four-day class and Capstone Paper
includes 32 CEU's and Certification.

For more information:
scottandclareloughrige.org

ALSO AVAILABLE FROM INTERVARSITY PRESS

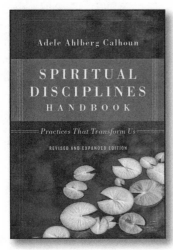

Spiritual Disciplines Handbook:
Practices That Transform Us
978-0-8308-4605-4

Invitations from God: Accepting
God's Offer to Rest, Weep, Forgive,
Wait, Remember and More
978-0-8308-3553-9

True You: Overcoming Self-Doubt
and Using Your Voice
978-0-8308-4315-2

Coloring Our Gratitude:
The Art of Everyday Thankfulness
978-0-8308-4630-6

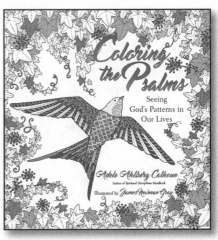

Coloring the Psalms:
Seeing God's Patterns in Our Lives
978-0-8308-4629-0

formatio

TRADITION. EXPERIENCE.
TRANSFORMATION.

Formatio books from InterVarsity Press follow the rich tradition of the church in the journey of spiritual formation. These books are not merely about being informed, but about being transformed by Christ and conformed to his image. Formatio stands in InterVarsity Press's evangelical publishing tradition by integrating God's Word with spiritual practice and by prompting readers to move from inward change to outward witness. InterVarsity Press uses the chambered nautilus for Formatio, a symbol of spiritual formation because of its continual spiral journey outward as it moves from its center. We believe that each of us is made with a deep desire to be in God's presence. Formatio books help us to fulfill our deepest desires and to become our true selves in light of God's grace.